NATIONS OF THE MODERN WORLD

AUSTRALIA	O. H. K. Spate *Director, Research School of Pacific Studies, Australian National University, Canberra*
CEYLON	S. A. Pakeman *Formerly Professor of Modern History, Ceylon University College; Appointed Member, House of Representatives, Ceylon, 1947–52*
MODERN EGYPT	Tom Little *Managing Director and General Manager of Regional News Services (Middle East), Ltd., London*
ENGLAND	John Bowle *Professor of Political Theory, Collège d'Europe, Bruges*
FINLAND	W. R. Mead *Professor of Geography, University College, London; Formerly Chairman, Anglo-Finnish Society*
MODERN GREECE	John Campbell *Fellow of St. Antony's College, Oxford* Philip Sherrard *Assistant Director, British School of Archaeology, Athens, 1958–62*
MODERN INDIA	Sir Percival Griffiths *President of the India, Pakistan and Burma Association*
MODERN IRAN	Peter Avery *Lecturer in Persian and Fellow of King's College, Cambridge*
ITALY	Muriel Grindrod *Formerly Editor of* International Affairs *and* The World Today *Assistant Editor of* The Annual Register
JAPAN	Sir Esler Dening *H.M. Ambassador to Japan, 1952–57*
KENYA	A. Marshall MacPhee *Formerly Managing Editor of* The East African Standard Group; *producer with British Broadcasting Corporation*

MALAYA — J. M. Gullick
Formerly of the Malayan Civil Service

MOROCCO — Mark I. Cohen
and
Lorna Hahn

NEW ZEALAND — James W. Rowe
Director of New Zealand Institute of Economic Research, Inc.
Margaret A. Rowe
Tutor in English, Victoria University, Wellington

NIGERIA — Sir Rex Niven
Colonial Service, Nigeria, 1921–59; Member of Northern House of Assembly, 1947–59

PAKISTAN — Ian Stephens
Formerly Editor of The Statesman *Calcutta and Delhi, 1942–51; Fellow of King's College, Cambridge, 1952–58*

SOUTH AFRICA — John Cope
Formerly Editor-in-Chief of The Forum*; South African Correspondent of* The Guardian

SUDAN REPUBLIC — K. D. D. Henderson
Formerly of the Sudan Political Service; Governor of Darfur Province, 1949–53

TURKEY — Geoffrey Lewis
Senior Lecturer in Islamic Studies, Oxford

THE UNITED STATES OF AMERICA — H. C. Allen
Commonwealth Fund Professor of American History, University College, London

WEST GERMANY — Michael Balfour
Reader in European History, University of East Anglia

YUGOSLAVIA — Muriel Heppell
and
F. B. Singleton

NATIONS OF THE MODERN WORLD

FINLAND

FINLAND

By

W. R. MEAD

FREDERICK A. PRAEGER, *Publishers*
New York · Washington

BOOKS THAT MATTER

Published in the United States of America in 1968
by Frederick A. Praeger, Inc., Publishers
111 Fourth Avenue, New York, N.Y. 10003

Library of Congress Catalog Card Number: 68–31441

Printed in Great Britain

Preface

THIS BOOK is neither a comprehensive study of Finland nor a compendium of knowledge about the country. Much of it is historical; but, as such, it can merely play the water beetle to the trout of Eino Jutikkala's *History of Finland* (1962) and to the lavaret of John Wuorinen's *History of Finland* from the following year. Some of it is geographical, but it can never approach the succinctness of Ilmari Hustich's *Finland förvandlas* (1967). Much of it is factual, but contemporary statistics have been generally omitted, because they are speedily outdated and are easily obtainable from the latest volume of the *Yearbook of Finnish Statistics* (*Suomen tillastollinen vuosikirja*). Finnish statistics are good and readily accessible – not surprisingly, for the tradition of handling and collecting them is two centuries old. The Finns are also great publishers; while as readers they seem capable of consuming a torrent of print.

Finland is an old nation if a young state. One object of this book is to draw attention to the variety of features and events that have made up the past feeling and enter into the present thinking of Finland. The approach is selective, intermittently evocative, occasionally analytical. It attempts constantly to see the present in the past: the past in the present. It looks regularly at everyday things, for everyday things mean more to most ordinary Finns than epoch-making events. In addition, it aspires to interpret a considerable range of literature not well-known or readily available in Britain. When outside events have stirred Finland or prompted debatable reactions, it tries not to take sides, for there are many sides to be taken in Finland. It is limited in its treatment of politics and passions. If there is something of the *touch-à-tous* about it, that is partly deliberate.

In Appendix A, there is a selected, but by no means comprehensive, list of publications which have been employed in the preparation of this book. Mention must also be made of regular reference to Finland's recently published encyclopaedia – *Otavan Isotietosanakirja*. This invaluable source of factual information also contains many helpful illustrations – from autographs of leading Finns (Vol. 1) to the typeface of historic newspapers (Vol. 8), from the full range of Finland's coats of arms (Vol. 1) to the changing character of its coinage and paper money (Vol. 8).

Few will have the time, energy or inclination to add Finnish – or even Swedish – to the list of languages that they read. But since the publication of Maija-Hellikki Altio, *Finnish for Foreigners* (Helsinki, 1964) and John Atkinson, *A Finnish Grammar* (Turku, 1961), Finnish is no longer so inaccessible. Place names beset anyone who writes on Finland. In this book the Finnish form is employed, except in the case of Swedish-speaking communes or settlements. In the index, both Finnish and Swedish forms are listed.

I have tried not to trouble friends in preparing this manuscript. The facets of Finland touched upon in it are so numerous that, had I begun to approach them, there is no telling when or where I should have ended. In completing this book, I am especially mindful of the constant help that I have received during twenty years from the staffs of Finland's research libraries and institutes. In particular, I should like to thank my many friends in the State Archives, in the various departments of the University Library of Helsinki, and the libraries of Åbo Academy and the Finnish Literary Society.

I am indebted to Kenneth Wass of the Department of Geography at University College London for drawing the maps. The quotations from *Kalevala* in Chapter 2 are reproduced by kind permission of Messrs J. M. Dent and Sons from William Kirby's translation in the Everyman Series (London, 1956). For the plates I am grateful to *Maanmittaushallitus* (The Finnish Land Survey), The National Museum of Finland, The Finnish Foreign Ministry, The State Archives of Finland, The Ateneum (The National Art Gallery of Finland), The University Library of Helsinki, the archive of the War Office in Stockholm, and to the Otava Publishing Company of Helsinki.

University College London W. R. MEAD
8 January 1968

Contents

Maps

List of Illustrations

(All are inserted between pages 128 and 129)

Acknowledgements

ACKNOWLEDGEMENT for kind permission to reproduce illustrations is made to the following, to whom the copyright of the illustrations belongs:

Ateneum, Helsinki: 5, 6.
The Finnish Embassy, London: 15, 16.
The Finnish Foreign Ministry: 19, 21, 23.
The Land Survey Office, Helsinki: 1, 2, 3.
The Museum of Finnish Architecture, Helsinki: 20.
The National Museum, Helsinki: 10, 11, 12, 13.
Otava Publishing Company, Helsinki: 17.
Radio Times Hulton Picture Library: 18.
State Archive, Helsinki: 14a and b.
The University Library, Helsinki: 8.
War Archives, Stockholm: 9.
The Wärtsilä Company: 4.

Chapter 1

A Land of Three Frontiers

THE HISTORY OF FINLAND is largely written in its geography. This is not to preach geographical determinism, but simply to underline the fact that the setting, size and resources of the land define the frame of opportunity within which Finns can effectively operate. In the study of any country, these three points call for immediate observation and continuous reference.

In setting, Finland occupies a zone of transition. It is poised on three frontiers. Latitudinally, it spans the cool temperate and sub-Arctic zones. In the first place, therefore, it is located on Europe's northern frontiers of settlement. Finland is the most northerly independent country in the world, its centre of gravity lies in higher latitudes than that of Iceland. The Arctic Circle runs through Finland's northern third, its southern boundaries hover around the sixtieth parallel. It is like Sweden shorn of its southern quarter: it is a counterpart of Swedish Norrland, with many of that northern province's attendant problems. Ilmari Hustich has pointed out that of the world population living north of the sixtieth parallel, Finland accounts for 35 per cent. In the second place, Finland spans a transitional zone between Atlantic and continental Europe. As a result it has a maritime frontier which looks to the west and to the world ocean. It has also a landward frontier which faces the east and looks towards the heartland of Eurasia. Finland is inescapably a marchland state between eastern and western Europe.

The land frontier on the east, the maritime frontier on the west and the settlement frontier in the north are inscribed upon the face of a country which is of average European size. Finland's surface area of *c.* 300,000 sq. km. is comparable to that of Great Britain or Italy. As with both of them, it has an elongated shape, stretching through ten degrees of latitude. The number of inhabitants is small in relation to surface area. But to counter-balance this relationship, the northern setting limits the opportunities of using a land, the resource base of which is modest and lacking in diversity.

The Challenge of High Latitude

Finns are first and foremost concerned with the challenge of high latitude. The principal consequence of high latitude is that winter prevails over summer. The words of the poet Eric Lindorm are even more appropriate to Finland than to neighbouring Sweden:

Vi födde mot norr, vår öden	In birth we are pitched against the north,
vetta mot vinden och döden.	Our wilderness looks to the wind and to death.

Under usual circumstances, south Finland is blanketed with snow and sheathed with ice for five or six months of the year: north Finland, for seven or eight months. 'This is a country of winter and crusted snow . . . and the frost drives deep into the ground', wrote the novelist Johannes Linnankoski. There is annual return to an Ice Age which may freeze the mercury in north Finland. It is a fact remarked by some geographers that the signs of the sub-Arctic begin in Sweden's province of Småland and that almost all of Finland is sub-Arctic by many standards. In this circumstance, the brief but intense summer shocks with pleasure. It is a season of prolonged daylight, when a virtually tropical sun can taunt, when cumulus clouds pile up and convectional thunderstorms spout. 'It might be the Bahamas or Bermuda', observed a visitor to north Åland in July 1966. The part of Finland that lies north of the Arctic Circle sees the 'midnight sun'; while for the same period the rest of the country enjoys the rare luminosity of the 'white nights'. Their atmosphere envelops the action of F. E. Sillanpää's novel, *People in a Summer Night.* Contrastingly, north Finland experiences a midwinter period when the sun does not rise above the horizon. For the northern Finn the winter twilight, which may be enlivened with pyrotechnic displays of *Aurora borealis,* is called *kaamosaika.* Spring is a surge of vegetation which rushes headlong into summer; everything blooms quickly in Lapland is the theme of Eino Leino's poem *Lapland Summer.* Autumn has a short, bright flush of colour – vivid in the Lapland fells, where it is known as *ruskon aika*, 'the red season'. In the south, there is usually a brief tawny period before October (*Lokakuu* – the month of mud) yields to November (*Marraskuu* – the month of death).

Finland's climate is also closely related to the interplay of continental and oceanic influences. The system of westerly cyclones which moves in a procession across the Atlantic and which has such a modifying effect on the climate of the neighbouring Scandinavian peninsula, also influences Finland, especially south-west Finland. So, too, do the powerful high-pressure systems which build up over the continent to the east. They result in clear bright weather instead of moist cloudy conditions, Siberian circumstances instead of Atlantic. Finland's winter weather is especially sensitive to the relationship between these air masses.

Climate is the more significant because Finland is located on the margins of the inhabited world. Exceptional seasonal circumstances or any long-period changes in climate will accordingly have exaggerated consequences. Plenty of evidence from the past indicates that since Finland was occupied by man its climate has experienced considerable long-period variations. Evidence is found in the pollen grains of peat bogs and in the shells of sea creatures, in the artifacts of prehistoric man, and at a later stage, in documents such as church records.

The outlines of Finland, in common with those of most of Sweden and much of north-west Russia, are inscribed upon one of the oldest areas of bedrock in Europe. It is the so-called Fennoscandian or Baltic Shield. As a result, Finland is a country of granites, gneisses, quartzes and other primary rocks. In spite of their uniform antiquity, the rocks vary greatly in appearance and in chemical content. For the most part, the bedrocks are resistant; but the rigorous glacial and postglacial circumstances have produced widespread local sheeting and shattering. Some granites also weather relatively easily because of their chemical composition. *Rapakivi* granite, 'rotten granite', is an example. It is widely distributed in southern Finland. Between the primary rocks and the youngest superficial deposits, almost all the other geological series are missing. For this reason there are neither coal-bearing nor oil-bearing rocks; though there are copper, iron and other ores.

The old and hard bedrocks of the Fennoscandian Shield have been subject to prolonged denudation. Accordingly, Finland is a low-lying country. Its features, usually smoothed and rounded, are inscribed *en bas-relief*. Only in the north and north-west does the land rise above a thousand feet. In later geological times, because of its northerly setting the territory that was to become Finland was subject to the full erosive force of the Quaternary Ice Sheet. Permanent ice retreated from it between 10000 and 7000 B.C., so that it was one of the last areas of Europe to be colonised by men.

On top of the bare granite the retreating ice deposited its debris. The results are seen in ramparts of moraine, such as those which compose the 500–600-feet high Salpausselkä that traverses southern Finland from eastern Karelia to the peninsula of Hangö; in boulder fields, such as those around Loviisa on the Gulf of Finland, which reminded earlier travellers of a battlefield of giants; in snaking eskers (or gravel ridges) such as those of Ruovesi and Punkaharju; in sandy heaths, such as those along the Maanselkä, which forms the watershed betweten Ostrobothnia and the interior.

In addition to its northerly setting and a background of primary rocks littered with Quaternary deposits, Finland is a country which has an extended seaboard. Its Baltic coast is officially estimated as 4,600 km. long. As with the coasts of most of Scandinavia, it is highly intricate, with many offshore islands. But the character and behaviour of Finland's adjacent sea differ greatly from those of the outer ocean. The inner recesses of the Gulfs of Finland and Bothnia are low in salinity and virtually tideless. As a result, when temperatures tumble, the greater part of the coast of Finland experiences winter ice obstruction of varying duration and intensity. In severe winters, even with modern vessels and technical aids, ferries and cargo shipping may be reduced to limited services from the extreme south-west of the country.

The form of Finland's natural drainage is also closely related to the consequences of the Ice Age. The elaborate interrelations between land and water which make Finland a land of ten thousand islands as well as of ten thousand lakes are partly the result of the obstructing deposits that litter the surface, partly the result of general absence of significant slopes and partly the consequence of the continuing upwarping of the land. The surface of Finland has many of the qualities of a drowned landscape in process of emerging from sea, lake and swamp.

Land emergence is one of the most fascinating physical phenomena of Finland. There are few occupied parts of the world where the postglacial adjustment of land and water levels have had such widespread human effects as in Finland. In archipelagic and coastal Finland evidence of former shorelines is seen in the rows of caves along the fissured *klints* of north Åland; in the raised beaches with their terraced boulder fields – the *stenåker* – which perplex geologists with their chronology; in the waterlines, now kilometres from the edge of the sea, that are etched on Ostrobothnia's rocks and boulders. Speed of uplift reaches a climax in Vaasa archipelago, where land emergence attains a maximum of 80 cm. per century. When changing water levels were first seriously debated in the mid-eighteenth century, Turku castle was one of the landmarks used by natural scientists. Vulcanists, who supported crustal upheaval, and Neptunists, who believed in diminishing water, argued over the causes of the apparent retreat of the sea from the castle's walls. Land surveyors and others who were curious about natural phenomena inscribed dated marks so that posterity might be advised of former water levels.

A country with an inclement climate living near in time to the Ice Age and experiencing a virtual annual recurrence of it, has correspondingly immature soils. They are frequently deficient in chemicals, cold and ill-drained. Extensive peatlands result in widespread humus soils, which have a surfeit of moisture and which are acidic. The soils of Finland have required and continue to demand heavy investment of capital and labour in order to produce the same as those in more favoured climates.

Cultivated land has been won almost entirely from the coniferous forest, with which Finland was largely covered in its primeval state. Spruce and pine remain the absolutely dominant trees; birch, alder, poplar are subdominant. Climax growth conditions for spruce occur across the southern half of Finland. In the north, the limits of coniferous woodland are set by climate. The frontiers of growth of pine push beyond those of the spruce both latitudinally and altitudinally. 'Southern Europe lacks a tree the proud strength of which can compare with our northern fir', wrote Zachris Topelius. On the southern flanks of Lapland are located some of Finland's oldest timber stands, the *urwald*, macabre primeval woodlands protected today in national parks. Elsewhere, circumstances of rock and soil control the detail of timber distribution – the acid peat bogs at the edges of which timber stands cease; the dry heaths, which the pine assaults with limited success; the bald granite, over which the roots of the conifers trace arabesques in search of a foothold in cracks and fissures; the tundra, with its stress of desiccation. Only in the extreme south-west of the country are there deciduous stands – residual oakwoods, the former more extensive distribution of which is reflected in place-names. An under-flora of berry-bearing shrubs – *Vaccinium* (blueberry) and *Myrtillus* (the bright red whortleberry) – rise through birch and alder scrub to the red-berried *Sorbus*, the mountain ash and the bird cherry. In general, however, the boreal forests have open stands, with relatively little undergrowth. Their glades support a variety of grasses. The lesser flora is most varied in the south-west, where it reaches its richest expression in the deciduous groves (Sw. *lövänger*) around the maritime fringes of the islands and peninsulas. In late May and early June, the *lövänger* are virtual Gardens of the Hesperides, with lily-of-the-valley (Finland's national flower) and anemone, primrose and dianthus, orchid and Solomon's seal beneath hazel bush and intermittent oak. Many are protected as nature reserves today. Linnaeus declared that no nobleman's park could be richer than these natural meadows of the *bönder*. Somerset Maugham might have been writing of these marginal lands where 'the everlasting youth of the oaks contrasts, like night and day, with the undying age of the firs'.

Their antithesis lies in the widespread open boglands, with their restricted plant species. Few countries have classified their boglands so carefully as Finland. *Sphagnum* moss is their most common plant. The tussocked margins around the spongy, tawny-green wastes yield cloudberries and cranberries. Mosses spread their variegated carpets through the woodlands – in cushions of green, gold and milky grey (the identifying colour of reindeer moss). They are beautiful to look upon, but hostile vegetable forces to man. Lichens scramble over the rocks beyond them – scabrous and brightly coloured. And, in the autumn, there is a veritable explosion of mushrooms and fungae. There are over a hundred kinds of edible fungus. They, too, can add their colour, from the favoured crocus-yellow *Cantharellus cibarius* to the red-and-white spotted *Ameneta muscaria*.

The long winter restricts the variety of fauna as well as flora. Finland's fauna is that of the boreal forest. Its fur-bearing animals – mink, marten, squirrel and beaver, preyed upon by wolf, bear and lynx, are what Auréléon Sauvageot calls collectively 'les fauves sylvestres' of Finland's woods. The gawky elk, with its top-heavy antlers, has always been widely distributed. So, too, the wild deer. They are the herbivors whose flesh remains most esteemed by hunters. The patterns of faunal distribution have changed and continue to change in response to both physical and human influences. The changing distribution of the polecat during the first half of the twentieth century probably reflected a cyclical improvement in winter conditions. The trapping lines of the 'fur princes' were already exhausted by the seventeenth century, while within living memory the frontiers where bear and wolf occur have retreated swiftly.

There is a large and varied bird population. Much of it is migratory, following *linnun rata* (as the old Finns used to call the Milky Way) from north-east to south-west to their southern homeland. Some are migratory from the east, adding yet another exotic element to Finnish wild life. Seabirds prevail around the coasts, nesting in impressive colonies in the outer skerries. The broad reedbeds of lake and seashore are rich in wild duck, divers and waders. The wild goose and wild swan are also migratory. Relatively few birds overwinter. Among winter residents the magpie is a distinctive farmyard visitor. So are the tits. The woods are plentiful in game birds. The hardier, such as the capercaillie and black cock, are better adapted to cope with the winter than the immigrant pheasant. The arrival and departure of swallow, swift and martin set the bounds to the northern summer. These birds are partly attracted by the immense clouds of midges and mosquitoes bred in the widespread swamplands. In summer, a rich insect life is born, so that the forest murmurs no less than in more southern lands.

Fresh-water fish predominate. The brackish sea has its harvest of Baltic herrings with limited cod and, in the south-western archipelagos, diminutive flatfish. Seals by the thousand prey heavily upon the fish of the Gulf of Bothnia. The salmon, also caught off the coast, is king of the river fish. Catches are greatest in the northern rivers – not least those draining from north-east Finland into the White Sea. The lavaret or whitefish and a small lakefish, called by the Finns *muikku* (*Coregonus*), are also members of the salmon family. Pike, perch and a miscellany of other bony and muddy-flavoured species are abundant. Stocks of fish are greatest in the northern rivers and lakes, which have been less extensively exploited. Crayfish are widely netted from 1 August, though stocks diminish both through overfishing and disease. Particular areas have their specialities, such as the lampreys of the Ostrobothnian rivers. Shellfish are very restricted in variety and coastal beaches lack their familiar litter, but fresh-water mussels yield their coveted pearls.

Changing technical facilities enable the diverse elements of Finland's natural environment to be viewed in different ways. At the scale of the atlas map, for example, it is possible to discern three principal regional divisions – the coastal plains and archipelagos, the lake plateau, the north country; though none of the divisions is clear-cut and broad zones of transition prevail. The regional diversity of Finland also becomes a visual reality when passed over at the speed of the aircraft. By contrast, earthbound or waterbound travellers sense a repetitive scenic experience. Morphologically Finland is the opposite of Norway, for the quiet intricacies of its local landscapes, seascapes and lakescapes rarely yield to striking contrasts of relief. Scenic variations in Finland are controlled by nuances and their details are multiplied in reflections and mirages. Familiarity with such a countryside yields much pleasure: unfamiliarity frequently breeds contempt. One of the first Europeans to capture its qualities was Bernardin de Saint-Pierre whose landscape impressions from the third quarter of the eighteenth century are scattered through his *Études* and *Harmonies*. Finland is also much in harmony with the spirit of Henry David Thoreau's book, *Walden*. Moreover, as with Thoreau's New England retreat, Finland displays the contrasts that are born of time rather than of place. The changing seasons yield the antithesis of a brief and florally exuberant summer (which foreign poets in their imagination have peopled with naiads and dryads) and the Arctic desolation of a winter in which Hans Andersen located the palace of his Snow Queen.

Dramatis personae

The nation of Finland has 4,600,000 inhabitants. By comparison, Sweden has 7,750,000 and Leningrad 3,500,000. The Finns call themselves *Suomalaiset* in Finnish; *Finnar* in Swedish. The constitution of 1919 guarantees the employment of two languages – Finnish and Swedish; while a succession of Language Acts, stemming from that of 1922, contains detailed stipulations about unilingual and bilingual administrative districts. Numerically, the Finnish-speaking Finns are absolutely dominant. The Swedish-speaking Finns, who total about 7.4 per cent of the population, occur principally around the Baltic coast. They are concentrated heavily in the south-west. The 25,000 inhabitants of the province of Åland are almost exclusively Swedish-speaking. The skerries of Turku province also have a heavy concentration. The Swedish-speaking belt stretches along the coast of Uusimaa through Helsinki and eastwards beyond Porvoo. It is complemented by another coastal concentration between Kristiinankaupunki and Kokkola in Ostrobothnia. The Swedish-speaking Finns are mostly descendants of immigrants who settled on the eastern shores of the Baltic in former centuries. In the northern fells there are about 2,500 Lapps. They call themselves *Saame* and although they are magnified in tourist literature, they are fast dwindling. They are restricted almost entirely to the parishes of Enontekiö, Inari and Utsjoki. Their neighbours are the considerably larger Swedish and Norwegian Lapp populations and the smaller Russian Lapp population in the Kola peninsula.

The lakeland provinces of Häme, Savo and Karelia are the essential homeland of the Finns. Finnish has always been their native tongue, though it is little more than two centuries since scholars began to transcribe it, not much more than a century and a half since it was first formulated in a grammar, and only just over a century since it was admitted as equal for official purposes to Swedish. Isolation preserved the Finnish language: the Finnish language, in turn, has isolated the Finns. International communication was originally in Latin, which was still frequently used for overseas communication two centuries ago. For the outsider, Finnish looks an unfamiliar language. In part, as a contributor wrote to *Chambers's Encyclopaedia* in 1862, this is explained by 'a copiousness of vowels'. At least one nineteenth-century environmentalist thought it 'a climatically influenced language'. 'At the very sound of *yö* (night) the imagination involuntarily transfers us to the dark north', he wrote. Lappish also belongs to the Fenno-Ugrian language group. Swedish usually provides the medium for communication with the rest of Scandinavia.

By comparison with the inhabitants of most European countries, the Finns are a relatively homogeneous people. It is a useless exercise to attempt to reduce their physical characteristics to common denominators. The unsatisfactory results of such an approach may be seen if the descriptions from a dozen earlier encyclopaedias are juxtaposed. Better by far take half a dozen worthy Finnish artists and turn to their portraits – to Albert Edelfelt's Karelians or skerry fisher folk; to Juho Rissanen's peasants (pictured *Fortune telling* or *Laying out the Dead*); to Hugo Simberg's thatch-haired, wrinkle-browed *Akseli* or to his potato girl; to Axel Gallén-Kallela's gipsy sketches and folk types from Vehmersalmi, Nurmijärvi, Kuusimäki, Kuolajärvi; to the vicars and country shop-keepers of Ero Järnefelt; to Pekka Halonen's mowers in the meadow, or men at mealtime; to the elect processions of Magnus Enckell's murals. Sculptors can also make their contribution: Gunnar Finne's *Engineer*, Sakari Tohka's

Britta, Väinö Aaltonen's *Aaro Hellaakoski* and *Jean Sibelius* are representative Finnish types. The presidents who stare down from schoolroom walls or whose faces give authority to the higher denominations of paper money provide another cross-section of Finnish profiles.

Most Finns are recognisably Finns because their country has not absorbed large numbers of immigrants. At the same time, the broad interior lake district where the Finns have been least disturbed, is an area of population outflow. Many of its tracts breed Finns with a remarkably similar cast of features. And today Finnish country areas combine a high birth-rate with a declining death-rate.

While cephalic or nasal indices, the form of a jaw or a cheek bone, the shape of an eye or an eyelid, the pigmentation of skin or the colour of hair may or may not be clues to remoter ancestry, contemporary physique is a surer guide to the vicissitudes through which a people have passed. Thus centuries of under-nourishment have affected the stature of many Finns. Biological reasons may help to explain the greater stature of the former inhabitants of the south-west and of the coast of Pohjanmaa; but the dramatic increase in the average height of Finns in the last generation is inseparable from dietary improvements. Again traditional deficiency diseases, such as rickets, have been brought under control – so that the misshapen bodies of older generations are rarely repeated in the young. Improved living conditions and new standards of hygiene are stamping out tuberculosis, so that sanatoria are emptying. Tuberculosis was still the principal killing disease of Tsarist Finland. Poets and artists have their few lines in encylopaedias to recall the fact that they succumbed to it, but most of those who contracted it in the dark, unhealthy homes of former times have no obituary. Only the novelist F. E. Sillanpää tells in the *Maid Silja* the story of many country people whose resistance was weakened by under-nourishment and over-exertion.

Other vicissitudes have left their mark. In historical times Finland can rarely have been without its army of those maimed in military combat. The wars of 1939–44 contributed the last heavy burden of wounded veterans – nearly 60,000 with permanent injuries. Wooden legs, armless sleeves and darkened glasses were more common in post-war Finland than in the England of 1919. Another cause of broken limbs and related casualties is the winter accidents resulting from ice and snow.

Today the streets of Finnish towns convey an impression of abundant and exuberant youth. Finland has more young people than old, and the modern nation of Finland is very much a country for the young. This, again, is inseparable from the nature of the countryside – and repeats the situation of Norway and Sweden. The ubiquity of water and of wild country has encouraged and permitted the release of energy. From an early age Finnish children learn to live with nature. There is also a cult of physical exercise – which is not entirely separable from national feeling. Pronounced seasonal contrasts encourage a range of sports not commonly enjoyed in more temperate climes. Water is so common that most boys rapidly learn to handle boats. The rise of winter sports in Finland is a saga in itself. It has undoubtedly made a significant contribution to the health of the nation – though people must be adequately fed before they can begin to think about squandering their calories on winter sporting. From the nursery slopes of the children's ice hill to the dizzy heights of hundreds of ski jumps, the country caters for youth in winter no less than in summer.

The time has almost passed when the young of Finland grow old before their time. Yet there remain plenty of Finnish faces which are heavily lined in middle age. The hardships of farmwork can still leave their mark in spite of the widespread availability of mechanical equipment. Most of the pioneers who opened up new land in the immediate post-war years show signs of their decade of hard labour. Some of them fought a double battle – that against the enemy on the eastern front and that against nature when clearing the forest. Thomas Hardy wrote of the Anglo-Saxon as 'the grey-haired enemy of the wood'. The epithet might apply equally to the tens of thousands of Finns who, during the last generation, have won new farmland from the forest. A number of observers have also written of the grey women of Finland. In rural areas they may still be encountered – prematurely aged with the double labour of work in the field and home and with frequent child-bearing. As one of a family of seventeen, Arvo Tuominen never remembered seeing his mother in bed in their Hämeenkyrö home. 'In the evening, we children went to sleep to the throbbing of the loom or the whir of the sewing-machine and the same sound wakened us in the morning. She could only have slept a few hours', he wrote in his autobiography.

The Problem of the Marchland State

A location on the northern frontiers of settlement in Europe suggests that isolation is a characteristic of Finland. Isolation is a theme which runs through Finland's story at large and in detail. At large, the country has lain aside from the main-stream of European contact and development. In detail, Finland has always had its isolated and inaccessible areas. Population has been and remains small in relation to surface area, so that there has been and remains ample opportunity to escape from the closed urban community into the open spaces. The hazards of the natural world are a risk to be taken by those who reject urban security, but Finns can cope with insecurity.

As a result, although the mid-twentieth century witnesses a retreat from the backwoods, small-scale advances into them proceed simultaneously. There is also a seasonal return to the isolation of the *korpi* or to the primitiveness of the *torppa*. Most Finns live in towns or urban areas today, but they are not by tradition a nation of town-dwellers. There is a widespread craving for isolation: for escape from the concrete (rather than ivory) tower of the town to the clapboard (rather than log) cabin of the countryside. Many Finns are natural solitaries. There remains a protective isolation for those who want it.

The Finns may have been principally concerned with the problem of winning a livelihood on the northern margins of settlement in Europe; but they have also been constantly beset by the relationships between their eastern and western neighbours. Both Russia, with its broad continental base to the east, and Sweden, with its diversified peninsula to the west, were politically organised before Finland. The experiences of Finland in history are inseparable from its buffer situation between them. Its fate has been partly an expression of the way in which their political energies have waxed and waned – in relation to Europe as well as in relation to each other. For Finland's maritime setting on the Baltic has also to be taken into consideration, and there have been other powers which for shorter rather than longer periods have challenged Russo-Swedish hegemony in this inland sea.

Not surprisingly, there has emerged in Finland a traditional view of the Baltic coast as a frontier of contact, across which commodities and ideas have been positively and generously exchanged. Contrastingly, the eastern and landward frontier has tended to be associated with memories of invasion, of armed conflict and of restraint. The

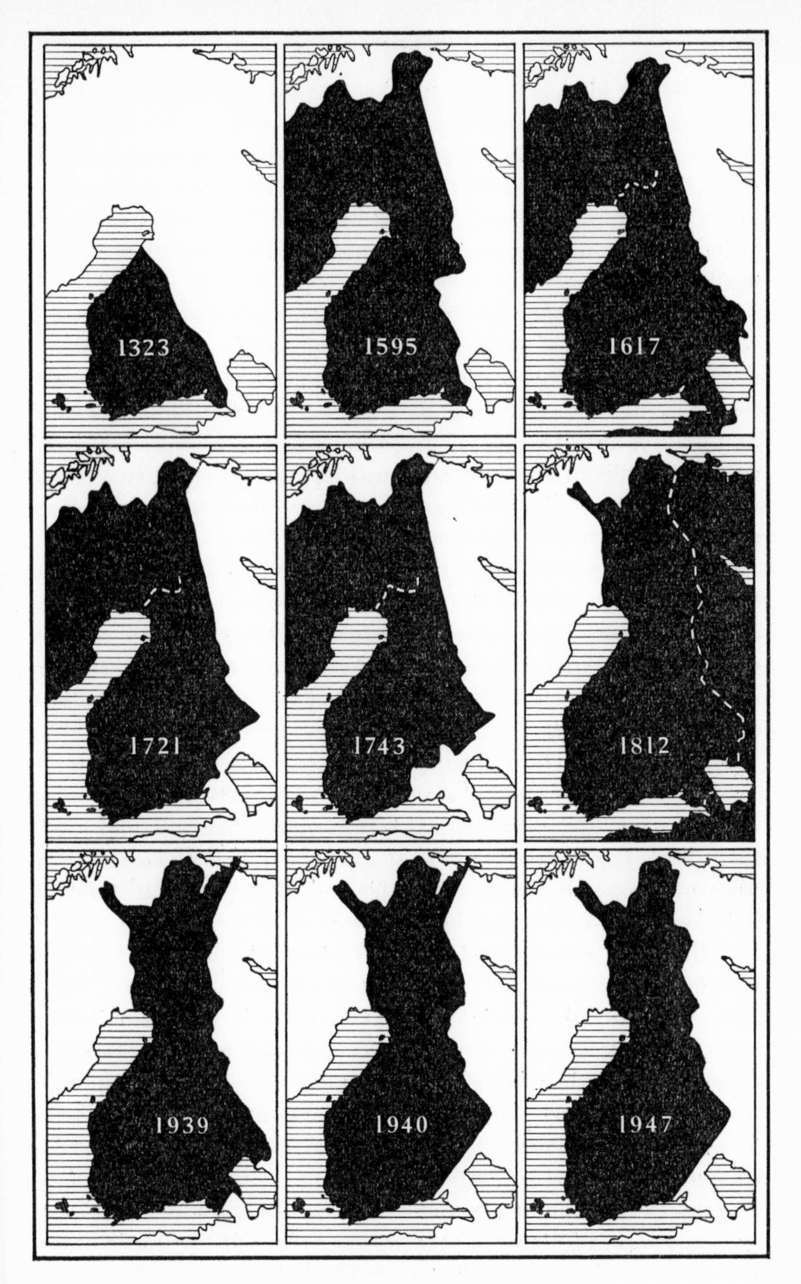

1. The Changing Shape of Finland

During the Swedish period it is difficult to give a precise form to the north-western frontier of Finland.

association of ideas is exaggerated because Finland's eastern frontier is also a part of the marchland of western Europe – coincident historically with a different religion, a different language and different script. Indeed, the first reference to Finland in any British document identified it as one of the outposts of western Christendom, ascribing to its monarch the responsibility of maintaining it inviolate against heathendom.

The land that became Finland was a part of Sweden from the twelfth century until 1809. Sweden emerged early as a strong maritime force and, in the days when movement across the sea was easier than movement across the land, it was natural that Finland should find itself absorbed by its more culturally and technically advanced western neighbour. By contrast it was separated from Russia by an extensive no-man's-land of forest, swamp and lake which strategists regarded as 'naturally demilitarised'.

Finland's political boundaries are traditionally unstable. During the course of its history, the shape of the country has changed frequently. Figure 1 indicates the principal changes. They are the consequences of an east European setting rather than those of a north European location. 'I am sorry, but we can do nothing about geography', Joseph Stalin is reputed to have said to President Paasikivi in 1940. The barbed apology accompanied substantial territorial demands. Yet Finland survived the loss – perhaps, also, because of geography. Finland's political fate has never been quite so harsh as that of its neighbours along the same parallels of longitude in eastern Europe. It is certainly explained in part by the country's isolation in the broader continental scene.

Perhaps the most critical fact in Finland's history was the final transfer of allegiance from Swedish to Russian sovereignty in 1809. From then until 1917 Finland was a Grand Duchy in personal union with the Tsar. The transfer occurred at a time when the forces of nationality were beginning to be felt in Europe. Their effects penetrated Finland slowly but surely. The nineteenth-century decline of Sweden and development of Russia eliminated any prospect of a Finnish reunion with Sweden. The spirit of the age encouraged Finland to turn misfortune to fortune by fostering a national identity. But national identity, in turn, was to be riven by inner differences before the independent state of Finland emerged from its tribulations. Ultimately divisions of opinion within – Swede versus Finn, White versus Red – were resolved in the face of pressures without. The resulting state bears two names. The outer world calls it Finland, in accordance with the old Scandinavian practice. Finnish-speaking Finns call it Suomi, strictly speaking *Suomen tasvalta.* Since recorded history, they have always called their country Suomi, though the origins of this patronym are as debated as the origins of the Finns themselves.

The Recognition of Finland

Finland became independent on 6 December 1917. Its political recognition was a slow process – largely because of the international entanglements which complicated the Finnish position. But the independence of the country was recognised by Germany, Sweden, France, Norway and Denmark by 23 January 1918, by the U.S.A. and Great Britain on 3 May 1919. At the Treaty of Tartu on 14 October 1920, the U.S.S.R. confirmed the allocation of an Arctic corridor to Petsamo, thereby according to Finland the most ample territorial proportions attained in its history.

Having gained formal recognition the next task was to establish Finnish identity in the comity of nations. Finland was only one among a group of new European states which had been born of the principle of self-determination and which were seeking to make their impact. The mid-twentieth century, with its studied care of national images, its public relations officers and its mass media, is a world away from the early years of independence, when flags and banners, music and selected literature were the principal features of the propagandists.

A commercial flag for Finnish shipping was suggested by Oulu ship-owners as early as 1862. The Finnish flag, a blue cross on a white ground, its colours proposed by Topelius many years before, was adopted in 1918. Although it is with nineteenth-century imperialists that flag-waving is most commonly associated, the younger nations lack nothing in the art. Their motives are naturally different. The Finnish flag flutters at the slightest ceremonial excuse, and the streets of Helsinki are slotted to receive their flag poles. The President's flag supports a rampant lion in the centre of the cross – a lion the earliest example of which is claimed to be on the arms of Gustavus Vasa's monument (*c.* 1570) in Uppsala cathedral, though there is mediaeval evidence of its appearance on the arms of the province of Finland Proper. The first postage stamps were to bear it and the first Finnish money. Provincial flags and coats-of-arms also play their role. The red and black flag of Karelia and the upraised weapons of its coat-of-arms are still powerful symbols. The Ålanders, sensitive about the use of the Finnish flag, pleaded successfully for the use of their own blue, yellow and red colours in 1954.

Music follows the flag, with national songs making an impact independently of national anthems. Sometimes the national anthem is adopted from among the existing corpus of national songs: sometimes, it has been composed specially. Finland's national anthem is not as well-known outside Finland as Jean Sibelius's *Finlandia*. Its Swedish words – *Vårt land* (Our land) – were written as a poem by J. L. Runeberg in 1846 before Fredrick Pacius composed the tune in 1848. In Finnish translation it bears the title *Maamme*.

Finnish concern about the way in which foreigners regarded their country is old-established. The editors of Finland's first newspaper, *Åbo Tidning*, reviewed a number of foreign texts in the 1780s and criticised them sharply for misrepresentation. 'We no longer live in the time of Tacitus', commented the most sardonic of them. C. C. Böcker in his statistical plan for a survey of Finland from the 1820s, included in his questionnaire items on what the outside world thought of his home country. Finnish educationalists were already emphasising the need to present a picture of Finland to the Finns a hundred years ago. Zachris Topelius, in his role as historian, never failed to impress the significance of the map for this purpose. The copy of M. K. Broström's relief map, dated 1858–59, that he used hangs on the wall of Oulu University. The map converted an infinity of scenic fragments into something finite and comprehensible. Finland became a shape in the mind's eye.

Given this interest it is not surprising that the Finns were the first people to produce a national atlas. The purpose of the *Atlas of Finland* (1899) was more than that of mere domestic enlightenment. It aimed to bring to the attention of the world the characteristics of Finland and the ability of its scientists to produce an informed survey of the land where they lived. In this, it achieved considerable success. Altogether four successive atlases have been produced – the latest in 1960.

The atlases played their own modest role in the international campaign for support prosecuted by the Finns during the difficult period of Russian pressure in the early years of the century. At this time, a not inconsiderable flair for public relations began to show itself. The Finns had their own pavilion at the Paris World Fair of

1900. In 1910, while still a Grand Duchy of Russia, Finland openly invited a party of British newspaper correspondents to examine its domestic circumstances. While without independent status, it was also permitted to send observers to the Inter-Parliamentary Union.

As with the other Scandinavian countries, Finland makes an impact out of proportion to its size and numbers. There are both positive and negative sides to this. Positively, the impact is rooted partly in the tradition of cultivating public relations; partly in the wide currency achieved by its artistic, intellectual and material contributions. Negatively, it springs from Finland's location next to a giant neighbour whose actions are always of world concern and whose second city of Leningrad is on Finland's doorstep. Fenno-Russian relations are a minor barometer upon which pressures of interest to many other areas are registered. In this system of pressures Finland has lived precariously but circumspectly since the Second World War. The studied care with which it contrives to maintain harmony with the U.S.S.R. may be interpreted as a new facet of an old policy.

The Public and The Private Face

Finland, then, has been born in an arena where there is an interplay of three principal influences. The strength with which physical and human forces from the west, east and north assert themselves varies in both the short term and the long term. Land and people continually mirror these variations – regionally as well as in the country at large.

In the physical environment three related facts have entered the conscious and subconscious thinking of the Finns. They are water, wood and winter. Finland, balancing seascapes and lakescapes, has been called an amphibious country. Its peoples have been distinguished historically from others of their ethnographic group by this association with water. James Latham, in his *Races of the Russian Empire* (London, 1856), wrote of the Finns as 'Ugrians in possession of a seaboard'. The seaboard is in many respects the public face of Finland. Its peoples tend to be outward-looking. The private face of Finland is turned inland; it belongs to the lakescapes. Time was when there was an element of truth in the division of the country into *Kirja Suomi* and *Runo Suomi* – the formal, bookish (and book-keeping) coastlands focusing on the metropolitan south-west, and the interior lands of oral tradition that were moved powerfully by regional loyalties.

The Finn of the interior no longer differs in literacy from his coastal compatriot, but he is pre-eminently a man of the forest. The Finnish word *metsänäjä* gathers together all the overtones associated with an existence in the greenwood – from lumbering to charcoal burning, from trapping to hunting. At the same time, as Finns have learned to live on the water and in the forest, they have accustomed themselves to cold – a characteristic personified by Zachris Topelius as 'the old giant of the north'.

Side by side with the natural features that have been born of inheritance are those in the human environment that derive from superimposition. Finns have been conscious of their relative weakness to resist the control of more powerful and better organised neighbours. As a direct consequence, Finland has suffered historical shifts of allegiance. Moreover, it has been subjected to geographical division. Finland is accordingly 'a little Balkanised' – with two languages, two Churches and pronounced ethnographic diversity. But if the divisions of the past are reflected in the present, contemporary Finland has also capitalised on the cultural diversity that they have imparted.

The features and symbols by which modern Finland is recognised are expressions of a small population operating in an environment of restricted opportunity. The chapters that follow will consider the way in which the Finnish homeland (*kotimaa*) has become the fatherland (*isänmaa*), and how it is supported and sustained.

Chapter 2

The Time Before the Records

The Pre- and Proto-Finns

There are three sources from which it is possible to glean a little about the 'pre- and proto-Finns' (as the Scottish ethnologist, John Abercrombie, chose to call them). First, there is the thin scatter of relics that have been left in the ground and on the ground. Secondly, there is the abundant, if fragmentary, folk poetry, that has been passed on orally from generation to generation. Thirdly, both the form of the language and the nature of the vocabulary are a guide to earlier Finnish links and associations.

The peopling of Finland has been less complex than that of many European countries; partly because it occupies a peripheral location in Europe and stands aside from any of the continent's major cross-roads; partly because of its somewhat discouraging climate; partly because the period over which settlement has taken place has been relatively short. Yet, although by external standards its prehistory is relatively simple and of short duration, men have lived in the territory that is now Finland for fully 8,000 years. Over this period, the ancestors of the modern nation entered by way of a variety of different routes from a variety of different places. They brought with them and received after their arrival a range of techniques. The nature of their entry into and occupation of the land is only beginning to be unravelled.

It will be clear from the introductory remarks on the evolution of Finland that the background to the daily life of its prior inhabitants cannot be conceived in terms of the contemporary geography. The shape of the land, the nature of the surrounding sea, the climate and the vegetation were all different from those in the familiar environment of today. Each phase in the evolution of the peopling of Finland has had its own distinctive physical setting. In re-creating the past, not only must the amenities of the present be stripped away, but the land must be reclothed with its earlier flora and fauna. At the same time, the whole tempo of contact and communication must be slowed down.

While the peopling of Finland may have been a more straightforward process than that of most European countries, investigations into Finland's prehistoric past are less easy than in many of them. There are two principal reasons for this. First, Finland's early inhabitants were thinly scattered and only left scanty evidence behind them. Secondly, the evidence is generally less visible than in countries where the landscape has been cleared of its original vegetation. For example the greater part of Finland's prehistoric remains are less visible than those of Denmark, where so many are clearly outlined on the face of the land or are detectable in the soil shadings and crop markings that stand out on air photographs. Finland's prehistoric sites are commonly cloaked by woodland.

Into the story of its prehistoric settlement are written features which continue as characteristics of present-day Finland. First, is its situation tributary to the Baltic Sea. Secondly, in and through this sea, it has sensed a powerful interplay of eastern and western European influences. Each influence has played a dominant or recessive role in turn – the impact being traceable in stones, bones, metals or artifacts of other materials. Thirdly, in the past as in the present, Finland has suffered deficiencies of strategic materials and luxury goods. Much that was fundamental to prehistoric cultural expression was drawn from outside the area – flint, slate, copper, tin, amber, gold, even durable wood. From the beginning of its settlement Finland has accordingly experienced dependence upon outside sources of supply.

Most of the influences affecting Finland have been seaborne. The western influences have been primarily of Scandinavian origin; the eastern have derived principally from the east Baltic lands. Eastern continental influences have affected Finland chiefly through the lands to its immediate south. Not until the so-called period of folk wandering (from *c.* A.D. 600–700) is there any significant evidence of trading links with central and eastern Russia.

The sea has borne a succession of colonial settlers to Finland. It is more likely that they entered in small groups than that there was any large migration. The successive coastal settlers have received and transmitted materials and techniques from overseas rather than disseminating their own products and ideas. Finland was not a hearth of diffusion in prehistoric times. Its coastal zone has shared with varying degrees of intensity in the waves of cultural diffusion common to the lands surrounding the Baltic Sea, but their impact has been weak in the northern and eastern interior. Increase of population and expansion of the occupied area have not been continuous. The answer to changes in population is probably to be sought in physical rather than human explanations. The clash of arms cannot have sounded often in prehistoric Finland, for there was space enough for all. But any minor cyclical changes in climate were likely to have a disproportionately hard impact upon the country as a settlement area.

The chronology of Finland's prehistory differs from that of western Europe and from that of the Mediterranean basin. For the most part, there is a delayed action which is largely the result of location and of environment. The terms of reference employed by the Finns are roughly the same as those employed in the neighbouring Scandinavian lands, but there are Finnish subdivisions which bear unfamiliar names.

The Evidence of the Earth

The earliest known settlements in Finland date from the Mesolithic Stone Age of northern Europe, somewhat earlier than 7000 B.C. They took place in a tundra environment, with a background to life similar to that of the earliest Danish settlers described by Johannes V. Jensen in the first volume of his novel *The Long Journey*. The oldest artifacts so far discovered have been from the parish of Askola near to Porvoo on the Gulf of Finland. A few scattered relics from peatlands in Kirkkonummi, Heinola and Antrea are also given a similar dating. Archaeologists associate these oldest discoveries with those of the Maglemose period in Denmark, the Komsa period of north Norway and the relics of the Kunda culture of the south-east Baltic. The earliest known finds merge imperceptibly into those of a culture named after Suomusjärvi, a site in south-western Finland. They are fairly widely scattered, with a tendency to concentrate along former shorelines of the Gulf of Finland, at sites between 90–130 metres above sea level. The distribution of the simple features common to this culture suggests that the sea was its route of diffusion.

The economy of the succeeding Neolithic Stone Age retained the same bases of hunting and gathering. There was hunting for seals (*Phoca greenlandica*, as is evident from a skeleton recovered in Närpes, Ostrobothnia) as well as for woodland animals and birds.

Fish, berries, nuts, roots and mushrooms were basic to diet. There was no agriculture and there were no domesticated animals other than the dog. But the Finnish Neolithic period was distinguished by the production of ceramics – after which its culture is commonly called the Comb Ceramic. Most of the ceramics recovered have affinities in form and design with those of an area extending to the south-east Baltic and eastwards into Russia as far as the Urals. It is not unlikely that the production of the ceramics from which the culture takes its name originated in the Ukraine. Although evidence of the Comb Ceramic culture has been assembled from places as widely separated as Åland and Rovaniemi, its fullest expression is found in Karelia, especially around the shores of the former Finnish parts of Lake Ladoga. Sufficient evidence has been left by the Neolithic peoples to enable the reconstruction of dwelling sites, though their graves have only yielded scanty information.

While the Comb Ceramic bowls two feet deep and fifteen inches across may be the most impressive relics there is a diversity of others. There are flint tools and arrow-heads deriving from both Russian sources (possibly the Valdai hills) and south Scandinavian sources; green slate, from the Onega area, has been worked into tools, handles, and ornaments, such as bear and elk heads. There are also slate implements of Scandinavian origin. Dolls and figurines of clay, sandstone and wood have survived, and a scatter of wooden artifacts. Oak sticks and staves are the most numerous among them. The parish of Ylistaro has yielded the runner of a sledge; while wooden spoons, made of Cembra pine from north Russia, provide clues to the extent of trading contacts or migration. Amber beads, possibly drawn from Jutland and east Prussia, have been found in all parts of Finland. Bone harpoons and arrow-heads are less common.

In their search for the origins of the Finnish people some students have invested the Comb Ceramic culture with a greater significance. They have suggested that its distribution coincided with the presumed area of early Fenno-Ugrian settlement. The culture prevailed from about 3000 until 1800 B.C., longer than the time span from early Viking times until the present day.

The end of the Stone Age witnessed a swing from mainland to maritime influences. Its most striking expression is seen in the period of Boat Axe culture (*c.* 1900–1600 B.C.). The relics of this intrusive culture, with its crouched burials and finely polished boat axes (made principally from a diabase and emanating from the Pori-

Rauma area), would seem to represent the advance of a seafaring people into the territory of a declining indigenous Neolithic settlement. The distribution of relics from the Boat Axe culture is essentially coastal, focuses upon the south-west, and stretches from the Kymi river on the Gulf of Finland to Kokkola in Ostrobothnia. This culture was one of the features that helped to fashion the differences in development between south-west Finland and the north and east interior.

Partly as a result of Finland's location between the Scandinavian and Russian hearths of dissemination, the differentiation was continued into the Bronze Age (*c.* 1300–500 B.C.). The earlier stages of the Bronze Age were to be characterised by a generous distribution of burial mounds, mostly circular in shape, constructed of boulders and situated upon heights of land facing the sea. Some 3,000 of these tumuli have been identified. They rim the entire length of the Finnish sea coast. They are removed in location from the Stone Age settlements, largely as a result of the change in sea level. The tumuli include some boat-shaped mounds and sites, similar to their Swedish counterparts. Remains of dwelling sites are uncommon. One of the best examples may be seen at Otterböle on the Åland island of Kökar, in a rocky cleft lying above the present fishing village. The plan of the site is readily detectable, though it has yielded little apart from fragments of pottery. Finds from some sites, for example Maaninka in Savo, suggest independent Finnish designs and castings.

The age of iron was slow to make an impact and the delay is inseparable from climatic considerations. Archaeological evidence for the half-century preceding the Roman Iron Age is rare. But during the first four centuries A.D., distant though it was from the cultural hearth of the western Mediterranean, Finland felt the influence of Roman civilisation. The remarks of Tacitus on the Finns as Finns may be dismissed, but the territory loosely called Germania, though but marginal to the provinces of the Roman Empire, was capable of transmitting its effects. The Vistula lands in particular became a focus of Iron Age culture – a fact inseparable from their situation on the north–south amber trading route. There was both a strengthening and a stabilisation of settlement in western Finland during the Roman Iron Age. Evidence from burial mounds suggests that there was a fairly steady infiltration of small groups of immigrants from across the Gulf of Finland. They may even have included merchants coming across to barter, as a find of older Roman Iron

Age implements and weapon heads at Malmsby in Pernå parish would indicate. Artifacts of foreign origin remain dominant during the period, but increase in variety. Weapons of war such as double- and single-bladed swords, spearheads, bucklers, knives and axes take precedence over implements of peace, such as reaping hooks and shears. Bronze prevails for the production of ornaments such as necklets, cylindrical bracelets and armbands, brooches and pendants. And products remote from the Baltic trading area begin to make their appearance – a glass drinking horn, probably shaped in the workshops of Cologne, is yielded by a burial site at Soukiainen; a bronze wine cup, bearing the inscription *L. Ansius Dindorus*, more certainly produced at Capua in Italy, is discovered at Pääkköönmäki in Vähäkyrö. The first Roman coins appear – a silver *dinar* on Sagu island and copper coins near Nykarleby, both from the time of Hadrian (A.D. 117–38).

Settlement sites began to stabilise in the later centuries of the Roman Iron Age. By then, the first seed grains had been introduced and there seems to have been incipient working of domestic bog ore. But there was little encouragement to settled farming, because rotational burn-beating of the woodlands provided a more rewarding and more easily worked seedbed than tilled land. By the late Roman Iron Age, coastal Finland was fully integrated with the Baltic arena. In addition to weapons, implements and such essential items as flint stones, Finnish exports of the time permitted the import of heavier ornaments. These included buckles and brooches from east Prussia, finer gold ornaments (from plain and spiral finger rings to at least one handsome snake-clasp chaplet) from yet more distant places, and enamelled metalware from Estonia, a product the technique of which immigrants introduced eventually into south-west Finland itself.

The occurrence of all these relics indicates a more vigorous occupation of the land, and there was active expansion into interior south-west Finland from the end of the Roman Iron Age onwards. The Kumo valley was the principal route of penetration. The distribution of burial mounds, readily dated from their contents, shows initial movement towards the area of present-day Tampere and southern Häme. Another concentration of rounded tumuli in the hinterland of Vaasa indicates a second and independent centre of development during the same period. The areas are commonly referred to respectively as the west Finnish and the south Bothnian cultural districts.

The break-up of the Roman Empire had no great direct consequences for Finland, but during the associated and ensuing centuries of folk wandering, the population of Finland grew apace. Both natural causes and immigration played their parts. In Finnish chronology, the period of the folk wanderings is divided into an older (*c.* A.D. 400–600) and a younger (*c.* A.D. 600–800) stage. The latter corresponds to the Swedish Vendel period (named after a site in Uppland) and is near contemporary with the English period identified by finds at Sutton Hoo. Evidence of the Folk Wandering Age is especially rich in west Finland, Ostrobothnia and the main island of Åland. It is even speculated that master craftsmen may have settled temporarily in Finland, to produce their highly individual Germanic ornamentation on button, brooch and buckle.

Some indication of the degree of population growth during this phase of the Iron Age is provided by the graveyards. In the older settled areas, isolated or clustered mounds are replaced or accompanied by concentrations of burial mounds. In west Finland, for example, a single site in Eura parish has 270 burial mounds and another at Rapola in Sääksmäki has about 110. But it is in the Åland archipelago, and especially in the main island of Åland, that the greatest density occurs. There are probably 10,000 burial mounds on the main island, and they occur in nearly 200 known localities. Some sites contain several hundred mounds and some must have been used throughout the better part of 500 years. In addition at least 200 Iron Age house sites have been located in Åland. These features are an integral part of the Ålandic scene and they give to it the same feeling of antiquity that prevails in the Swedish island of Gotland. In the vernacular the burial sites are known as *ättenhögar* (ancestral mounds). Limited excavation suggests affinities with counterparts in central Sweden.

The pressure of population growth no less than the superior attractions of hunting in interior Finland prompted a parallel though distinctly less spectacular colonisation of the more easterly parts of the lake district. The movement is discerned in the west Finnish grave forms found in Sysmä, Heinola and on the Karelian isthmus. Although ornaments recovered from Eura parish suggest contact with the Kama and Perm areas of Russia, Baltic controls prevailed. Southern Ostrobothnia and the Kokemäki valley found themselves drawn into a common unit with lower Swedish Norrland, and they may have had some contact with the North Sea by way of the Storlien gap and Trondheimfiord. Military equipment, almost exclusively Germanic in design, accounts for a substantial part of Finnish Iron Age finds. There are occasional silver ornaments. A fine brooch from Korpolaismäki near Turku has an east Baltic form; while animal designs on buttons and clasps found at Karja in Uusimaa and Ylistaro in Ostrobothnia, suggest a link with the North Sea area. But the continuingly peripheral position of Finland in the Baltic arena is clear from the poverty of precious metalware at a time when the graveyards of Gotland, of Öland and of the Swedish provinces of Västergotland and Södermanland contained so much.

Change was in the air. The Baltic Sea, which had been marginal to European activity until nearly the end of the first millennium A.D., became central to it with the rise of the Vikings. In Finnish terminology, the Viking period dates from A.D. 800–1050. The Baltic coastlands and islands became points of receipt and departure in their own right. Finland and its inhabitants shared in the trading and raiding. At the same time its archipelagos and coastal channels emerged as routeways of consequence in their own right. They lay between Birka, Lake Mälaren's focal point of settlement and exchange, and the more northern routeways into Russia. Finland's coastal routes were also only a short sail from Gotland and, by way of the Bothnian Gulf, opened up Lapland trading points.

Merchants came to Finland from farther afield. Possibly the Frisians and Rhine mouth sailors, who came regularly to Birka, travelled on to its shores. Their heavy *Kugger* remained as familiar vessels in Finnish eyes for generations. Some of the place-names which recall them (Kuggsundet, Kuggevik, Kuggholm) probably date from the Viking period, while they are recorded in wall paintings from mediaeval churches such as Korppo and Finström in Åland. Among commodities entering Finland were an increasing variety of refined metal goods. More than fifty swords of Rhenish origin have been attributed to the period. Improved bills, reaping hooks and shears are complemented by scissors and flax combs. Wooden ploughshares are iron-tipped, so are spades. A site in Kumo parish has yielded weights and scales. Another, in Åland's Saltvik, has produced some fine silver pins of Anglo-Norse origin. There are also hoards of coins, which indicate the extent of broader Baltic trading activities. They have been recovered from sites scattered along Finland's south coast from Åland to the Karelian isthmus. The coins bear Arabian as well as German and Anglo-Saxon imprints. One of the richest hoards discovered was at Bertby in Saltvik. It consisted of more than 800 coins contained in a bronze flask of oriental origin. Not surprisingly, the people who had enough enterprise to acquire these implements and monies expanded inland as well as operating beyond the seas. In particular, they pioneered Savo province.

In keeping with the spirit of the time, the Younger Iron Age had its fortified sites. *Linna* (= fort), which is the place-name associated with them, is clearly among the oldest Finnish toponymical elements. The fortified places were usually located on sites that were naturally protected. The two main concentrations occur in south-west Finland and along the north shore of Lake Ladoga, between the parishes of Kurkijoki and Impilahti. The main island of Åland has at least half a dozen, and another loose concentration occurs along the shores of the south-western lake system tributary to the Kumo river. These hill forts (as they might be more familiarly known in Britain) sometimes occupy heavily wooded heights composed of glacial materials, as with twin ramparted Rapola in Sääksmäki parish; sometimes, they sit on bald rocky heights, as with Vanhalinna in Lundö near Turku; sometimes, they look down from powerful eminences as at Sulkava in south Savo. Sometimes, they have an island site and are protected with water and rough boulder walls, as with Tiurinlinna on a Vuoksi river island in the parish of Räisälä. The fortified sites have made a continuing impression upon men throughout the intervening years. So, too, have the stone circles that occur in a number of places in south Finland and which may be from the same period. They are generally regarded as former meeting-places rather than the relics of burial sites. The Younger Iron Age, a marginally heathen period, also bequeathed a scatter of offertory stones. Not surprisingly, some of the sites of their occurrence are traditionally associated with the devil (in Finnish, *hiisi*) and his works. The place-name element *hiisi* is frequently attached to natural landscape features. So, too, are the names of some of the early deities.

There was some differentiation between the expression of the Iron Age in south-western Finland and that in the south-east. The climax of development in the south-east was around Kexholm, with a fair measure of continuous and inter-linked settlement for a hundred miles eastwards to Sortavala. The settlements were stimulated by close trading links with Novgorod, by way of Lake Ladoga and the Volkov river. The proto-Karelians who lived here became

Finland's *coureurs de bois*, gathering together the harvest of squirrel, sable and other skins by their thousand and trading them through the mart of Novgorod. It was an expansive period and outliers of Karelian settlement were established north in Savo, west in parishes as far as Nastola, south in Ingria and east towards the White Sea lands. Local craftsmen, fashioning their ornaments, not only elaborated indigenous designs such as the horseshoe, chain and spiral, but beat into their motifs the exotic shapes of acanthus and palm leaf. Their work represented the farthest north echoes of Byzantium at that time – and perhaps the bird-shaped pendants, trailing clusters of bells, had yet more distant origins. (The designs of the Karelian Iron Age have been adopted by those who fashion present-day 'Kalevala' jewellery.)

Already before the end of the Viking period, the signs of Christianity were appearing in Finland. Ninth- and tenth-century swords are sometimes chased with crosses and at least one has been recovered that bears a Christian inscription – *Innomnedmn* (*In nomine Domini*). Such weapons are from the same time as Ansgar's missionary journeys into the Baltic (A.D. 830, 850), during which he reported upon a flourishing city, deemed to have been Birka, on the island of Björkö in the Swedish Lake Mälaren (then, still a gulf of the Baltic). So, too, it would appear, are silver crucifixes, such as that inscribed with the image of the Virgin Mary found in Taskula or the superbly chased cross from Halikko. It is difficult to determine whether relics of this character were carried by the vanguard of early converts or were simply the plunder brought back from Viking forays.

Christianity did not exactly arrive in Finland at the point of the sword, yet the formal conversion of the Finns was not achieved without resort to arms. The so-called 'Time of the Crusades' lasted for a full century in western Finland (A.D. 1050–1150) and much longer in Karelia and eastern Finland (A.D. 1050–1300). It is usually dealt with as prehistory because historical documents rarely refer directly to it. A considerable body of legends has grown up about it. Among them is that which centres upon Bishop Henry – a twelfth-century martyr of the Church of Finland at the hand of 'the worst of the pagans', Lalli. The stone church built 'on the sands of Nousiainen', and the ark in which his presumed relics repose in Uppsala cathedral, may still be seen, but the incident rests upon no more secure foundation than the copy of a folk poem recorded in the seventeenth century. Documentary evidence of precise crusades into the heathen territory of Finland is equally absent. Nevertheless several generations of Danish and Swedish churchmen and warriors were probably engaged in the expeditions. Among the crusaders who gave their lives was Egil. He died in Tavastia – Tafstalonti, as it is pricked out on a runic stone raised at Hämlinge near Gävle in Sweden by his brother – sometime between A.D. 1030–50.

In the context of the broader Baltic arena, it was logical that there should be an advance into Finland by the Swedes. The contest between the eastern and western branches of Christendom was partly played out in Finland. Excavation of burial sites slowly reveals the distribution of early adherents to the different Churches. Those who belonged to the western faith were buried with their crucifixes and amulets of readily identified design, those of the eastern faith might be recognised by a Russian Byzantine cross or a miniature ikon. Still others, conforming to west–east Christian burial, nevertheless retained their pagan grave goods. Before Swedish records are available, there are early thirteenth-century records from Novgorod that confirm the baptism of Karelians into the Orthodox faith. The oldest Finnish words dealing with Christianity – cross (*risti*) and pagan (*pakana*) – are of Russian provenance. Possibly the peaceful penetration of monastic cells proceeded simultaneously from west and east before temporal power entered the scene. The Swedish forces that campaigned in Finland probably included few recruits from beyond the Baltic – no one comparable to Chaucer's knight, for example, who had 'reysed in Lettowe'. But the equipment of the 'crusaders' derived from Europe as well as from the homeland. It is seen in the religious motifs engraved on the swords, in the ornamented battle-axes and in a solitary knightly shield, found in Nousiainen and regarded as of Norman design.

At the time of the Christianisation of Finland there was little permanent settlement save in the southern third of the country. Occupied Finland lay essentially in the south-west of a line linking present-day Vaasa with Sortavala. And even within this frame, permanent settlement was thinly scattered. Back from the coast the modest concentrations of people were separated by extensive waste-lands. Their settlements were oriented to the lakes and river valleys. The two principal groups of inhabitants were centred in Häme and south Karelia. The former bore the name *Hämelaiset* or Tavast-landers; the latter, *Karjalaiset* or Karelians. The level of culture was similar to both groups, with minor variations as already indicated in Karelia. At the time of the Swedish advance into Finland, native Finns had little if any form of administrative or political cohesion. There may have been some loose local tribal organisations, but there was no military organisation. There may have been trading places at which people intermittently assembled. Hiitola, with its concentration of burial mounds, suggests the beginnings of a village, but there was nothing in size approaching a town. The social hierarchy was little developed. The farmer was basic to a peasant society in which some farmers were naturally richer than others; but in which there were no aristocrats. The association of weapons with burial sites implies no more than that the owner was a free man who might bear arms. Feudalism did not penetrate far into Finland, though in the marchlands of east Finland there were forays by Russians (Novgorodians) in search of slaves.

Although north Finland lacked settlement apart from its Lappish communities (the total population of which is more likely to have numbered hundreds than thousands), there was evidently movement to it and through it during the 'crusade' period. A site at Marikkovaara near Rovaniemi, for example, has yielded a sword and a fine damascened spearhead from the time. Treasure trove, consisting of silver coins, bracelets, buckles and collars, has been found in Kuusamo. Silver collars have been discovered in Ylitornio. Again, the discoveries can only be understood in a broader context. North Finland formed a part of the transitional territory between Finnmark and the south-western reaches of the White Sea, which was known as Biarmia, the country of the hunters. Biarmia, or Bjarmland, is familiar from both the Norse sagas and from the Journals of Orosius as reported by King Alfred. It was a territory into which outsiders conducted trading – and raiding – sorties. Swedes who moved into Finland and Finns themselves shared in these activities. And there emerged a specialist group of indigenous traders, possibly concentrated in the western interior, to whom the name *Pirkkalaiset* (Sw. *Birkarlar*) was given. Place names such as Birknäs, Pirkholm, and Pirkkala (in Harjavalta parish) recall them.

The foregoing seven or eight pages cover seven or eight thousand years of Finland's prehistory. The story remains sketchy. Yet limited though the discoveries may be upon which it is based, they are sufficient to provide at least the main outlines of Finland's early evolution. Far more remains to be revealed than is known already. In many cases, this is even true of known burial and settlement sites. Åland provides the outstanding example, with less than five per cent of its Iron Age burial mounds and less than a third of its house sites investigated.

What is the relevance of archaeological investigation to the modern Finnish nation? It confuses as much as it clarifies the issue of Finnish ancestry, but two points are clear. First, unless some waves of immigrants were much more powerful on their arrival and more prolific after their arrival in Finland, it is not easy to explain the present-day Finn as springing from anything other than a somewhat mixed stock. Secondly, though they may raise as many problems as they solve, prehistoric remains add a new dimension to the appreciation of the land that was to become Finland. The fragments of early life and art in Finland, cased behind glass and mounted beside speculative time charts, push the story of the occupation of the land back fully eight thousand years. At the very least they underline the integration of Finland with lands bordering the Baltic Sea, convey a sense of union with their historical evolution and indicate a continuingly common heritage with them. The future may reveal other sources of information that suggest closer Finnish links with the continental heartland than with the neighbouring coastlands. If that is so, it seems unlikely that the links will belong to the more recent centuries of prehistoric experience.

The evidence of the earth has been seized upon by amateur enthusiasts and sifted by professionals. Observations go back to the foundation of the Swedish *Collegium Antiquitatis* in 1667, to which twenty Finnish parish priests sent returns. Topographical literature from the succeeding century incorporated many references to local curiosities, from interior hill forts to seashore labyrinths or mizz-mazes. While J. R. Aspelin is generally acknowledged as the founder of academic archaeology in Finland, Carl Axel Gottlund also initiated a record of relics in the mid-nineteenth century. Gottlund's enquiries were part and parcel of his concern with Finnish ethnography and his antiquarian interests belonged to his later years. The manuscript volumes of his incomplete parish-by-parish survey indicate the energy that he devoted to his self-appointed task. The contents of his notebooks range from proposals for a grand tour of the prehistoric sights of Denmark and Sweden to the practical details of equipment assembled for field surveys in Finland – compass, umbrella, thigh boots (for use in traversing swamps), a saddle ('to ride through woods and heaths') and an English spade. The tightly-packed observations, with their scattered field sketches, might indicate a magpie-like mind, but they also provide some measure of the variety of remains that could be gathered from Finland's past. Little by little, they were mustered by Aspelin in the National Museum or protected as antiquities in the field.

Archaeology is a relatively young field of enquiry in Finland. If it owes much to Scandinavian example, it stands to benefit much from Russian discovery. For the pre- and proto-Finns, no less than their descendants, can only be fully appreciated in the broadest possible Baltic context.

The Songs of the People

The story of this field of enquiry belongs to Chapter 5, but it is relevant to juxtapose with the archaeological remains another body of Finnish material that has its roots in the prehistoric period. These are the Finnish collections of folklore, heroic poems and epic songs. They may not unfittingly be called voices from the past, because they belong to a pre-literate people and have been transmitted orally through successive generations. They consist of an extensive and extraordinary collection of material which has been painstakingly assembled throughout more than a century and a half. Best known is *Kalevala*, the collection assembled and arranged by Elias Lönnrot. It is only a fragment of the whole; but its fifty *runot*—or poems—totalling over 22,000 lines have been most thoroughly analysed. Students of language and literature believe *Kalevala* to contain three essentially different constituents. In order of age they consist of the proto-Kalevalan poems, the epics and lyrics that form the core of *Kalevala* and the concluding fragments which constitute the mediaeval Kalevalan poems. In an attempt to give some temporal setting to the Kalevalan sections of the text, the standard history of Finnish literature (*Suomen kirjallisuus historia*) employs as illustrative material archaeological finds from the period A.D. 600–1200. The span of years is important, because in all assessments of the contents of *Kalevala*, the accumulation and change of centuries must be remembered.

The oral poetry of the Finnish-speaking peoples, an object of curiosity for at least two hundred years, is undoubtedly deeply rooted in antiquity. The richest collections of it derive from eastern and south-eastern Finland and beyond the border in the Russian provinces of Archangel and Olonetz (present-day Karelian S.S.R.). The origins of the poems and their migrations have been the subject of much scholarly debate. The materials are evidently of widely diverse origins in time and place and it is this fact which gives to them their extraordinary richness. The bulk of them are pre-Christian, but pre-Christian in Karelia could mean as late as the thirteenth century. Some of the poems appear to have had their origins in south-western Finland and to have been preserved in the interior fastnesses after having retreated before intrusive peoples. Other poems are probably of remoter eastern origin and have affinities with the folk materials of related Finnic peoples in Russia.

The events and adventures of *Kalevala* took place in a setting that is described in considerable detail, for the singers of the Kalevalan poems had a good eye for landscape. In addition to an acuteness of observation, the poems reflect the attachment to locality that remains an enduring Finnish quality. To gather together the manifold references to the country of Kaleva is to sense something of the mediaeval appreciation of the natural scene. The word pictures in *Kalevala* are the Finnish counterparts to the miniatures painted in western Europe's books of hours or embroidered on its tapestries.

The country was believed to be the creation of an all-embracing water mother. The poet had been able to witness the geological process of land being born of water. He had seen 'marshy land' emerging first from sea and lake to be succeeded in turn by islands in 'a sea of swamps', and by 'points and capes a thousand' thrusting out their 'shingle shores' and rocky promontories to unite island and mainland. Islands in the Kalevala country were so numerous that most were nameless: lakes were so broad that they embraced islands by the hundred. Great rivers beset with 'foaming torrents, cataracts and rapids', fed by the 'snow slush' into 'spring flood', coursed a country which was ill-defined in relief. 'Void and barren', 'steel-hard' mountains of copper, iron and granite rose above the 'pine-clad' hills.

The pioneer among the trees was the willow, which was both marsh-loving and tolerant of cold. 'The hundred-needled' spruce, the 'grey-headed' aspen, the birch, oak and 'holy' mountain ash were each associated with particular types of countryside. The 'hills of sand' supported pines on their 'sunny slopes' and 'broad extended heathlands'. In the south, more fertile soils had linden, maple, nut trees and 'cherry thickets'. 'Berry-bearing bushes' mingled with timber trees, while juniper pointed out the stony land. In the natural clearings 'plumed grasses' mixed with bedstraw, 'the thousand-headed yarrow' and 'herbs of every species'. Wild rose and honey-suckle bloomed on their drier margins and lakewards they yielded to reeds, rushes and water-lilies. Bilberry, cranberry, strawberry, raspberry – each had its appointed habitat.

Wild life ranged from lesser rodents such as the titmouse, long-eared mouse, martin and squirrel, through badger, otter, hedgehog and hare ('white in winter') to fox, wolf, lynx, glutton, elk, deer and bear. Lesser creatures, such as toads, frogs and worms, were observed, but vipers and adders played a role in Kalevalan country out of all proportion to their numbers. Among insects, the bee entered actively into the poets' plots and metaphors. Birds around the homestead included the sparrow, pigeon, dove, raven, crow, magpie, lark, linnet, bullfinch and goldfinch. Many beside the swallow, fieldfare and plover were birds of passage. Game birds included teal, grouse, and capercailzie; waterfowl included moor-hens, ducks, geese, swans and cranes; among birds of prey were eagles and hawks. No bird was more popular than the cuckoo, a bird of good omen. The waters had their store of fresh-water herring, roach, perch, chub, bream, trout and salmon; while to 'the huge and scaly pike', a veritable 'water-dog', was accorded a cardinal role in 'the land of heroes'. Round the coast were seals. Walruses and whales were also mentioned – perhaps springing from experiences of White Sea or Arctic Ocean origin.

A simple farming life was pursued in this world of nature and the Kalevalan people, for all their adventurings, were of unassuming peasant stock. Their homesteads were small, isolated, often no more than clearings in the wood. They were owner-farmed and the patriarchs who tilled them owed no feudal allegiance. Homes and farm buildings were built of timber; and though reference was occasionally made to a stone fortress, a stone-built church was never mentioned. The dwelling, with its smoke-hole in the roof or rarer stove, was constructed of broad-planked 'fir-wood', with 'rafters of oak'. Sheds and storehouses clustered about the yard; birch trees shadowed them. The whole was hedged with a stake and twig-bound fence, sometimes wattled, beyond the gate of which were the bath-house, the boat-house, the fishing huts and the 'barns along the forest border'.

The 'home fields', which were regularly fallowed, grew oats, barley, beans, peas, cabbages, turnips, flax, hops and mustard. They were steadily extended through new clearings. The 'hard stumps of the clearing' were usually left to rot slowly in the ground. 'The stiff clay of the cornfield' was not easily mastered. As acre was added to acre, the frontiers of farmland reached the 'stony places', which were yet more laborious to reclaim. Praise was bestowed upon him 'who first prepared the marshland' and opened up a new kind of cultivable land. Forests were burnt in a shifting agriculture.

Cattle took priority over other farm stock, and the singers symbolised the cattle culture of eastern Finland in the minotaur-like 'bull of Karelia'. Sheep, pigs, goats and poultry occupied a lesser place; while horses were employed only for riding or driving. Reindeer replaced other domesticated animals in the north. Pastoral life reached its fullest expression where herdsmen and dairymaids sounded the cowhorn in the summer groves, and sought from the sound of their cowbells the herds which grazed 'in the tangle of the forests'. Bonfires were lit so that smoke clouds would keep insects at bay while the 'golden herd' yielded its milk for making 'summer butter'. Only the bears, sometimes bewitched by Lapland enemies, destroyed the peaceful idyll.

Although the Finland of Kalevalan times had vast uninhabited areas, as in all communities where arable husbandry runs side by side with animal husbandry, there were bound to be disagreements. Problems of trespass gave rise to family feuds, as when Untamo's sheep 'browsed the oats of Kalervoinen'. In some parts, the poets recorded that the land was completely occupied. Lemminkäinen commented of one island:

> All the land is now divided
> And the fields in plots are measured
> And allotted are the fallows.
> Grassland managed by the commune.

Where land was fully occupied, an incipient system of taxes and land dues had come into being.

After water, fire was the most significant element in the cold country of Kalevala; but it was peculiarly fickle, hard to capture, even harder to control. Uncontrolled in the forest it could wreak untold damage. Eventually fire was imprisoned in the tinder box; forced into the stove, turfed over in the charcoal pit. Fire was represented as the enemy of iron, which took refuge 'amid the quaking marshes'. Ilmarinen, 'the primeval craftsman' and prototype of

Finnish ironmasters, was 'born upon a hill of charcoal' and, 'seeking a wide place for his bellows', set them upon a 'windy land ridge'. Ilmarinen had an eye trained to detect the traces of iron, even in the spoors of wolf and bear. Iron was a controlling element in daily life. It was beaten into hatchets to clear the forests, axe blades to trim planks, rowlocks for oars, neck chains for cattle, wire hoops for barrels, shoes for horses, muzzles to set upon hogs, rakes for farmland, tools for flax-scraping, runners for the sleigh, kettles for the stove, spears and swords, knives and scythes, crossbows for the chase and fetters for felons. Copper, lead, gold and silver were also smelted; but the Kalevalan world was bound together by iron.

Among other crafts, wood-working took precedence. Planks were trimmed for houses and boats; tubs, casks, buckets and barrels 'hooped with copper' were made for milk, butter, rye and barley; the birch yielded many products, from arrows for hunting to birch-bark shoes. The 'tarry-sided' boats used were made of 'pine from which the pitch is rising'; though oak was used where available. Different types of boats were constructed for lake and sea and they were hauled across portages on wooden rollers. For six months of the year, the sleigh replaced the boat and *Kalevala* discloses a whole sleigh culture. Another domestic task was to prepare pine slivers and 'to trim them into torches'. Weaving of flax, hemp and wool was widely practised and, beside homespun clothes, 'seaborne raiment' was worn. Nets of linen or bast thread, hempen cords and metal lines were produced for the fisheries. Leather was tanned for clothing and for the bellows of forges. 'The earliest pots were of stone', but dye pots and butter jars were kilned. Stones were trimmed for hand mills; but the mason's skills were only modestly developed.

The people of Kalevalan times had a virtually self-sufficient economy; but there was a little overseas trading. Salt and 'wheat from foreign countries' were necessities. The incipient Hansa people sent luxury goods: 'Saxon boots and shoes', 'the finest soaps' and furnishings of 'Saxon timber'. Transport of goods was difficult, for forest pathways were 'full of windings' and river journeys interrupted by rapids. It was easier in winter when frost opened the 'extended surface' of the lakes.

The singers identified Finland as a land of hardship. Their plots turned upon the hazards of the land – landslips, bogs, forest fires, wolves, bears; the risks of the waters – 'ice when rotten', whirlpools, cataracts, gales, storms. The evils of the flesh were attributed principally to the evil influence of the people of the north land. Armed 'hosts from distant countries' brought war, laid 'their homes in ruins', 'wasted all their holdings', and sometimes carried the Kalevalan people away as prisoners to Russia. Famine, always near at hand, was witnessed in place-names such as 'the hungry promontory' and 'the cape of hunger'. Sometimes it resulted from lack of foresight ('the smallness of the storehouse'); more often it was a consequence of 'the mighty droughts of summer' or of frost.

The struggle with frost took the forefront of the stage. There were summer frosts as well as those which followed 'in the pathway of the spring wind'. Frost was depicted as 'wandering through the swamps in summer'. The winter progress of frost's journey from its attack on the shallow margins of the bays and lakelets to its challenge of the deeps was told with acute insight. The ferocity of frost was most intense during the 'open nights of winters', when ice floes choked the seaway, fused into bridges and piled into ice packs. In the woodland, frost

> 'Grasps the aspen till it murmurs,
> Peels the bark from off the birch tree'.

In the homestead, frost could freeze the 'coals upon the hearthstone'. When the thunder rains of summer and the 'iron hails' of the equinoxes became the snows of winter, 'spearshaft' deep from mid-February to mid-March, the Land of Suomi submitted to 'mighty cold's dominion'.

But if the shadow of hard times hung persistently over 'the land of heroes', there were times of rejoicing, when wheat bread and ryebread were baked from fine-sieved flour, when bark bread or oat cake mixed 'with chaff and straw' were forgotten; when honey was there for sweetening and mead was drunk as well as beer. Then, the vision of the paradise of the people of Suomi was revealed by Väinämöinen. It was a pastoral paradise through which 'rivers of milk' flowed from 'plains o'erfilled with milk cows'. And the poet, if he had the ability, would sing the sea to honey, the sea sand to malt, the gravel to salt, the forests to grainland and the wasteland into wheatfields.

The Speculation of Scholars

Kalevala provides scholars with endless opportunities for speculation. Speculation ranges principally around people and places. The place of origin of the legends and poems and the place in which the episodes of *Kalevala* had their setting raise two different, though related, groups of questions. Nor is the function of the different kinds of oral material free from debate.

Place-name evidence makes a strictly limited contribution towards the understanding of Kalevalan localities. Only a handful of names are employed – the historic provinces of Karelia, Savo and Häme; Vuoksi river with Imatra torrent, Kemi river, the falls of Hälläpyörä in Häme and Kaatrakoski in Karelia; Neva, the Cape of Neva, the Cape of Suomi, the Sound of Salt (Öresund?) and Sound of Sariola; Sweden, Russia, Viro (Estonia), Ingermanland and Saxony. The lands of the north command most attention – 'the barren treeless tundra', 'the wastes where grow no bushes', 'the desert's borders' and 'the country where they plough not'. But there is no precise indication as to where 'Pohjola's dark regions' are located.

The natural background of *Kalevala* provides argument for a Karelian setting, perhaps more narrowly the White Sea slope of Karelia. One hypothesis limits Kalevalan origins to Uhtua and Vuokkiniemi in east Karelia; another identifies Viena with the Dwina lands and sets *Kalevala* in the Archangel area. A third theory uses linguistic evidence and suggests a west Finnish setting. In this context the Darwinian theory of survival is called in to explain how either the runes migrated as their originators migrated or older ideas were transmitted to the east as the pressure of new ones forced them out of the west. A fourth theory gives to the Kalevalan world an island location and a Baltic hearth, and hints that it might be equated with the island of Gotland. A fifth thesis locates the 'land of heroes' in the coastal marchlands between Estonia and Latvia, around Väinäjoki the boundary river, possibly with the islands of Hiiumaa (Dagö) and Saaremaa (Ösel) beyond. Francis P. Magoun in his splendid edition of *Kalevala* sets the entire action upon a much more restricted stage. He reflects the school of thought which sees in the conflict with Pohjola evidence of antagonism between Finns and Lapps. For him Pohjola is simply the North Farm and the action centring on it is no more than the simple feuding that might take place between local families. Certainly, in interpreting *Kalevala*, the social setting of the Viking world with its family feuds cannot be disregarded as offering a parallel. It may be concluded that 'the land of heroes' is best regarded as a composite work and that elements of truth are to be found in all of the theories.

The inhabitants of the Kalevalan community were neither historical characters nor pagan gods. In most translations of *Kalevala*, the leading characters are described as heroes. The Finnish word is *urho* – not strictly speaking 'hero' in the sense of the heroes of classical epic or mediaeval lay. The principal characters are Väinömöinen, Ilmarinen, Lemminkäinen, Joukhahainen, Kullervo and Louhi, the mistress of Pohjola. They are distinguished from the more ordinary mortals of the land of Kaleva not by any kinglike qualities or aristocratic lineage. They are the more colourful and gifted members of the community, each being endowed to a certain extent with magical powers. The experiences through which they pass are such that they may best be described as shamans – perhaps comparable to the Samoyed shamans. They are not eclipsed by the coming of Christianity. Priests do not enter the Kalevalan community, though there is both direct and indirect reference to biblical stories. Indeed, the adventures of the Kalevalan heroes are heightened as a result of the absorption by the singers of biblical knowledge. Apocalyptic utterances have an especial appeal.

The heroes are distinctive types as well as characters in their own right. The central figure is Väinömöinen – the 'eternal sage' or wise man, as he is identified by Martti Haavio. He is the primeval maker of music, singing his poems to the zither-like kantele. Väinömöinen combines the qualities of Orpheus and Prospero. Ilmarinen, somewhat like Vulcan the smith, is the technological hero. Kullervo is the hunter. Lemminkäinen is the eternal, but not very successful, lover – a Don Juan who suffers the fate of Balder.

To the Pantheon of heroes must be added the spirits of nature, who play an important part in the ethos of *Kalevala*. Indeed an entire animistic community enters into the plot – from Ilmatar, the spirit of the air, to Aalotaar, the spirit of the water, from Etelätar, the spirit of the South Wind, to Pihlajatar, the spirit of the rowan tree. The spirits of the ethereal world may have their moments of influence and the heroes may vie with each other in their bizarre adventuring, but in the text of *Kalevala* neither claims more space than the earthy activities and pursuits of day-to-day living in which the lesser mortals engage. Always assuming that he remembers the way in which the songs have been accumulated and the centuries through which they have been transmitted, it is in these latter facts that the student of prehistory may employ *Kalevala* to throw an occasional shaft of light upon Finland's dark ages.

While the contents of *Kalevala* and of *Kanteletar* (The Old Poems of the Finnish People) are of intrinsic and possibly historical interest, the function of the poems is of independent concern. The Finnish ethnographer Kustaa Vilkuna believes that many of the Finnish folk poems were employed to celebrate the beginning and ending of certain kinds of work. While some may have had an appointed place in the seasonal activities of the farming year, others may have been linked with cooperative work such as fishing. There are recorded instances within living memory that this has been the case in parts of neighbouring Russia.

In the light of archaeological discovery and folkloristic speculation, the panorama of Finland's past has acquired and continues to acquire new dimensions. On the one hand, archaeological finds indicate the association of the early occupants of Finland with a growing variety of distant places. On the other, the contemporary approach to folkloristic studies reveals complementary Finnish links with incidents and ideas distant in time and place. The evidence of the earth and the songs of the people have new meanings as Finnish enquiry is integrated with international scholarship.

The Words that Speak

There is a third bundle of tenuous links with the world of shadows – the words that are used by the people. *Sanat puhuvat*, 'the words speak', is the apposite title of a book by Y. H. Toivonen which extends the thesis that vocabulary in its own right provides clues to the evolution of the pre- and proto-Finnish peoples. Although, by comparison with many languages, Finnish is relatively pure it contains words of many origins. These words were absorbed into the language at different times. It is suggested that they might derive from the successive areas where the prehistoric ancestors of the Finns halted on their migrations to the west.

In the same way as Axel Gottlund began to assemble archaeological facts in a systematic manner and Elias Lönnrot to encourage the systematic collection of oral poetry, a group of philologists and ethnographers emphasised the significance of the diverse Fenno-Ugrian vocabularies for the fuller understanding of the Finns. Their studies began in the first half of the nineteenth century and at least one of them, M. A. Castrén, acquired an international reputation. Although it was Castrén whose writings made the greatest impact, P. A. Sjögren probably had a more thorough appreciation of the place of broad humanistic studies for an understanding of the Finns. Sjögren, sometime professor of philology at St Petersburg, made a number of journeys into Finnish-speaking territories of Russia. His travel diaries reiterate the importance of linguistic, toponymic and ethnographic studies for unravelling the prehistory of the Finns. At an early stage in his argument, Castrén had written, 'In Karelia we have not only the word but also the thing'. The Finnish language contains many words which no longer apply to objects in the contemporary environment of the Finn. In eastern Finland, however, it was frequently possible to find the objects which had disappeared among the western Finnish peoples. Out of these approaches has evolved a thesis which marries narrower philological and broader environmental considerations.

The oldest identifiable words in the Finnish language appear to have Indo-Iranian roots. Scholars associate them with a time during which the Fenno-Ugrian peoples lived in the southern Urals. Many words applied to food, fauna, flora and topographical features are both old and of enduring quality. *Jousta* (cheese) and *kalastaa* (to fish) appear to be primeval words associated with Uralian times. *Mehilainen* (bee) and *mesi* (honey) are words closely related to languages employed by other Fenno-Ugrian peoples who appear to have had their original home in the Urals.

With the dispersal of Finnish groups from this area, some migrated westwards to occupy a zone of contact between the woodland and southern steppe zones of Russia. *Hevonen* (horse) and, more particularly, *varsa* (a young horse) are key words which derive from the equine culture of the Russian steppe and have been absorbed by Finnic groups. *Vehnä* (wheat), *pähkinä* (hazel nut tree), *jalava* (elm) are attributed to the so-called Permian phase of experiences; to be supplemented with *lehmä* (milk cow), *vasara* (hammer), *sika* (pig) and *vene* (boat) from the Volgan phase. As settlers advanced towards the Baltic, they encountered new crops, new creatures and new experiences. *Herne* (pea) was an addition to the range of crops; *härkä* (draught ox), to stock; *harakka* (magpie), to familiar wild life; *halla* (summer frost), to the realm of climatic experiences. The sea coast being reached, a maritime vocabulary akin to that of the south-east Baltic peoples was adopted – *meri* (sea), itself for example. The first centuries after the birth of Christ witnessed a rapid multiplication of Germanic words. They were especially strong in the agricultural area, and indicative of increasingly permanent farming settlement. *Kaura* (oats), *ruis* (rye), *humala* (hop), *lammas* (sheep) and *aura* (plough) provide examples. Farms of different sizes – *kartano* (estate), for example – began to be distinguished. Finnish words applied to metals had Germanic roots – *kulta* (gold), *rauta* (iron). So had a variety of administrative words, for example – *hallitse* (government) and *tuomitse* (judge). To the varied substantives was added one adjective – *kauni* (beautiful). Baltic and German words were the last groups acquired by the Finns as they filtered into Finland. But the process of word accumulation continued in Viking times – principally with navigational terms, though agricultural words were also added. While Viking words indicated western contacts in the time before record-making, a variety of words from the language of commerce also derived from contacts with the east. To the area between Novgorod and Pskov are attributed *tavara* (merchandise), *turku* (market) and *saapas* (boots). Words are light baggage and easily carried. It may be unwise to hang too much upon them. But at the very least they open up an interesting area of speculation.

So do place-names. Finland lacks early documents comparable to the charters and taxation records of most of western Europe. Its studies in place-names accordingly follow a different approach from those in, for example, England. But place-names tell many facts about the emergence of the country. Sometimes, they are writ large on the map and are indicative of a major stage in the occupation of the land. Nyland (Uusimaa), for example, was the new land on the frontiers of Swedish mediaeval settlement that was taken over in the so-called period of the crusades. Satakunta was the old hundred (Sw. *hundre*; F. *sata* – hundred, *kunta* – an administrative unit) on the northern marches of the Swedish colonial settlements. Sometimes, place-names reflect the changing distribution of different ethnographic elements in the countryside. In the broader national picture, for example, it is possible to speculate upon the former distribution of Lapps in the light of Lappish place-names or place-name elements. Lappeenranta and Lapinlahti are the names of two parishes which formerly contained Lapps. T. Itkonen has mapped the distribution of many similar settlement names. An example of a different character is found in areas where the frontier of settlement has shifted between Finnish- and Swedish-speaking groups. This is especially evident in parts of coastal Ostrobothnia. Place-names may also reflect changing morphology. This is particularly the case along the Ostrobothnian seaboard where land upheaval has converted

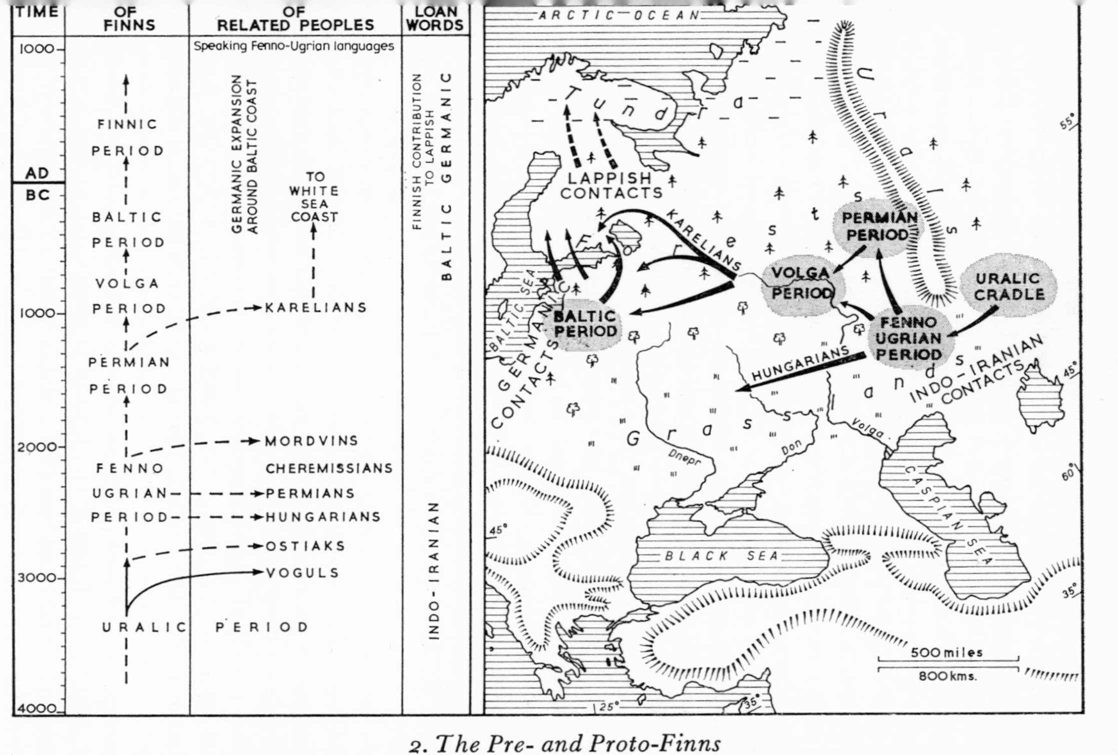

2. *The Pre- and Proto-Finns*

The origin of the Finns is speculative in the highest degree, and no diagram can acceptably interpret the evidence put forward. The facts incorporated in this diagram attempt to put some of the speculations into space and time.

extensive areas of sea floor into dry land. Words of insular or peninsular meaning may be found several kilometres from the seashore. Earlier vegetational features may also be reflected in place-names, for example the recurrence of the element *tammi* (Sw. *ek* = oak) along the littoral of Uusimaa. Changing land use has also left its legacy of place-names and changing land ownership.

'The Strawberry Land'

Map 2 summarises some of the speculations of scholars about the Finns during the time before the records. *Ur-Finland* has been described by Ilmari Hustich as a country having its nearest contemporary counterpart in interior Labrador. Its story begins when the Finnish people entered the land that was to bear their name; but it is difficult to deny the contribution of the unknown settlers of diverse origins who peopled it before the arrival of the Finns proper and to exclude from the ancestry of present-day Finns the many immigrants who came from Sweden. When they eventually reached Finland, the proto-Finns, who had hitherto led what Zachris Topelius called 'a knapsack life', entered into a more sedentary phase of existence. As with the Mormons in their journey through the American West, they passed through more geographically favoured territory before they reached their home land. Yet primeval Finland had its own particular attractions for them at their stage of its occupation. Fish, fowl and flesh were relatively abundant, and fauna meant more than flora. Slowly the home country was made to yield cultivated harvests in spite of the physical restraints. And no matter how lean and hungry it might appear, it was christened *maansikka maa* (strawberry land) at an early stage in its settlement.

Academic journeys back to Methuselah arouse limited interest in the average Finn. Yet the facts which are assembled from these journeys of exploration into the past are a part of the subconscious of most Finns. They also contribute to Finland's *genius loci* and the majority of Finns are peculiarly sensitive to the local atmosphere. They help to account for local customs such as the midsummer bonfire (*Juhannuskokko*), which burns all over Finland today but which was formerly an Eastertide feature in the south-west. They help to explain the names which are applied to the features of place, and which in their own right are evocative of a multitude of personal experiences. They provide the terminology of time and place, and they lie behind the language through which the Finns love and live.

Chapter 3

The Saga of the Spacious Days

THE LAND that was to become Finland was an integral part of Sweden from the time of the mediaeval Swedish campaigns until 1809. Sweden gave to it unity; but in the earlier stages of the Finnish story it was a unity that was one with that of its western neighbour. The territory to which this unity was given was subject to recurrent attack from Muscovy. Accordingly the rudiments of Finland's history are to be gleaned from both Swedish and Russian manuscripts. The position of Finland remained vulnerable until that of Sweden was strong. And it was not until the sixteenth century that Sweden escaped from internecine conflicts with a powerful dynasty and a strongly centralised government. Thereafter the Gothic north emerged from its world of shadows to play an impressive role in European affairs. The emergence was based upon a new order – in the Church, in the army and in the administration.

The order that Sweden eventually created had both domestic and international consequences for Finland. It knew the same law, the same religion, the same system of taxation. When called together the four estates (which consisted of the nobles, the Church, the burghers and the peasantry) were common. Domestically Swedish organisation opened new horizons and spurred forward the colonisation of Finland's extensive backwoods. Internationally it gave to the Finnish half of the Swedish realm new interests beyond the narrow seas. As a result Finland became a confirmed part of the European community as distinct from an uncertain appendage of it.

Throughout, Finland shared the fortunes and misfortunes of Sweden. It experienced the exhilaration of the conjunction of circumstances that transformed Sweden into a great European power in the seventeenth century, and it contributed substantially to the Swedish achievement. But, although the European environment has been a forcing house of great powers, the spacious days of most of them have been brief. Finland consequently suffered more grievously than Sweden proper from the eventual demise. It is another of the paradoxes in its history that it flowered most freely during the last sixty years of its 600-year association with Sweden.

Points of Reference

For more than a century, Finnish historians have debated when the history of Finland began. The point is partly academic. Did Finland have a history before it became an independent state or was its history previously a part of the history of the states to which it owed allegiance? More fundamentally, did Finland have a history before it became aware of the fact that it was a nation? Certainly the territory occupied by the Finns had a history, and for the descendants of those who shared in its earlier experiences, the history has become a part of their consciousness.

History begins with historical facts and historical facts begin with documentary evidence. There is no point in time when Finland as Finland sprang into existence. In the first instance, Finland was no more than Sweden's *Österland*, the land in the east. It was a part of the territory beyond *Östersjön*, the East Sea, and was akin to the Easterlings, the lands on the Baltic seaboard of Muscovy. For contemporary Finland, the Baltic Sea, although on the west, remains Itämeri (the East Sea).

Mediaevalists have teased out the earliest references to Finland from both eastern and western manuscripts. The clear calligraphy of the Novgorod Chronicles recalls early sorties into Finland in 1186, 1191, 1228 and 1311. The counter-campaigns of Birger Jarl and Tyrgils Knutsson are also recorded. Erik's Chronicle touches upon Birger Jarl's campaign of 1249. The rampant lion of Tyrgils Knutsson's seal is still attached to parchments which have survived the damp and fires of centuries. The seal confirms the lion as central to Finland's heraldry at an early date. With these and later scraps of information, Finnish historians, such as Jalmari Jaakkola and Martti Kerkkonen, have sought to reconstruct early frontier lines upon the map of the country, groping for points of reference along the borderlands of eastern Uusimaa and south-western Häme before the first boundary was established by the Peace of Pähkinsaari in 1323. The Peace Treaty is one of the oldest Finnish documents in the Swedish State Archives.

Church and state were closely allied in the mediaeval life of the area that was to become Finland. On horse as well as on foot; with a growing weight of armour and variety of weapons; with trumpet, drum and bagpipes, a succession of intruders (to whose enterprise posterity has applied the name crusades) pressed eastwards. They came from Denmark as well as Sweden. At the end of the twelfth century, indeed, Danish missionary rivalry reached a peak. By 1216, the King of Sweden was accorded formal papal authority to take over the heathen lands of Finland. Granite castles, planned by military architects who knew the bastions of western Europe, marked their progress – Kastelholm on the main island of Åland, Turku (Åbo), Hämeenlinna (Tavastehus) and Viipuri (Viborg); lesser strongholds were constructed – Raseborg (Raasepori), Kusisto and Kexholm (Käkisalmi). To incipient military organisation were added the beginnings of civil law. The roots of Finnish law belong to the fourteenth century, and although they were Swedish the very phrase *Jus finnonicum* breathes a precocious distinction.

The Church took its tithe but it contributed much to the land and to the people. It may have reduced much that was pagan and colourful, but it replaced it with much that served the body as well as the soul. It was a handmaiden of the forces of military and civil order, but a builder for posterity.

The outward and visible signs of the plantations of Christendom remain. They are most evident in the durable granite churches which often sprang out of the foundations of earlier wooden structures. Architectural designs followed those of Gotland and Sweden. Granite was less easily worked than the building stones used for most of Europe's churches. Nevertheless buildings began to soar in a characteristic Gothic manner. And even if stained glass and precious metals were less abundant than in the wealthier lands of western Europe, imagination in the decorative arts knew little restraint. Brick and tile patterned and complemented the granite. Tarred shingles served as roofs. Inside, lime-washed walls lent themselves to the artists' skills. Patient restorers in present-day Finland have uncovered the mediaeval heritage on the walls of scores of churches. Lohja, Hattula, Rymättilä, Taivassalo, Nousiainen, Ingå, Kumlinge, Finström and Lemu are names with which mediaevalists conjure. The leaves and branches which twine their interminable patterns over the spacious walls and broad columns unite the lives of saints and the punishments of sinners. Luther sits uncompromised between the two groups in Lemu church. The tasks of the seasons and the amusements of a primitive age stand in juxtaposition. The historian can see the merchants in their ships, the farmers with their ploughs, the young bloods jousting as they were seen in the eyes of the people of their day. Smith and carpenter gave of their best work to the buildings which were least likely to destruction and decay. Woodcarvers modelled their saints – Olav, Lawrence, Anna and Martin of Tours. And, since the Catholic Church of Finland was the Catholic Church of Europe, vestments and plate as well as bibles and missals were imported from abroad. The churchmen brought the first books to Finland – *Missale Aboense*, printed in Lübeck in 1488, for example. And some of the oldest words inscribed in Finland are found on their memorials. Ulvila churchyard has a granite headstone with a fourteenth-century inscription.

Religious houses never multiplied in Finland to any great degree. The remains of the Franciscan friary at Kökar in the Åland islands lie on the leeward side of the churchyard. Turku still has its Luostarinmäki or Klosterbacken, the name of which recalls the site of a monastery. At nearby Nådendal (Naantali), there were both a monastery and a convent. The religious houses were of modest size – their communities numbering tens rather than hundreds. In the same way as their mainland Europe counterparts, they wedded practical with spiritual pursuits. Eric's Chronicle refers to the Cistercians at the time of Birger Jarl:

De munkar de äro grå — The monks are grey
Och bo å land, ärja och så — And live on the land, plough and sow.

In the wilderness that was mediaeval Finland, their impact was slight, but they must have introduced new ideas to the generations of anonymous land-breakers beside whom they worked.

The new Church meant the twilight of the old gods; though the dawn brightened only slowly into day. A cult of saints was initiated, chief among them were Erik, Olaf, George, Michael and Sweden's Birgitta. Through the canonisation of 'Bishop Henry', Finland acquired its own saint, which made Turku a place of pilgrimage. Religious ballads and didactic poems were composed. Some conceived apocryphal stories from the New Testament. The celebrated *Luojan virsi* transferred the birth of Jesus from a stable to a *sauna*. Invocations to Catholic saints to help in the day-to-day activities of hunting, trapping and fishing were introduced to challenge pagan incantations. Rhymes were invented to fix the new gods in the memory:

Anna, Antti ahvenia, — Ann, Andrew for the perches,
Pekka, pieniä kaloja. — Peter, for the little fishes.

But the churches could scarcely keep pace with the steady expansion of settlement into interior Finland. As the wilderness (*erämaa*) or hunting-lands were slowly converted into settled lands, parishes the size of English counties emerged. Their boundaries were zones drawn through the no-man's-land of wood and swamp, their core areas lay upon the lake terraces below which waterways opened communications. In such a land the Church's difficulty lay less in conversion than in the maintenance of a state of grace among the converted. Not surprisingly the Christianisation of the nomad Lapps presented the greatest problem. W. Canton in his *History of the British and Foreign Bible Society* (1904) hinted darkly that the interior and north of Finland 'had drunk deeply of the cup of infidelity'.

Through both Church and state, people and place were being slowly recorded. Although there are between six and seven thousand documents in Swedish and Latin which make reference to Finland earlier than the 1520s, only a modest harvest of place-names and personal names can be assembled from them. But christenings, marriages and funerals began to fix names and places. Christian names derived increasingly from those of the saints. The saints' days of the holy calendar were attached to the secular calendar: the Latin forms were gradually translated into Finnish – Antti for Andrew, Juho for John, Kertto for Gertrude, Pentti for Benedict, Marja for Mary. 'Name days' entered the social scene in the seventeenth century and continue to have social importance in Finland today. There was no significant substitution in the name-day calendar of more modern names for the picturesque older names (Hyginus, Polykarpus, Perpetua) until the twentieth century. A child who lacks a name day loses a second birthday (though perhaps he would willingly forgo the pleasure if he had to be called Narcissus instead of Alfred in order to benefit).

Surnames grew mostly out of the land where people lived. They were both given to and taken from farm holdings. 'Because I was born on a farm called "Tokoi", that became my surname, after the custom of the time', wrote Oskari Tokoi in his autobiography. Although no one knew how the family farm got its name, most surnames sprang from meadow and field, from the clearing in the wood (*aho*), from lake (*järvi*), river (*joki*), island (*saari*) and sound (*salmi*). Another group of names were rooted in agricultural practices, such as firing the woodland (*kaski*). The present-day telephone directory has extended lists of surnames which derive from natural features of the landscape. They may be compounded as well as in the singular, e.g. Rautavaara (iron ridge), Rantavaara (the ridge by the lakeshore). The suffix *-la* or *-lä* is a common extension of these names, e.g. Ahola, Salmela. So are the possessive suffixes *-äinen*, *-enen*, which may be traced back in documents to the fourteenth century in such names as Hännikäinen and Killinen. Karjalainen (a man from Karelia), Hämäläinen (a man from Häme) and Pohjalainen (a man from Pohja – Pohjanmaa, Ostrobothnia) are readily explained. More interesting, and rooted in the circumstances of the changing political frontier, is the profusion of Ruotsalainen and Veneläinen surnames. They arose in the eastern lake district and recall the former division in allegiance of the people between Sweden (Ruotsi, in Finnish) and Russia (Venaja).

The outer world scarcely knew the name of Finland until the sixteenth century, and until much later its people were confused with those of Finnmark. Because of the confusion, many Europeans attributed to the Finns the qualities of Lapp and Quain. They were known to occupy a world the physical nature of which had been twisted, perverted and contorted. It was genuinely believed that something of this had entered into both the physical frame and the mental condition of its inhabitants. In addition to being a haunt of necromancers and a haven of heathendom, Finland was also partly regarded as the home of the Goths – a notion which ecclesiastical apologists magnified and perpetuated.

A Gothic Image

The Scandinavian dignitaries Johannes Magnus and Olaus Magnus were among those who fostered most powerfully the Gothic image of the north. It was largely due to Olaus Magnus that the character of Finland first began to make an impact on western Europe. It was a twofold impact – for Olaus Magnus began by presenting the north in a map and subsequently published an immensely influential book. Western Europe's cartographers were slow to escape from the Ptolemaic tradition and, although the lineaments of the north were being recast in maps such as those of Claudius Clavus and Jacob Ziegler, it was the *Carta marina* of Olaus Magnus dated 1539 which first shed more accurate light upon them. This richly pictorial document, which he affectionately called 'my Gothic map', was the first to give an outline of Finland that is recognisable today.

The text was translated into English a century after its original Latin edition (1555) as *A Compendious History of the Goths, Swedes and Vandals and other northern Nations* (London, 1658). Both map and text gained wide currency and remained primary sources of knowledge – and misconception – about Finland for several generations. Information from them was speedily embodied in a variety of atlases, geographies and histories. The Finnish part of Olaus Magnus's map and text were compiled from a variety of sources. From his youthful journeys in his native Sweden, and his later residence in north Germany, Olaus Magnus had ample opportunities of meeting merchants, ships' captains, churchmen and scholars who came from or who had visited Finland. Two types of information dominated the text – Finland's experiences as a military buffer and its resources as a trading land. Map and text brought out clearly that Finland was a land of three frontiers and of 'a multitude of waters'.

Interest was focused on the south of the country and, in particular, upon 'peninsular' Finland. The Gulfs of Bothnia and Finland were represented as opening trading highways north and east respectively, despite their ice obstruction. Beyond the conventionally represented lake district, the marchlands of the interior led to a *terra incognita* where the distribution of land and water owed more to speculation than to knowledge. Trading and raiding were symbolised by the products of exchange and the weapons of war respectively. The liveliness of Finland's contacts with the Baltic Sea and the importance for its economy of the western approaches stood in antithesis to the role of the eastern frontier as a frontier of conflict. Along the eastern face Swedo-Finnish cavalry in battle array confronted the troops of Muscovy, while a cannon directed its fire eastwards from Viipuri. The troops who were pitched against each other in the northern marchlands were complemented by Orthodox monks proselytising the Lapps. The western coasts of Finland were scattered with barrels of pitch and tar, 'cleft boards of pine', 500 lb. bundles of dried fish, and skins (especially ermine, 'in bundles of forty and carried to far distant countries'). Seals were being hunted on the ice floes for their skins and oil, the peltries of the forest were represented, boats were being constructed, 'ranged deer, yoked like oxen' drew travellers, merchants (Russian as well as Finnish) portaged their vessels. Finland was also depicted as a winter land on the sub-Arctic frontiers of European settlement. Ice bridges spanned the neighbouring gulfs, ski and sleigh speeded movement over them bringing to such winter markets as Tornio 'a rich confluence of merchants'. The graphic woodcuts of J. B. Fickler's German edition of the *History* illustrated the ways in which the cold of winter was turned to good effect in resisting the assaults of the enemy.

At the time when Olaus Magnus's book was circulating, there were about a quarter of a million inhabitants in Finland. Farming was the predominant activity. Forestry, fishing, hunting and occasional mineral-working supplemented the virtually subsistence economy. For most of the farming community, the money economy meant little. Barter was widespread; trading, very restricted. When the spring thaw's 'infinite swift torrents' opened water routes, a minority dispatched their refined forest products to the limited number of coastal trading places. Some sent fish, such as those along Torni river, where, according to Olaus Magnus, salmon were 'like soldiers in bright armour' and so abundant that they broke the nets. Some exported 'summer butter' and 'aromatical' cheeses. Among minerals, locally smelted with charcoal, iron was chief. Iron ore was 'hooked out' from the lakes (as the early atlas-maker Moses Pitt put it) and iron nodules were recovered from the bogs. Salt was the principal commodity needed – generally deriving from overseas because of the low salt content of the surrounding waters. It entered in Dutch as well as Swedish vessels. Travellers went to the coast in winter to fetch it. There is still a local saying in Savo – 'to go to Oulu to fetch the salt'.

From his log cabin, constructed of fir trees rudely squared by the axe, insulated with moss, with smoke-hole in the roof, and little or no glass for the low slit windows, the *talonpoja* (or *bonde* as he was called in Swedish) would have seen the forest both near and far. Its presence was comforting, for its trees were the source of shelter, light, heat, fodder for beasts and food for man (in time of need). The *talonpoja* was usually the owner of that which he surveyed, and into the loosely claimed hunting-lands that lay beyond it he could spill his offspring to recreate his circumstance. Gunvor Kerkkonen quotes an example from Kyrö:

> Henrik Riikalan hade ett erierum vid Visu insjö 20 mil från hans hemman. Och där är ett borum, som hans sjalv skäll besitta och hans eldre broder skall förestå hemmanet har hans fader.

> (Henrik Riikalan had a pioneer homestead by Visu lake, 20 miles

from his home farm. And there is a dwelling which he himself will occupy and his older brother will keep the home farm at his father's place.)

The *talonpoja* was more than 'peasant', as the word was used in western Europe, but he was frequently less than yeoman, as the word emerged in England.

Domestic animals came up to his threshold and frequently shared a common building. Not surprisingly, garden plots were rare; fruit trees and bushes rarer. Olaus Magnus wrote of fruit which would 'dull a sword's edge with its juice'. Animals were relatively abundant. Cattle, including draught oxen, sheep and goats, were found on most properties. Horses, basic to both the economy and the army, were carefully bred. Pigs and chickens were also kept. Winter fodder came principally from natural meadows; bundled leaves and sedges were collected. Since taxes were frequently paid in kind, it is known that oats and barley were the principal crops on cultivated and on burnt-over land. Rye and turnips were also staples. Flax was widely grown for domestic spinning and weaving. Fish, fowl and flesh – dried, smoked and salted – were stored against winter. Brandy (which, as ever, continues to be illegally distilled) was the chief medicine. The seasonal round, as described by topographers for the depths of north Finland at the end of the eighteenth century, must have been very similar over the greater part of the country in Olaus Magnus's time. The limited infield area was divided into strips (partly by drainage ditches), the commonlands were shared with neighbours or other members of the family, and there were hunting and fishing rights.

The *talonpoja*, who had a place in the lowest of the country's four estates, slowly emerged as the fundamental constituent in the social structure of Finland. His long-suffering qualities had already been identified by Olaus Magnus. He knew how to live off the land; his whole existence was tailored to its meagre resources. Intermittently, life was Hobbesian in character – 'nasty, brutish, short'. In his study of Akaa (Vamala) parish, S. Suvanto wrote of the church bell cracking because of its ceaseless tolling during the famine of 1696–97. Yet there were compensations. For this was a struggle with nature rather than with fellow men. By comparison with country people in most of Europe, the Finn was relatively free from human interference and restraint. He acquired an independence of outlook because independence of action was constantly demanded of him. And this resistant and resilient force in the countryside, who was the salt of the Finnish earth, was a natural pioneer in an area that needed pioneering, a generous breeder in a country that needed men for the army, and a safe source of taxation for an exchequer that was expanding in its demands.

While the *talonpoja* was numerically dominant in Finnish society, a number of estates of manorial pretensions had also emerged in Finland by Olaus Magnus's time. They were to multiply with the expansion of Sweden. The owners of these estates, whose family vaults are ranged in and around Turku cathedral and whose coats-of-arms (resplendent with helmet, plume, gauntlet, spur and sword) add an unexpectedly feudal touch to its gaunt walls, were among the earliest to keep longer-term records of their properties. Eric Fleming of the Quidja estate in Parainen parish and Ivar Fleming of the Sundholm estate in Kalanti parish provide examples. A register (*Jordebok*, as it was called) from Quidja estate has survived from the years 1420–1551: another, from Sundholm, covers the greater part of the sixteenth century. The Quidja manuscript, 262 pages long, contains the first written reference in Finland to a sawmill. The Sundholm register opens with a description of a farmstead which, by Finnish standards, must have constituted a desirable property.

<table>
<tr><td>Akrr land, litidh . . .
richt engiss bool . . .
nok wedha skogh . . . .
till gehielp löff skogh nog . . .</td><td>A little arable land . . .
rich water meadows . . .
sufficient firewood . . .
enough leaf woods to provide supplementary fodder (for animals)</td></tr>
<tr><td>En timber skogh sunnligit, dok död wedha skog till behielp . . .</td><td>A timber stand lying to the south with fallen wood useful for fuel . . .</td></tr>
<tr><td>Gaatt ffiskerj medh not, nät och kattisse stand . . . Kittama öö, ther all molke boskapen haffver thera sommar beet upa.</td><td>Good fisheries for both netting and trapping . . . Kittama island (also belongs to the farm) where all the milking cows have their summer pasture.</td></tr>
</table>

It is interesting that many of the Swedish words in the original text speak for themselves without translation. The austere, factual statements of these registers, recorded in the vernacular, provide a marked contrast to the observations in church Latin of Olaus Magnus's picture of the Gothic north.

The Introduction of a New Order

Olaus Magnus was the last Roman Catholic archbishop of Uppsala, but his map was the representation of a see over which he never held sway. For the years of his office paralleled those of Gustavus Vasa. Gustavus Vasa initiated a new age in northern Europe. As an integral part of Sweden, Finland benefited from the new orderliness that emanated from his rule and shared in the new horizons associated with his dynasty. Once Gustavus Vasa had overthrown the Danish Baltic hegemony, established his autocratic regime and acquired the material means of support for it, Finland's fishermen, farmers, burghers and traders were slowly drawn into a fuller community with Sweden.

The first and in some respects most critical action of Gustavus Vasa was to seize the resources of the Church in order to establish the authority of the crown. Relations with Rome were ruptured, Gustavus Vasa assumed the role of head of the Church of Sweden, and the ensuing Reformation set a pattern which was to become familiar in other parts of north-western Europe. By the so-called Västerås Edict of 1527, church lands were transferred to the crown. Subsequently, mass was forbidden, ceremonial was abolished and Latin was replaced by the vernacular in church services. In the process, the door was opened to the adoption of the Lutheran faith, though its official acceptance was delayed until 1593. Finland was the less wealthy half of Sweden and the Church was less entrenched within it, but the effects of these acts were speedily felt.

The Reformation brought Finnish churchmen to the fore: in turn, it gave rise to the first book to be printed in Finnish. It was the work of Michael Agricola (1510–57), a disciple of Martin Luther and bishop of Turku. Agricola's statue, standing on the green embankment at the east end of the great Gothic cathedral of Turku, commemorates an outstanding Finn who helped to usher in the modern era. His prayer book (*rukouskirja*) and A.B.C. book both appeared in the early 1540s. They complemented each other and a jingle began to circulate:

Kun ABCkirja ensin on,	When the ABC book came into being,
Siitä alku opista uskon.	Then people began to learn the faith.

Agricola added his New Testament in 1548. Altogether ten works were published in Finnish during his years at Turku. The orthography common to Swedish and German publications was employed in them.

A century was to pass before the first Finnish translation of the Bible was undertaken by Eskil Petraeus (1593–1657). This weighty and generously illustrated volume, published in Stockholm in 1642, was additionally significant because it established the form of printed Finnish for the next two centuries. The Bible adopted the west Finnish linguistic form (in contrast to the east Finnish form, which eventually made its impact in the printed version of *Kalevala*). Accordingly, it represents a stage in the crystallisation of written Finnish. Philologists identify three different written forms of the Finnish language – a mediaeval form (until 1543), an old written form (from 1543 to *c.* 1800) and a new written form in which elements of east and west Finnish are blended.

The Reformation both opened and closed doors to Finland's churchmen and students. Choice of European universities at which they might study was reduced in number, but those that remained available were hearths of considerable intellectual ferment. North Germany provided natural places of pilgrimage. Indeed, it was at Greifswald in 1582 that two Finnish students first published in Latin their *Piae cantiones*, a collection of spiritual and secular songs from the 'Island of Finland'. The songs are still among the best known and frequently performed of any in the musical literature of Finland. In *Tempus adest floridam* is the air of *Good King Wenceslas*. Britain also attracted students. Jacobus Langius and Abraham Alanus were at Oxford. So, too, was John Gezelius whose studies in oriental philology and rabbinical literature were cut short because of his father's suspicions of England's religious loyalties. Partly to provide training grounds for its clergy, Sweden established a number of new universities in the seventeenth century. Among them was the University of Turku in 1640, the initiative for the foundation and endowment of which came largely from Per Brahe. Its natural scientists made an early impact – Ellias Tillandz, for example, anticipated Carl Linnaeus with his *Catalogus plantarum* of 1673.

Numerically, the yeoman and small-farmer class should have given disproportionate weight to the fourth estate of the realm. Yet for a variety of reasons, control was vested solidly in the nobles, clergy and burghers, shifting according to circumstance and as the monarchy wished to strike a balance of forces. Moreover, when the estates were called, Finnish representation tended to be modest because of the cost and difficulties of travel. Nor did the representatives tend to function as Finns speaking for Finland.

Among the nobility, a considerable number had acquired extensive fiefs in Finland. None had larger Finnish estates than Per Brahe, sometime governor of Finland. Per Brahe is usually regarded as one of the most able administrators who have served Finland. Memorials to him are widely scattered and his name is commemorated in the Bothnian town of Brahestad – Raahe, in its Finnish form. Some of the military aristocrats who settled in Finland received grants of land for services rendered to the crown on the field of battle. Twentieth-century Finland has a fair sprinkling of families who are the direct descendants of mercenaries ennobled by the Swedish monarchy. Their names may be French, such as Charpentier or de la Chapelle; Scottish, such as Bruce or Ramsay; or German, such as von Born or von Essen. Interest in genealogical trees is livelier in contemporary Finland than in most countries – and *Finlands Adels Kalender* (Finland's Calendar of Nobility) is probably consulted almost as much as *Kuka on Kuka* (Finland's *Who's Who*).

The foreign-born estate-owners introduced a cosmopolitan element to the Finnish scene. To half-manorhouse, half-castle – such as Louhisaari in Askiainen and Qvidja in Parainen – they brought trophies of war. Military coffers, furniture, apparel, trinkets, snuff-boxes, goblets and other souvenirs may still be found in the homes of some of their descendants as well as in museums. Oak, ebony, walnut and pearwood were carved and inlaid by cabinet makers. New fashions from the outside world – tobacco-smoking, wine-drinking, coffee-drinking – were introduced. Some even sought to explain to themselves and to others Finland's position in the world – for geographical globes began to appear, as at Viurila estate in Halikko. They spread methods of time-keeping, as witnessed by sundials from Urjala (1564) and Pernaja (1580), by hour glasses in churches and, eventually, by the bell on the estate building that was rung to assemble the work people to meals.

Some of the retired mercenaries were encouraged to settle on the frontiers of Finland. The governor of Käkisalmi, an Ogilvie of Scottish descent, was among them. His son, Patrick, not only retained contact with his homeland, but also kept the English tongue alive. He bequeathed his impressive library to the University of Turku. It included English texts, among which were treatises on artillery and 'the making of extraordinary artificial fireworks' – appropriate, perhaps, for a frontier guard. But for each of the mercenaries who settled on their Finnish estates, several elected to reside in metropolitan Sweden and to live on incomes derived from their Finnish properties. Such absenteeism was bound to have undesirable effects.

As early as 1542, Gustavus Vasa had proclaimed all of Sweden's unoccupied land as the property of God, the crown and the state. He thus confirmed a principle which gained currency at the end of the Middle Ages, that land was only held by its owners on title from the crown. This principle was basic to the confiscation of church lands at the time of the Reformation and, in the 1680s, to the reduction of fiefs. Finland has much state-owned land today and its origins are a direct result of crown policy in the sixteenth century.

The principle also provided good grounds for elaborating the taxation system. Payments in kind, especially the percentage of skins, was slowly transformed. *Skattskinnet*, the pelt tax, and *oravainen*, the squirrel-skin tax, were subordinated to property taxes. Among the earliest tax books was that initiated by Gustavus Vasa for the province of Åland in 1537. The refinement of land taxation had already been carried far by the end of the sixteenth century. Thus, the surveyors who were concerned with the property inventories of Viipuri province from 1588 onwards not only indicated the different kinds of land use, but recorded taxable fishing rights, watermills and windmills. Qualitative considerations were introduced at an early stage, and some assessors even paid sympathetic attention to 'frost-bitten' land. The taxation of land continues as an integral feature of the fiscal structure of twentieth-century Finland. It is basic to the elaborate records of land use and land value that are invaluable to those who work with the history and geography of Finland. Against the background of these early land records, with their complementary administrative correspondence and court rolls, it is possible to reconstruct much from the Finnish scene of the sixteenth and seventeenth centuries. At the same time the exchequer, as well as military enterprise, encouraged the opening up of mineral deposits. The age saw the establishment of local iron-working plants – Fagervik, Skogby, Antskog, Dahlsbruk, the descendants of some of which still function today.

The new order soon resulted in a tug-of-war between centralisation and decentralisation. No matter how strongly government might be centralised in the person of the crown, some delegation of authority was unavoidable. The creation of the title of Duke of Finland in 1556 and of the appelation 'Grand Duchy of Finland' in 1581 was little more than playing with words. But by the 1620s, the Swedish chancery had established a special official to deal with Finnish affairs. Provincial governorships were being established and they still bear the same title – Sw. *landshäradshövding*: F. *maaherra.*

A court of appeal was established in Turku. The role of Turku was also strengthened by the creation of an office to deal with Finnish finances in the 1630s. On the other hand, the Stockholm administration pressed for identity of organisation in Finland and Sweden. This had both positive and negative consequences for Finland. It enabled certain Finnish-born nobles to rise to some of the highest offices in the land. Contrastingly, it meant that Swedish-born officials, lay and ecclesiastical, tended to outnumber Finnish-born officials in Finland itself.

A concomitant of the new order for Finland was the expansion of its political frontiers. Finland's eastern border had been defined in European terms for the first time in 1323 by the settlement of Pähkinsaari. The boundaries were redefined in 1595 at the Täyssinää settlement, and in 1617 by the Peace of Stolbova they marched eastwards to include the provinces of Ingria and Käkisalmi (Kexholm). Sweden's territories across the Baltic Sea reached their maximum extent at the same time. Evidence of boundary changes may still be seen on the ground. Three Swedish crowns chiselled into a rock serve as a boundary stone at Ohtansalmi in Tuusniemi parish. The three crowns were repeated in other places in other ages. Virtelä village in Salmi used to claim the distinction of a royal marker – *Hic regni posuit finus Gustavus Adolphus rex Sveonum, fauste Nomine duret opus.* During the time that Sweden was a great power, the buffer zone between the older settled parts of Finland and the marauders of Muscovy was pushed hundreds of miles farther eastwards. For nearly a century, there was greater security. No settlement benefited more from this situation than the fortress city of Viipuri. During the spacious days of the Swedish period, its hinterland stretched deeply into Karelia, its shipping looked beyond the Baltic to the coasts of western Europe and its merchant community acquired a more cosmopolitan character.

Finnish merchants also benefited from another consequence of Swedish policy. Despite the prevalence of mercantilist philosophy, a number of new cities were founded in the sixteenth and seventeenth centuries. They were located principally on the coast; though Lappeenranta, Savonlinna and Kajaani (all appropriately fortified) were established in interior Finland. Among others, Raahe, Oulu, Kokkola, Pietarsaari, Uusikaupunki and Kristiinankaupunki came into being along the Bothnian coast. On the south coast, Helsinki was raised from the status of a village in 1550. It was auspiciously conceived as a rival to Reval; though, in the context of the time, it was helped little by either site or situation. Gamla Helsingfors was awkwardly removed from the sea, at a site which strode a modest waterfall but was fed by a non-navigable river. It lacked a richly timbered hinterland with the freely flowing water necessary for the movement of softwood products.

The Broadening of Horizons

The broadening of horizons for the people of Finland took place in four directions – in the interior of their own land, in Sweden proper, on the European mainland and beyond the seas. In Finland and Sweden, pioneers pushed back the frontiers of settlement. On the banks of the Delaware, they shared in the establishment of a short-lived Swedish colony that was absorbed by the British. Mainland Europe opened to them intermittent military adventures, where their troops constituted a formidable component of the Swedish army.

The thrust to the interior of Finland was an intensification of an age-old process. Beyond the developed coastal zone of settlement stretched broad hunting lands and fishing waters, which were extensively employed by those who inhabited their margins. These lands were loosely defined, generally recognised as private property and may have been as much as fifty or more kilometres from the home farm.

They were penetrated seasonally as grazing lands, for cattle were proportionately more important on immature holdings than on established farmsteads. They were also basic to extensive cultivation by various methods of rotational woodland burning. Particular methods employed in different localities are recalled today in the legacy of place-names. *Huuhta* is an element recalling a cleared coniferous or mixed forest: *tulimaa* is a reminder of fired, half-grown deciduous woodland. The process of firing gave rise locally to a number of different forms of cooperative endeavour – *talkoot*, as it is still called. In his study of northern Savo, Arvo Soininen has estimated that 40 per cent of the farming units appear to have been operated by some kind of team combination. The land was frequently managed in common, if not owned in common. Groups of farmers banded themselves together into burn-beating organisations which might be semi-permanent as well as temporary.

Pioneering, though favoured by the crown, was not exactly encouraged by it. Evidently, a primary motive prompting migration was tax avoidance. The increasingly elaborate organisation of taxation in established areas of settlement – and its progressively heavy incidence – caused many to seek a more relaxed way of life away from the frontiers of authority. There was a second advantage in the earlier stages of settlement in new areas. Wood and water yielded a higher return of wild life than those in longer settled areas. On the debit side of the account were climatic uncertainties. New land was unknown land and the risk of crop failure on it was also higher. The colonial country was traditionally 'bark bread' country, where the pulverised phloem of trees was mixed with ground grain to make it last longer. Proverbs grew up among the backwoods people to echo down the generations – 'Go not to the larder when bread is in the log'.

As the hand of the administrator and tax gatherer stretched into the colonial lands and the boundaries of administrative parishes were cast around them, new generations of pioneers broke loose and sought escape as had their forbears. By the time the process had brought colonisation to the fringes of Lapland, an age of enlightenment was dawning and the pioneer was encouraged by favoured taxation rates.

The reindeer-breeding Lapps retreated before the intrusive pioneers. In 1649, the Kemi Lapps were complaining to Queen Christina that 'Many rich peasants leave their fat and fruitful properties in Savo and Oulu provinces, and pass over the borders of Lapland into our country'. The Savo colonists brought with them farming practices inimical to those of the indigenous graziers. Especially disastrous was the introduction of woodland burning, for it destroyed the reindeer mosses. The intruders also took over the trapping and fishing preserves of the Lapps. In the face of better equipped trappers and fishers, many Lapps adopted a sedentary life and intermarried with the Finns. In the words of Pastor Lagus, writing from Kuusamo in 1772, they were 'converted to farmers'. The process continues, though for more complex reasons.

A second group of Finns, numbering several thousands, migrated westwards into the largely uninhabited Swedish borderlands of Värmland and Dalarna. They moved in the early years of the Vasa dynasty, principally from parishes such as Puumula and Rautalampi in Karelia and Savo. Some settlers penetrated into the Norwegian no-man's-land that came to be called Finnskogen. Their absorption was slow and their language lingered for two centuries. When C. A. Gottlund visited these tracts in the early nineteenth century, he tried to resuscitate their Finnish sentiments. But the links with the past had already been severed. A sprinkling of place-names, associated principally with natural features and homesteads, remains today and local museums have contrived to assemble a few relics. Otherwise, little more than the ghost of a dialect word or a design unwittingly reproduced by a local craftsman remains of a migration that took place four hundred years ago.

The third group of migrants only numbered several hundreds. They moved yet farther west, to the tidewater lands of North America's Atlantic seaboard, where they helped to found the colony on the Delaware promoted by the New Sweden Company between 1638 and 1656. Among the directors of this enterprise was Klas Fleming, who was born at Louhisaari manor in south-west Finland. A sprinkling of Finns continued to go there even after New Sweden became English -- the pietist Peter Schäfer, for example, who knew William Penn.

A fourth group of Finns, serving as mercenaries rather than conscripts in Sweden's armies, shared experiences in a different theatre of activity. More than 10,000 of them were involved in the campaigns of the Thirty Years War, familiarising themselves with the character and customs of mainland Europe, witnessing the splendours of Breitenfeld and the miseries of Lützen. Swedish canvases of the day depict their pikemen and swordsmen following blustering commanders rampant upon heavy chargers. Popular textbooks have represented them as embracing total war in the cause of Protestantism (though the issues were less clear-cut than religious propagandists might aver). The war cry of the Finnish cavalry – *Hakkaa päälle* – found its way into European historical texts, while Finnish regiments became sufficiently renowned to claim a place on cartographers' cartouches. London's *Swedish Intelligencer* (1632–34) recounted stories of their prowess. Daniel Defoe attributed to 'Peter Alexowitz, Czar of Muscovy' the urge to conquer Finland because it would 'draw a vast number of good soldiers; the Finlanders always being esteemed the best men in the Swedish army – and especially the horse, it being a country for breeding horses'. Fiction soon began to mingle with the fact of their reputation. 'Six-foot tall Laplanders' were numbered among the ranks of those who marched with William of Orange's troops when they advanced on London from the West Country; while Lord Macaulay, in his *History of England*, gave the Fynlanders (perhaps, from Denmark's island of Fyn?) a role to play at the Battle of the Boyne. Nor were the Finnish mercenaries less resolute in defeat. C. G. Granfelt was among those captured and imprisoned after Poltava. Thirteen years later, in March 1722, he arrived safely back in Åbo (Turku). The last entry in his diary reads 'Till Åbo i Jesus namn' (To Åbo in Jesus' name).

'A Province large enough to be called a kingdom'

Five hundred years passed between the Swedish conquest of Finland and the climax of the spacious days – twice as long as the span of time between the climax and the present day. The civilising process was slow until the rise of the Vasa dynasty; but with the expanding horizons of a people on the move Finland responded accordingly. Land and population relations changed. At its most extensive, following the Stolbovan Peace, Finland was no less in geographical extent than Sweden proper. But, Sweden changed shape on the west as well as the east and the absorption of the Danish provinces altered the population balance so that peninsular Sweden had almost twice as many inhabitants as Finland by the 1670s. The size of Finland began to make an impact outside the north. In his *History of Peter the Great*, Daniel Defoe saw Finland as 'a province of itself large enough to be called a kingdom'. The qualities of Finland were presented by atlas makers in an increasingly favourable light. 'Finlandia dicta est pulchra terra, quod pulchrior et amaenior Suecia est', wrote Sebastian Munster. And Gustavus Adolphus helped to extend the image through his sponsorship of the magnificent baroque map of Anders Bure. The end of an epoch was portended in Dahlberg's *Suecia antiqua et hodierna*, a pictorial miscellany of Sweden's cities. This formidable propaganda piece, with profiles of fortified towns such as Viipuri and Hämeenlinna, was intended to leave no doubt of their capacity to withstand aggression.

It was a logical consequence that the tightening of the bonds within Sweden-Finland should lead Finland to be pressed increasingly into a Swedish mould. The process of Swedification that was applied to the ceded Danish provinces of south-west Sweden was inevitably felt in Finland. This is not to say that the application was deliberate or even conscious. Certainly, the Swedish language was given new emphasis. It was used to the disregard of Finnish in the army and in the civil service. Locally, this produced irritation, even opposition. Yet, Finland had few administrative growing points and no consciousness of a separate identity which prompted any organised resistance. For a minority, the tightening of Swedish bonds offered the ultimate in opportunity; while larger numbers found it convenient to adopt the Swedish tongue and Swedish names. It was above all in Per Brahe, the governor of Finland from 1637 to 1640 and from 1648 to 1654, that such Finnish feeling as there was found expression. But Brahe's motives in encouraging this were personal and national rather than provincial. Finland's history is scattered with examples of men with a powerful Swedish background who in word and deed have proved themselves to be more Finnish than the Finns.

Chapter 4

The Paradox of the Apocalypse

FINLAND HAD SHARED the benefits of Sweden's ascendancy. It had been a springboard for advance; its lands had been bestowed as estates to officers and mercenaries who had served the military cause; its men had been a part of Sweden's legendary vanguard in the field. It had now to be converted into a territory of defence – to resist, to absorb and to suffer the attacks made upon the parent country in decline. The blows aimed by Russia under Peter the Great and his successors were received first upon the Finnish shield and upon the Finnish hearth. From the demise of Charles XII until the dotage of Gustavus IV, Finland was ridden hard by the horsemen of the Apocalypse. Yet in the intervals between the nightmares, there is evidence of remarkable resilience. From the latter half of the eighteenth century onwards, a new spirit of enquiry seized the leaders of its community, a new intellectual and administrative advance was registered, a new assessment of the country was urged forward. The most powerful impetus for advance came from Sweden or through Sweden; but it would not have made progress had it not been for the inherent qualities of the Finns. Robert Ker Porter, commenting on them in 1808, discerned an 'alloy of inquisitiveness' within them, 'a sign of their being on the alert' and 'a sure promise of future improvement'.

A Cockpit in the North

The nadir of Finland's fortunes was reached during the Great Northern Wars between Russia and Sweden – years of wrath preceded by the hard famine of 1696–97. The wars lasted twenty-one years and their effect upon Finland was especially hard after 1710. Only two decades after the armistice of 1721, Finland's experiences were repeated through a retaliatory attack started by Sweden between 1741 and 1743. In 1788–90, Gustavus III's war afflicted Finland's south-eastern margins. Finally, in 1808–09, the country was overrun from the Torni river to the Åland islands and Sweden was driven from the eastern shores of the Baltic Sea. Nor was there any atmosphere of relaxation between these open hostilities. A cold war continued largely unabated.

As a result of the wars the frontiers of Finland experienced a succession of changes. The Peace of Uusikaupunki (Sw. Nystad), concluded according to the copperplates of the day by periwigged plenipotentiaries in unlikely baroque surroundings, bisected the province of Karelia and inscribed in 1721 a boundary roughly similar to that at present prevailing in the south-east. By the settlement of 1743 the Russian boundary was advanced westwards to the line of the Kymi river and north-westwards into the Saimaa Lake district. Lappeenranta fortifications were taken over by the Russians; great star-shaped bastions, accommodating several thousand troops, were built beyond them. The *status quo* was maintained as a result of the inconclusive engagements of 1788–90. Taavitti (R. Davidov: Sw. Davidstad), which boasts the ruins of an impressive fortress, is among present-day Finnish hamlets on the south-eastern borders. In September 1809, by the Treaty of Hamina (Fredrikshamn), Finland became a Russian dependency.

The fate of Finland hinged upon the opening of Peter the Great's window on the west. St Petersburg was established in territory which had originally been occupied by Finnish-speaking peoples. The Ingrians, one of the Finnish groups which the Russian chauvinist Polewoj later likened to ethnographic 'thistles and weeds', remained a significant minority group, organised into their own Lutheran church parishes, until the present century. They were Russianised without great resistance. But if the swampy site of St Petersburg was slowly given security against the Neva, its setting was regarded as insecure unless the Finnish frontier to its north was forced back. 'We must pray God that Russia will succeed in situating its capital in Constantinople. Then it might leave Finland in peace . . .' wrote the ageing Chancellor of Turku University, H. G. Porthan. But Russia's second city was to remain on the Baltic and the unfortunate juxtaposition of Finnish territory was to bedevil Finland to the present day.

The entire sequence of military engagements in which Finland was involved must be seen in its broader European perspectives. First, they were in part an expression of Sweden's politics – the eighteenth century being a period of tension in which domestic rivalries overflowed into the international arena. The challenge to the authority of the monarchy and the struggle for power between rival factions had direct repercussions on Sweden's external relations. An example is provided by the fierce differences between the party of the Hats and the party of the Caps: in the 1740s the Caps were especially active in their manoeuvres to sustain Finland's position *vis-à-vis* Russia. Secondly, Finland's experiences were inseparable from the grouping and regrouping of the systems of European alliances. The resulting system of checks and balances might be based upon major international events – such as the successive Russo-Turkish engagements in the eighteenth century or upon such minor manoeuvres as the appearance of a west European fleet in the summer waters of the Baltic.

There is another perspective from which the Finnish military engagements must be viewed. In absolute numbers, the Finnish army was small; as late as the 1780s, it only totalled 22,000. Accordingly, the scale of its operations was modest. By comparison with the vast engagements on mainland Europe, many Finnish battles were little more than skirmishes. The plaque at Porrassalmi, a tranquil isthmus south of Mikkeli, commemorates one of the best known Finnish actions in 1789; but it was very modest in size. The Swedish General Staff has issued a many-volumed history of the war of 1808–09. The painstakingly detailed record of the campaigns underscores the very limited scale of most of them. In his *Atlas of Finnish History*, Eino Jutikkala has indicated by a series of arrows the courses of the major operations in the succession of wars. But for the layman, it is the impact of fiction that takes precedence over fact. For example, the war of 1808–09 has become a part of the national *légende* principally because of J. L. Runeberg's *Songs of Ensign Stål*. These long narrative poems have immortalised the heroes of the last military incidents in which Swede and Russian were involved.

'Like one of those moving bogs in Ireland, (Russia) comes slowly, but surely on, threatening to overwhelm the country', wrote the Cambridge mineralogist Edward Clarke in 1800. It was less than a decade after he passed through Finland that Russia made its final bid for Sweden's eastern wing. Even then the eccentric Gustavus IV declined the offer of the substantial British help which had arrived in Gothenburg under the command of Sir John Moore. ('Twenty thousand Englishmen who could come neck and crop' to Turku, was the way that it was expressed in C. N. Klercker's letters.) The transfer of Finland's sovereignty in 1809 was confirmed by the dynasts of the day when they recast the map of Europe in Vienna in 1815.

As Russian pressure on Finland had mounted, the Swedish army had taken increasingly elaborate precautions for defence. When outposts in the Karelian isthmus and the Ladogan lands were lost, strongholds such as Olavinlinna were strengthened. Loviisa became the easternmost strong point after the line of the Kymi became the new frontier in 1743. The differences in the attitudes of the people and the appearance of the countryside on either side of the boundary gradually sharpened. They were recorded by most foreign travellers who followed the route between Stockholm and St Petersburg in the latter half of the eighteenth century. The gaunt granite fortifications on the eastern side of present-day Loviisa are a memorial to the time. Meanwhile, August Ehrensvärd, his lively pen writing and drawing with equal facility, was supervising the construction of an elaborate fortress at Sveaborg (F. Suomenlinna), on the island approaches to Helsinki. Its monumental façades, grassy embankments and shipyards, faithfully recorded in the detail of canvases by the Swedish painter Elias Martin, were intended as an impregnable stronghold to complement the defences of Hämeenlinna to the north. Its stone walls are a constant reminder to the Finns of the weakness of men, for what was once called 'The Gibraltar of the North' yielded without resistance in 1809. Today, as Jacob Bonsdorff observed of it in 1799, 'flowers sprout beneath the lips of cannons', but the present lips (first pursed in Russian foundries) have been long since silent.

Finland and the Finns were viewed differently in the context of a defensive situation. The organisation of the army was modified, provincial regiments came into their own, battle colours and standards acquired new meaning. From the 1760s onwards, military surveyors began to record the detail of the topography; to identify highway, byway and bridle path; to pinpoint defensive sites, fords and beacon hills 'for signals of smoke by day and fire by night'. In the process, soldier-farmers were encouraged to take up holdings in the frontier lands. O. E. Wetterhof conceived them as similar to the Romans on the *limes* of the antique world. Moreover, he wrote, 'Strange armies from the west can never grow to know the countryside in the same way or to care about it to the same degree' as those who live in it. Local guerrilla fighters had always played a useful role in Finland's wars. In the last half of the century, reconnaissance maps and texts multiplied to give a remarkable record of southern Finland. 'It is in the calm of peace time that a country should be studied', Sprengtporten wrote fatefully in his *Military Description of Savolax* in 1799. 'When war breaks out, victory is then so much more certain.'

The coastal waters as well as the land needed reconnaissance. Survey of the critical waterways of archipelago Finland was hastened after the war of 1788–90, when naval actions such as that of Svensksund (F. Ruotsinsalmi) off the Kymi estuary illustrated the urgent need for a record of local channels. Flamboyant canvases of the sea battle and of its accompanying storm were painted by artists such as J. L. Desprez and J. T. Schoultzin. The incident also remains vivid for the people around Kotka Bay, for in the summer months, amateur divers comb the wrecks in the shallow waters for treasure trove – cannons, cables, glass, porcelain, even bottles of wine.

The survey of Finnish waters was energetically conducted by C. N. af Schultén, a personable character and a prolific correspondent, whose descendants retain their links with Turku archipelago. His neatly-drawn working charts, their data plumbed with the lead in summer and through the ice in winter, are among the abundant family papers in the *Åbo Akademi* archives. As a result of land and coastal reconnaissance, Finns began to acquire a fuller appreciation of the shape and content of the southern part of their country.

But as a consequence of the events which prompted this knowledge, land and people suffered grievously. During the Great Northern Wars and during the wars of 1808–09, there were major migrations to Sweden proper. Extensive areas were deserted and formally organised life ceased within them. Property was reduced to ashes, stock was destroyed, arable land reverted to the wilderness, churches were desecrated, the very tongues were torn from bells. Sometimes, occupying Russians deported entire communities from Ostrobothnia and Karelia. 'Woods spread over the fields, wild animals spread through the woods, those who owned a cow or a couple of sheep were accounted rich', was the graphic description given by Zachris Topelius to his students. The desolation was echoed in Book I of Wordsworth's *Prelude*. The ultimate simile for the winter wind in Esthwaite hills was a loud

> 'Protracted yelling, like the noise of wolves
> Howling in troops along the Bothnian main'.

The incidence of invasion was the harder because of the inherent physical condition of Finland. It is not a country where it is easy to live off the land. Only when cultivated and organised with the greatest care can the bare minimum of food be obtained to meet domestic needs, and war interrupted food production and distribution. It also interfered with the channels of trade. The problems of trading during the anarchy of the Northern Wars are illustrated by the fragmentary commercial correspondence dated 1718–19 of Thomas Dunn, an English merchant resident in Finland. Domestic products entering his trade were in short supply, imports had to run the gauntlet of enemy patrols; while the pack and sleigh horses that were vital for commodity transport were everywhere pressed into military use. He lamented the early appearance of his 'grey hairs'.

And, as if to try still further the patience of such youthful Jobs, the eighteenth century experienced a cyclical worsening of the climate. Evidence is found in occasional local meteorological observations, such as those of J. Leche for Turku (1750–61). Church books also yield evidence. The vicar of Saltvik in Åland, for example, recorded in his church register in 1785 that the ice lay on the north shore until two weeks after midsummer. In October 1761, winter had already arrived. *Lumi-talvi* (snowy winter) and *sula-talvi* (hungry winter) are other notes encountered. A legacy of country phrases was passed on to posterity – 'It was so cold that the fire froze in the hearth.' But it was not only the severity of the winters which discomfited the Finn, it was the delaying action of hard conditions on springtime ploughing and sowing. Agriculture, too, passed through the valley of the shadow of death.

The direct impact of the war and the indirect effect of the climate upon food supply took their joint toll of Finland's population. At the end of the seventeenth century it is estimated that the population was about 400,000. A generation later, at the conclusion of the Northern Wars, it had probably fallen by nearly a quarter. It was slow to recuperate; but by 1809 it had reached nearly 900,000. As today, it was concentrated in the south-west of the country. It found its focus in the provincial capital of Turku – an older Turku, the bridgehead and principal point of entry into Finland of ideas and innovations from the outside world, which had yet to suffer its devastating conflagration.

A View from the Bridge

Turku also included a northern coppice of the groves of Academe. In keeping with the spirit of the age, the University of Turku was moved both by the curiosity about natural phenomena and by political arithmetic. As a source of illumination in Swedish Finland, it reached a climax under the rectorship of Henrik Gabriel Porthan. In addition to being an able administrator, Porthan knew Finland widely and deeply. His publications included an anonymous *Geography of the Grand Duchy of Finland* (Stockholm, 1795). It provided a view from the bridge of a country which was not yet a state and not yet a nation.

The geography, which he was prompted to compose as a result of the ill-informed nature of much that was written about Finland, summarised settlement and activity on a provincial basis for the whole country. It made use of many new sources of information and, in particular, it cast new light on the interior of the country. In its introduction it identified Finland's perennial problems – war, famine and pestilence. Yet the very fact of Porthan's book reflected the paradox of the situation. It was a well-arranged and scholarly statement, printed with a touch of the rococo for the rector of a university which Cambridge visitors in 1799 esteemed above that of Uppsala. The century of the visitation of military wrath was also a century of considerable enlightenment in Finland. While the spread of enlightenment was inseparable from the growth of European interest in the natural and applied sciences, the stimulus of what Voltaire called 'the luminaries of the north' was no less compelling.

Thus the detailed estimates of people, land and resources which were initiated in the mid-eighteenth century were closely related to the need to know the availability of man-power, of foodstuffs and of materials for war or the purposes of the tax gatherer. Indeed it was already acknowledged in mid-eighteenth-century Finland that a substantial population was a country's principal wealth. Optimists were intimating that Finland should be capable of supporting three million inhabitants, when England (which was not as big as Finland) had seven million. In order to make assessments, the need for a fuller organisation became manifest. The organisation was common with that of Sweden, and when Finland was separated from Sweden it retained the established structure. Accordingly much that has meaning for modern Finland is rooted in this critical age.

Attempts had been made to codify population recording in the Church Laws of 1686, but it was the preliminary work of the Swedish Academy of Sciences that eventually gave rise to the central commission of *Tabellverket* in 1748. Thereafter, from every parish and town a three-yearly return was made until 1775, after which a quinquennial return was continued until the end of the Swedish period. On the rough paper of the printed forms, enumerators were required to identify a range of age groups and to distinguish over thirty different causes of death (including 'of hunger and unsuitable food'). As a result, Finland has, like Sweden, some of the world's most complete demographic materials. Both Thomas Malthus and the Scottish political scientist, Thomas Thomson, paid tribute to *Tabellverket* (as the population tables were called). Not surprisingly, Finland has a continuing tradition of statistical excellence. Another feature of the modern state is the continuing responsibility of church officials for the maintenance of population statistics. The parish, both Orthodox and Lutheran, remains the unit of collection. A lay population register – *henkilökirja* – has also been kept by each local government authority for the last thirty years.

In the later eighteenth century, a return of 'classes' and professions was added to the census. The 'classes' conformed largely to the four estates – nobility, clergy, burghers and yeomen, each of which had its own house of representatives. The return of households by professions and pursuits was carried to a considerable degree of refinement. If a sample return be taken for 1795 from Nurmes, on the frontier settlement in north-east Finland, it will be found to include fifty colonists (Sw. *nybyggare*) as well as the 330 established farmers. A special category was introduced for Lapps in 1760. Urban occupations identified in the return ran from furriers and curriers to pinmakers and spurmakers. The products of eighteenth-century workshops may still be found. The passage of time is still marked by birch and pinewood grandfather clocks, such as those produced by Master Widlund of Kokkola.

From 1802 onwards, *Tabellverket* included a simple census of crop returns; stock was to be added from 1805. Not until the 1860s was a formal collection of farm statistics initiated, but the incipient crop and stock returns indicate an additional aspect of responsible thinking in the parish communities.

While military mapmakers were committing their reconnaissance surveys to paper, Finland's farmland was also being mapped and its use recorded for different reasons. In 1747, Sweden initiated a land reorganisation programme (*Storskifte*) which encouraged the unification of fragmented farm holdings. The following year, the first land survey officers went to Ostrobothnia to set in motion a scheme which was to have a fundamental effect upon the structure of Finnish farming and to strengthen the system of assessment for land taxation. The maps that resulted were the Finnish counterparts to Britain's Parliamentary Enclosure Awards. The present-day Land Survey Office (F. *Maanmittaushallitus*: Sw. *Lantmäteristyrelsen*) houses the original copies of thousands of them. As befits a social group upon which maps have been imposed, Finnish farmers are continuingly map-conscious.

Behind the surveys and property reorganisations lay a new attitude to the land – an attitude which owed much to the school of natural scientists at Uppsala. Carl Linnaeus, its primary instigator, sounded the keynote of his approach in an inaugural lecture entitled *Oratorio qua peregrinationum intra patriam asseritur necessitas* and delivered on 17 October 1741. Already by his time provincial governors were making their intermittent reports to Stockholm and assembling a miscellany of facts about the economy and society of their territories. Already, mineralogists were making their perambulations and looking for the believed counterpart to Sweden's Bergslagen. Daniel Tilas, who undertook a journey along Kokemäki valley into Häme in 1737–38, was among them. He produced a model report with lively field sketches, but could forecast no more than limited prospects. Linnaeus and his disciples gave a new meaning and a new impetus to the collection of information. There were at least two results. First, there arose a school of topographers who set about describing the nature and classifying the features of the parish scene. Secondly, financed by the Swedish Academy of Sciences, a generation of disciples journeyed to the four corners of the earth bent upon discovering new and useful plants.

The influence of Uppsala bore fruit at Turku in schools of both natural philosophy and natural husbandry. The natural philosophers speculated upon broader as well as deeper matters. Johannes Browallius, sometime bishop of Turku, added his arguments to those upon the causes of land upheaval; others, such as J. H. Colliander, lowered their gaze to a catalogue of native medical plants. The zoologists debated the habits and habitat of the beasts of the chase, pondered upon variations in the numbers of river fish, and discussed the characteristics of caterpillars and mosquitoes. The natural husbandmen turned principally to the economics of farming – to such topics as the suitability of fell tracts for colonisation, the economic consequences of Finland's climate and the problems of a grazing husbandry. Economic considerations reached their climax in the work of Anders Chydenius, sometimes called the Adam Smith of Finland, who formulated a series of precepts in keeping with the new age. Largely due to his initiative, economic liberalism gradually succeeded to the old mercantilist doctrines.

Although it drew its inspiration principally from Uppsala, the Finnish university community also struck contact with the Academy of St Petersburg when Fenno-Russian relations permitted. Some Finnish scholars migrated to the Russian capital. Among the most distinguished was A. J. Lexell, a student of Turku who gained European renown in the field of astronomy.

Most of the teachers at Turku University were churchmen and most of the students were destined to follow the same calling. The physical circumstances of Finland implied that they were likely to live isolated lives and that, as with their congregations, they were likely to be most successful if they were practical husbandmen. Their church farms, frequently some of the largest and oldest in the community, were often central to parishes as large as English counties. From them, they surveyed the gathering momentum of interior colonisation – especially along the northern valleys. In addition to their spiritual calling, country vicars were also expected to be sources of practical enlightenment. They were the remote channels of communication between the educated minority and the uneducated masses. They spread the ideas of innovators to country people – partly by exhortation, partly by precept. It was usually the vicars who introduced new crops and practised new methods of cultivation or stock management on their own holdings. They also had the advantage of pulpits from which to preach potatoes, Spanish ewes or English rams, and the virtues of conserving the dwindling timber supply. Their office enabled them to urge the moral of Joseph in Egypt and to store grain in years of surplus against years of famine. Some of the sturdy parish store houses – granite-hewn and shingle-roofed – remain today as testimony to their effectiveness. Not infrequently the vicars were at the same time teachers – extending the knowledge of Swedish, carrying the cadences of Latin to the frontiers of inhabited Europe, committing the occasional Finnish to paper. Many Finnish churches have monuments to spiritual forefathers who were at the same time mindful of the body as well as the soul. A. A. Parvela has intimated something of their contribution to field crop, kitchen garden and cottage window in his history of plant cultivation in Oulu province. The rural clergy were also the natural progenitors of phenological observations.

At the same time the country vicars educated the administrators and university men of Turku about the nature of the distant parishes where they served. No one knew the problems and potentialities of the countryside as well as they. Their reports described parishes as remote as Kuusamo, in the sub-Arctic attics of the north-east, and Sagu in the kindlier archipelagos of the south-east, Enontekiö in the piedmont of the Scandinavian keel mountains and Laihela in the level and fertile plains of southern Ostrobothnia. They contributed scores of topographical accounts (mostly 20–25 pages long) and, for personal as well as public reasons, maintained records of many other features. Not least they set in motion the building of new churches and the improvement of old. The parish churches of the Ostrobothnian littoral reflect their influence – as well as the relative affluence of their communities. Their furnishings include handsome ship models that recall safe landfalls from perilous seas.

These developments were inseparable from the expanding horizons of the coastal inhabitants consequent upon relaxed trading relations. The demand for greater freedom of trade was urged for both domestic and international reasons. From 1765 onwards direct trading between Ostrobothnian harbours succeeded to the monopolist control of the staple ports. 'Stockholm tar' (although its name was to linger for two centuries) became literally what it was – tar from the round pits and sturdy barrels of Ostrobothnia. From the copy books of trading houses such as Hackman of Viipuri, which have been maintained almost continuously since the 1790s, it is possible to appreciate the growing diversity and strength of overseas trading relations. Trade in eighteenth-century Finland was restricted by both the limited number of market towns and the control of goods exchanged at them. In the 1740s there were only sixteen market towns. Local customs offices levied tolls on goods moving in and out of them. The site of Helsinki's toll gate is commemorated by a restaurant named *Tullinpuomi* (Sw. *Tullbom*) at the north end of the principal city street, Mannerheimintie.

In the limited trading scene, fairs assumed a correspondingly greater importance. Local fairs, dated according to the Julian instead of the Gregorian calendar after 1751, multiplied considerably in the later eighteenth century. They continued to be held with greater frequency in autumn and winter than at other seasons of the year. Easier communications favoured winter fairs. Foreign observers such as Edward Clarke described the remarkable distances covered by some vendors who brought their refrigerated products to Turku market: John Atkinson has drawn illustrations of others. In his description of Kuusamo in 1772 Elias Lagus spoke of winter travellers in his parish as reading their way by the stars – 'Ursa major and minor, with Orion, served them as a compass'. Even reindeer carried them at 20 km. an hour.

Easier domestic movement of people and products pressed hard. There might be routemaps and guides to posting routes such as C. P. Hasström's *Vägvisare* of 1807, but most ordinary travellers paid small heed to them. Some new roads were built in the eighteenth century, partly for military reasons – and south Ostrobothnians still call one of them by its early royal name. Most travellers' accounts were unflattering about Finnish roads and the posthouses or *gästgiveri* that were strung along them like beads on a thread, but they were complimentary about the briskness and energy of Finnish posting horses. Poor highways were to remain until new machines and new methods of construction were to revolutionise road-making after the Second World War. The travelling tinkers and tailors, soldiers and sailors, gipsies and Karelian pedlars, administrators and strolling players (they carried *Romeo and Juliet* to Oulu in the 1780s) simply complained and accepted the rude highways.

The problem of communication between the interior lakes and the coasts grew increasingly. None of the interlinking rivers was easily navigable; though there were boat stations along them and their rapids might be shot 'with adroit men at the helm' (as one of Klercker's reports put it). Not surprisingly the canal mania which swept western Europe in the eighteenth century had its distant Finnish echoes. Finnish businessmen, such as C. F. Bremer, corresponded about the economics of inland waterways with constructional engineers, such as Edward Thomason of Birmingham. Academics spoke of the gods of English navigation – Bridgewater and Brindley. Schemes proliferated, though little was achieved save for some rather energetic digging along the course of the Kokemäki river in the last few years of Swedish rule. The corps of engineers who constituted the *Strömrenssningskommitté*, in which all improvement of watercourses was centralised, were mostly concerned with local projects. Two centuries of their accumulated efforts have done much to bring new land into cultivation and to improve the drainage of old.

None were more eloquent in advocating the liberalisation of trade than the leaders of Ostrobothnia. Already by the mid-eighteenth century, trading establishments such as that of the Malms in Pietarsaari had come into existence. Its shuttle of wooden vessels, consisting of a fleet about a score in strength and mostly less than 140 tons in size, was plying the summer waters with cargoes of tar to the ports of western Europe. The vessels were built locally, for the seaports of Kokkola, Vaasa, Kristiina and Uusikaarlepyy all had their own wharves. Sometimes, shipbuilders brought their skills from abroad. In Turku, for example, Robert Fithie was elected chief of the shipbuilding wharf in 1737 and the yards blossomed under his son. Tombstones to the Cowie family, also shipbuilders, remain in the old burial ground of Turku. Some of Pehr Malm senior's captains had already taken to 'tramping' and building up credits by the 1790s. And Finnish seamen who served them had spiritual as well as material needs. The Swedish church of Ulrike Eleanore, established in Wapping in 1713, included Finns in the succession of its resident chaplains. Among them was the provocative A. N. Matthesius, a member of a prolific and gifted Ostrobothnian family.

The handful of Finns who had sought their fortunes in distant places included P. A. Bladh, an agent of the Swedish East India Company in Canton. On his return to Finland, Bladh took up residence on his estate, Bennäs in south Ostrobothnia. In furtherance of his commercial aims, he established the port of Kaskö (Kaskinen). Like Thomas Dunn, he was to suffer personally under the scourge of war. Souvenirs from China (punch bowls, smelling of arak, and Cantonese lacquerware) and the decorations of a trader's household (from European manufactures to gift-framed silhouettes) disappeared when Bennäs was destroyed in the war of 1808–09.

Pehr Kalm, one of the most influential of Linnaeus's 'wandering scholars', might also have gone to China. When the botanical journeys for Linnaeus's students were planned there was an initial proposal that Kalm should follow in the footsteps of Marco Polo. Eventually he went to North America. Kalm, son of an Ostrobothnian vicar who had fled to Sweden during the Great Northern

Wars, graduated from Turku University and eventually returned as Professor of Natural Husbandry to his *alma mater*. His three-year North American sojourn yielded a rich harvest of botanical observations, a memorable diary and an abundance of inspiration to at least a generation of students. Under Kalm's supervision more than a hundred academic dissertations were written. Kalm also succeeded in establishing his own *hortus botanicus*. Both in the precinct of present-day Åbo Akademi and in the garden of Maaria vicarage to which he retired, there are mature trees which tradition ascribes to his planting. Kalm's tradition lives on; Finland's horticultural research institute is located at Pikkiö (Pikkis), thirty kilometres to the south-east of Turku. It is an institute which carries on at least some of Kalm's ideas. In a letter to C. F. Mennander, Kalm wrote of his North American apple, cherry and plum trees fruiting with as much flavour at Sipsalo as in their native habitat. Present-day Pikkiö has Ottawa apple stock, New England tree blueberries and a terraced vineyard of hardy Canadian grapes.

While Finland's eighteenth-century academics were practical men of action, they also heeded the importance of the printed word. A steady stream of student dissertations emerged under their supervision. Most of them were modest contributions – a score of pages long, preyed upon by dedications, decorated with woodcuts, printed upon rough rag-and-straw paper. The printed dissertation was an early tradition. As a result, Finland has been able to keep a virtually complete collection of them. The tradition continues, for all doctoral dissertations must be published before they are formally disputed.

Most publications circulating in eighteenth-century Finland emanated from Sweden. But by the 1770s, Finland had its own periodical – *Tidningar utgifvna af ett Sällskap i Åbo*. It was the work of the Aurora Society and provided a forum and a focus for the university world. Turku University had its own printing machines at an early stage. Turku's Royal University Press was associated with the names of master printers from the mid-eighteenth century onwards. The family Frenckell (whose name, ennobled by *von*, is still well-known in present-day Finland) made an especially powerful contribution to the printed word from the 1740s onwards.

Until the 1750s, as many dissertations appeared in Latin as in Swedish. Other than the Bible, hardly any publications appeared in the vernacular. Daniel Juslenius, already known for his remarkable *Aboa vetus et nova* and *Vindiciae Fennorum*, juxtaposed Finnish with Swedish and Latin for the first time in his dictionary, in 1745. Christfrid Ganander gathered together material for a Finnish dictionary, which was not published until the fat manuscript appeared in facsimile in 1937–40. Foreign tongues additional to the classical languages began to be taught. German took precedence over English. French, the language of diplomacy, was learnt by the nobility and military officials. Some families, such as that of Gustav Mauritz Armfelt, employed French tutors. If his son, Alexander Armfelt, was representative of their charges, they were not unsuccessful teachers. After Stockholm ceased to be the court circle to which Finland's administrators moved, French served no less well in St Petersburg.

Libraries also began to multiply in private homes. They consisted mostly of Swedish publications to which were gradually added domestic journals such as *Åbo Tidningar* and, later, *Finska Hushållningssällskapets Berättelser.* In 1801, the first attempt at a husbandry book for farmers appeared – *Försök till lärobok i landthushållningen för finska bonden.* It was, incidentally, among the first publications to urge the improvement of the existing arable land rather than to extend intakes from the wasteland.

Books from abroad began to appear. Eighteenth-century property inventories of deceased Finns indicate the relative breadth of reading. The contents of libraries belonging to estate-owners ranged from historical texts and studies on canal construction to racing calendars and cookery books. Books in English and French were to be found in the homes of merchants, customs inspectors, soldiers and priests. The poets and dramatists of other lands began to make an impact, in the original as well as in German and Swedish translations. They included Shakespeare, Pope, Milton, Goldsmith, Fielding, Montaigne, Molière, Rousseau and Boileau. Söderman's bookshop in Turku advertised in 1789 that French, English and Danish books were available for customers. Their customers must have included Franz Michael Franzén. Franzén, the young poet from Oulu who later became a Swedish bishop, was well acquainted with the plays of Shakespeare before he wrote almost intoxicatedly of them during his visit to London in 1796. His poem, *Finlands Uppodling,* published in *Åbo Tidning* in 1800, was a hymn on the birth of a new century. In it he displayed the fervour and forward-looking qualities of the best of his west European contemporaries. To the age of reason and to the concept of utility he added a breath of romance.

In fact the ripples of a variety of movements which stirred western Europe lapped upon the remote shores of Finland. They included the romantic movement and its associated attitude to the landscape. British poets such as Thomson and Gray were discussed in Turku, while A. N. Clewberg was translating Ossian in the 1770s. Undertones of sentimentality moved polite circles through such artists as J. C. Linnerhielm, A. F. Skiöldebrand and A. G. Silverstolpe. The circles were restricted because late eighteenth-century Finland had no more than 260 large estates. All of their families did not react equally strongly to the romantic movement, but when it was translated into terms of landscape gardening it became a more easily appreciated applied art. Parks were planned in which deciduous trees were planted to hide the encompassing pines. They were identified as 'English parks' from the fashion of the time and the literature from the English age of landscaping. In the intervening 170 years, the parks have attained maturity. Åminne, near Salo, in south-west Finland, provides an example. Viewed from its terrace, oaks of 'the umbrageous English style' dominate. They are called *ädelträ* in Swedish (*jalopuu*, in Finnish) – noble trees. Russia as well as western Europe contributed exotics. It matched the deciduous hardwoods with the *Larix sibirica*; though the original object of planting it, as at Raivola in the Karelian isthmus, was to ensure future supplies of ships' timbers. The lesser farmers might not be able to introduce foreign trees to grace their properties or to afford panorama wallpapers to enliven their living-rooms, but aesthetic ideas spread down to them. Avenues of the native birch and rowan at the approaches to their holdings and the warmly-coloured *ryijy* or wall-hangings were pleasant substitute features – and still are.

Few Finns communicated the mood of sentimental romanticism better than Jacob Bonsdorff. *Sommar resan*, printed in Turku in 1799, is his record of an unashamed pleasure journey. At Fagervik estate, where he contemplated 'an island landscaped in the English style', a Chinese pleasure garden, and 'a hermit's simple abode . . . in an icy and lovely grotto, all nature's colours seem(ed) to be united through art to awaken gladness in the eye of the beholder'. Later as he drifted along Borgå river, the sounds of his flute answered from the trees by invisible birds and echoed back from the hard rocks, he sensed a veritable summer ecstasy.

Others, too, romanticised their ideal. Such was the anonymous author of *Mit Wal* (published in *Åbo Nya Tidningar*, 1798) who described a small estate 'in imitation of the English'. The description descended to the detail of the library 'where one might read how nature overcomes art'. The occasional late eighteenth-century farmer came near to achieving his ideal. This is testified by advertisements in *Åbo Tidning*; though Finnish *fermes ornées* were rarities. Yet if the romanticists of six or seven generations ago could be transported to the byways of metropolitan Finland today, they would rejoice in the widespread occurrence of trim and fruitful holdings which conform to the ideal.

While there were Finns travelling abroad in search of education (such as Franz Michael Franzén and Carl Fredrik Bremer), of scientific knowledge (such as K. D. von Haartman and C. J. Gadolin) or trade, European travellers began to leave an increasing record of Finland. Usually they followed the established route between Turku and St Petersburg. They were few and far between compared with the stream that followed the Grand European Tour, but their observations were a useful addition to the limited knowledge that the outer world was able to assemble about Finland. The accounts of British travellers such as Marshall, Swinton, Wraxall, Barrow and Clarke, are collectors' pieces today. Others such as the earlier accounts of the French travellers Maupertuis and Outhier, are significant for Finland, because they contribute footnotes to the history of science. Some travellers were more lively with their sketch pads than with their pens. No foreign visitor recorded everyday Finnish activities more appealingly than John Atkinson, though Robert Ker Porter supplemented his details. Carl von Kügelen, their slightly later German counterpart, focused his attention on landscape. All these books commanded respectable subscription lists; but it was war and trade which stirred more popular interest in Finland. The earliest comprehensive account of Finland for British readers appeared in the *Atlas Commercialis et Maritimus* in 1723. By the end of the century, under the surveillance of C. P. Hallström, the magnificent Atlas of the Grand Duchy of Finland was published as the second volume of the Atlas of Sweden in Stockholm by Baron Hermelin. It was the first bound book of maps to be devoted exclusively to Finland and marked a milestone in the appreciation of the country. It must have served as a basis for a number of the professional soldiers who paid heed to the war of 1808–09 – a war reported for the English in regular dispatches to *The Times*.

The Partition of Sweden

It might be assumed that the physical detachment of Finland from Sweden, the ferment of ideas which began to work in the Grand Duchy as the century advanced, and the spirit of the age which moved the continent after 1789 would prompt particularist tendencies in Finland. Such an assumption might be strengthened by the fact that Finland as a country began to have a fuller and more personal meaning as a country for the Finns. Yet during the Swedish period, Finland displayed no pronounced consciousness of its own individuality and its leading figures sensed no great urge for an existence independent of Sweden. True, they began to speak and write in terms of a fatherland and to cultivate patriotic fervour as a commendable virtue. They also began to demonstrate sensitivity to any remarks that were derogatory or belittling to their country. Lord Baltimore's *Gaudia poetica* (1769), in which he confused Finns and Lapps, and the Liège *Encyclopaedia* of 1756 were cases in point. Again the name of Canada was sometimes mentioned by the outer world in the same breath as that of Finland. H. G. Porthan derided those who urged the comparison. 'It is not agreeable,' he wrote, 'when we are set side by side with such a wild and uncultivated land.' F. M. Franzén wrote an anonymous contribution to *Åbo Tidning* in 1800 on the attitude encountered among the Swedish *beau monde* when confronted with Finland. 'To Finland? Over the sea,' cried all the young ladies and took a step backwards. '... The Lord help you, sir, on such a journey.' Such reactions may perhaps be better interpreted as those of slightly affronted provincial pride rather than of offended national feeling. Down to 1808–09, Finland and Sweden remained very much one land.

Yet the later eighteenth century witnessed a growing awareness of the differences between the Swedish and Finnish languages and between those who spoke them. Two contrasting features became manifest. First, the significance of the Swedish language in Finland was increased. This was a natural development rather than a contrived situation. To a large extent it was explained by the increased means of integration and communication between the two halves of the nation. Those who wished to advance themselves had to learn Swedish, in the same way as those who wish to advance themselves in Finland today have to acquire at least one of the major world languages. Partly with the object of advancement, many people with Finnish family names changed them for Swedish.

Secondly, and in contrast to these tendencies, the great mass of the people living in Finland remained Finnish-speaking only. Their attitudes slowly changed as did that of others to them. For example Finnish-speaking Finns became increasingly critical when administrators with no knowledge of Finnish were appointed to districts which were entirely Finnish-speaking. Although interpreters were employed in the courts this was no final solution to the problem. Complaints were not unsympathetically received in Stockholm, but trained administrators with a knowledge of the Finnish language were limited in supply. There was certainly no bar to their recruitment. Johan Matthesius and Johan Arckenholz, both of whom rose to leading positions in the central administration, were representative of Finns recruited to the service. Eventually Matthesius lost his office in the intrigues which surrounded the political rivalries between Sweden's 'Hats' and 'Caps'. But involvement was neither because he was a Finn nor because he had a Finnish axe to grind.

Nor can the most serious division of opinion with Sweden that disturbed Finland in the eighteenth century be ascribed to ethnographic feelings of distinction. There is a long story leading up to the events which culminated in the Anjala incident in 1788 and they have been much the object of Finnish enquiry and interpretation. Suffice to say that opposition to the policies of Gustavus III came to a head on Finnish soil. The instigator was G. M. Sprengtporten, a Swedish officer who together with his half-brother J. M. Sprengtporten had been rebuffed by Gustavus at an earlier stage in his career. An important related consequence of their action in 1772 was the new Form of Government accorded to the Grand Duchy. When Gustavus launched his war of aggression in 1788 a mixed group of Swedish and Finnish officers attempted to call a halt to it. Overtures were made to the Russians, the conspirators were arraigned by the King, and in their defence they produced a document which set out their case. The document was signed at Anjala, the frontier town in the Kymi valley, after which the incident usually takes its name. Subsequently, Sprengtporten manoeuvred for an independent Finland under Russian protection. Though he and his companions claimed to speak for 'the whole nation and especially the people' (which might have been the Swedish independently of the Finnish nation), it may be fairly asserted that the action was personal and opportunist rather than rooted in popular feeling. Porthan dismissed the Anjala League as a group of 'witless adventurers and windbags among our nobility'. Only one head fell – that of Colonel Hästesko.

Those members of the nobility who had their roots in Finland were, in any case, divided along Swedish political lines. Some, who attained and maintained high office, were remarkable in their own right. From Count Arvid Horn in the earlier years of the century to Gustav Mauritz Armfelt at its close they supplied astute leadership. In another setting Armfelt might have become a second Metternich. So far as the Finnish people themselves were concerned, the clearest testimony of their attachment to Sweden would appear to be their unanimity in the war of 1808–09 – though a cynic might proclaim that it was the traditional hatred of Russia that was fundamental to their resistance.

Be that as it may, the consequence of defeat in 1809 was the partition of Sweden. Yet the partition of Sweden did not give reality to the dreams of the ageing Sprengtporten. Through it the Finnish half of Sweden became a part of the Baltic foreland of Russia – a political entity constitutionally guaranteed by the Tsar. Finland escaped the government 'on the Livonian or Courland model' that Porthan feared. Moreover, its constitution was strengthened through the old-established contacts between the coastal Finns and the peoples of western Europe. These counterbalanced any new economic pull to the east. 'The Finlander', wrote James Latham in 1856, was 'united with the Swede rather than subjected to him . . . (Therefore) his civilisation that of western Europe rather than eastern Europe. His alphabet is Swedish and Roman, not Russian and Greek . . . in the way of intellectual development, Finland stands to Sweden as Spain and Gaul to Rome.' These facts are still relevant for any explanation of the life and attitude of the present-day Finn.

If Finland received much from the mother land, it suffered much for her sake. 'This country, Finland, has belonged for 700 years to the Swedish crown', complained a deputation from Finland to the Swedish Parliament in 1746–47, 'but has not known 25 years' uninterrupted peace.' It was ironical that the eventual transfer of allegiance to Russia, so abhorrent to Finns, was to give to them a longer period of uninterrupted peace than they had known in their entire history. The irony was intensified, because the long unbroken peace that Sweden was to experience after the loss of Finland would have been impossible if Finland had continued to be a part of the Swedish realm.

Chapter 5

A Grand Duchy of Russia

AMONG EARLIEST EXPERIENCES which Finland underwent as a Russian Grand Duchy there were three that were to have an immediate impact and continuing consequences. The first, and most immediate, was a new constitution – later to become one of the most disputed in Europe and central to the rupture of Fenno-Russian relations. The second was a change in the shape of the country – or, rather, the restoration of a former political outline. For, in 1812, *Gamla Finland* (Old Finland) as it was known was reunited with the remainder of the duchy. From this new outline (to which there was some opposition at the time) were to arise eventually the principal problems of the republic of Finland. The third was a change in the site of the capital city. In 1812, the Russian government also set in motion the transfer of the powers of administration from the historic Swedish capital of Turku to the small south-coast settlement of Helsinki. The different development of the two cities was accordingly sealed.

These immediate and tangible experiences were followed by the stirrings of political, economic and social change which were moving western Europe at large. There was a considerable time lag before Finland was able to share fully in these changes; but the foundations of the modern industrial and commercial state were firmly laid while Finland was still a Russian dependency. The Grand Duchy also became a nation. It could not anticipate a return to the Swedish realm, it did not wish absorption in Russia. Accordingly, it had to become Finnish. In his colourful letters on Finland, Xavier Marmier wrote of Helsinki society in the early 1840s as 'Finnish at heart, Russian by circumstance'. The growth of national feeling had parallels in many parts of nineteenth-century Europe, but the process in Finland had highly distinctive characteristics. And in some respects it became a nation in spite of itself, for there were deep divisions within – of the hungry and the filled, of the property owner and the property-less, of the Swedish-speaking Finn and the

Finnish-speaking Finn. The climax of the situation was largely precipitated by events on a higher plane. Finland was not directly a party to the First World War, but its declaration of independence was inseparable from it and the recognition of this independence was related closely to the international alignment of the European powers and their various allies. Nor was Finland able to escape the upheavals of the Russian revolution. They cut clean through the fabric of its society.

The Grand Duchy of Finland

On 28/29 March 1809 the Emperor Alexander convened the Diet and in an Act of Assurance created the autonomous Grand Duchy of Finland. An oath of allegiance was taken by the estates to Alexander as the new Grand Duke of Finland, and the decrees of agreement were read from pulpits throughout the land. A formal government was eventually organised, the central body of which took the name of the Senate. In general, the new administration grew organically out of the pre-existing Swedish order. A Supreme Court took over the functions hitherto performed by the Central Swedish Court and the Swedish Law of 1734 became the basis for the codified law of Finland. The new Finnish laws also applied to the reunited south-east of the country. The Tsar appointed his own personal representative as Governor-General in Finland. In theory, the Governor-General was the chairman of the government, though in practice he only performed limited duties in this office. Apart from the first year, when G. M. Sprengtporten held this office, the Governor-General was always a Russian. The full powers of the office only became manifest during the last twenty years of the Russian régime. In St Petersburg, a Finnish Affairs Committee provided the direct channel of communication between the Finns and the Tsar. It was headed by a Finnish Secretary of State with a resident Finnish staff.

The immediate consequence of the new constitution was that the Finnish people became Finns. They were no longer Swedes. Nor were they constitutionally Russians. The Finnish army was disbanded, though its officers were generously treated with retirement pensions. Although a school for officers was established at Hamina in 1821 (and remains there today) and although a token militia came into being in 1878, those who wished to make a career of soldiering commonly joined the Russian Imperial army. Russian troops were garrisoned in Finland, but their numbers were modest – even during the First World War. Foreign affairs remained in Russian control. So did consular matters. As with Norway in relation to Sweden, this was among the acerbating factors at the end of the century. In the domestic sphere, Finland had complete liberty of action. Above all, taxation was raised for domestic purposes only.

Alexander's liberal settlement with Finland seemed entirely out of key with the traditional behaviour of Russia. The purpose of such generous treatment was probably to pacify Finland and to woo it from Sweden. The policy achieved a considerable degree of success. For two generations Finland remained a peaceful buffer; the Finns, a peaceable people. The settlement was not entirely out of context with broader north European policies. In 1812, Alexander concluded an agreement with Sweden, pledging his support to the attempt by Carl Johan (formerly Count Bernadotte) to unite Norway with the Swedish throne. It was assumed that a sympathetic Russian attitude to these aspirations would offset any Swedish expectations for a re-union of Finland.

The new duchy had to have a new capital. Helsinki grew slowly, but splendidly. Some services, such as the Post Office in 1811 and the Board of Health in 1812, were established in it before the formal construction of the new city area. When Colville Frankland visited it in 1830, he remarked that the Finns were 'converting a heap of rocks into a beautiful city'. From a settlement of 4,000 inhabitants in the lee of Suomenlinna fortress, Helsinki was converted into a city of Baltic consequence within two generations. The city centre was planned in imperial terms. It was carried out under the surveillance of J. A. Ehrenström and designed in the neo-classical style by C. L. Engel. Their contribution is commemorated in a plaque on the granite wall below the university library – itself a part of the complex. To the stone-built quarters of the city were added stucco sections and, eventually, timber sections. The official plan was not completed until the 1870s.

The association of a garrison with the city and the rapid growth of trade speedily gave to Helsinki cosmopolitan qualities. The disastrous fire suffered by Turku in 1827 spelled its eclipse. The university, located in Turku for nearly two centuries, was shifted to spacious premises on Helsinki's great square in 1828. It received the name of the Emperor Alexander's University. In modern Finland, it remains a state university with professors appointed by the President.

The city's ornaments did not stop with its first planners. Helsinki was among the vanguard of cities in Europe to establish a park. Kaivopuist (Brunnsparken), already conceived as a minor spa in the 1830s, became a formal park in the 1850s. The development was partly conceived by Henrik Borgström, who was much influenced by the early ideas for the establishment of city parks on Merseyside. Kaisaniemi followed in the same decade, complete with its verandahed restaurant. The different quarters of the city began to acquire distinguishing names, and a photographic record was made of them in 1866 from the tower of Nicolai church. To concentration succeeded decentralisation with the coming of the railways, so that by the time the population of the city had reached 100,000 decentralisation was pronounced.

The Elevation of the Language

In the rise of modern Finland no single fact has been more important than the cultivation of the Finnish language. Although spoken by a majority of the inhabitants, it had no status in the administration and education until the nineteenth century. It even lacked formal grammatical expression. The first attempt at a Finnish grammar book was published in Viipuri in 1818, by Jaako Juteini. Within a generation of its publication, a score of other Finnish grammar books appeared. Their abundance expressed both the extent of the curiosity in Finland about the language native to the country and the recognition that the Swedish language could no longer serve the needs of the country. The formulation of the Finnish language laid the basis for its employment in the public life of the Grand Duchy.

The promotion of Finnish-language studies sprang from the concentrated endeavours of a small group of scholars and publicists. It was a group that was almost exclusively Swedish-speaking by upbringing and, despite their personal enthusiasm for the work, some of them never acquired fluent Finnish themselves. Individually, some were conscious of the nature of the forces that they were fostering by their actions: some were not. And, even if some of their actions were harmless in the setting of their time, they were to have profound consequences at a later stage in Finnish history. They taught the Finns to speak their old tongue with a new voice; they gave to it form and resonance.

Finland had been nurtured in Sweden, but its nature was now

being given the means of self-expression. In the literary and romantic stage of its development, the features associated with Finndom had a fascination that appealed beyond the bounds of Finland itself. As a political force cultivated to strengthen resistance to Russia, it had sympathetic support. As a domestic attitude calculated to replace old-established systems, it was to lead to serious divisions within. The formulation of the language, which was the beginning of its academic apprenticeship, anticipated its gradual official acceptance. Intellectual appraisal anticipated popular appeal. When the language as a patriotic instrument was allied to politics the stage was set for a new chapter in the life of the nation.

Already by the 1820s, there were those who began to urge a frame of mind which thought of Finland for the Finns. Adolf Ivar Arwidsson was among the early leaders. He was well aware that he was preaching the doctrine of nationalism, though he could scarcely foresee that his approach was likely to complicate the entire Finnish national issue by proclaiming the need for a single unifying language. He was a lively protagonist of Finnish as a language of education. Like many others, whose attitudes were unacceptable to the authorities of the Grand Duchy of Finland, he left the country and took up residence in Sweden.

It was evidence of the strength of feeling existing in his time that the School Commission should be encouraged by the Chapter of Turku cathedral to go ahead with the establishment of Finnish-language teaching. In 1824, the Church was sensitive to the need to have Finnish-speaking clergy in Finnish-speaking parishes. Partly in response to this need a special lectureship in Finnish was created when the university was shifted to Helsinki in 1828. A chair of Finnish language was eventually established in 1851, to which the ethnographer and philologist M. A. Castrén was appointed. Thereafter, developments followed thick and fast – the demand for Finnish-speaking judges, the use of Finnish for local record keeping, and in 1858 the first Finnish-language high school in Jyväskylä.

Although these developments were not anti-Russian in attitude, some of those who encouraged them regarded them as a counterweight to the possible challenge of Russification. Castrén himself was among those haunted by 'the terrible barbarism' of Russia and was conscious of the need to build up reserves of 'spiritual and intellectual power' in case the threat became a reality. These fears were expressed in the early 1840s at a time when all was outwardly relaxed. They constituted a theme that recurred in Finnish publicity. They had an appeal for an international audience –

> Fastän ett ringa folk, vår vakt
> mot vildhetens och mörkrets makt
> Är mänsklighetens egen strid
> för ljus och liv all tid.

(Although a poor folk, our watch against barbarism and the powers of darkness is really mankind's own continual struggle for light and life.)

Such was the conclusion to a greeting to Sweden in *Helsingfors Tidning* in 1857.

The Finnish language was given a completely new appeal through the work of Elias Lönnrot. He was not the first to penetrate the backwoods of Finland and to transcribe the oral poetry of the countryfolk. But he was the first to make it available to an influential group of countrymen at a moment in time when such material had a critical impact. His selected poems appeared as *Kalevala* in 1835 and were enlarged in a second edition in 1845. *Kalevala* had a threefold importance. First, by adopting east Finnish forms, it introduced a new printed form to the Finnish language. Secondly, it gave a new depth and a new breadth to Finnic studies – by developing the idea of ethnographic connections in the east and by adding a new dimension to the concept of Finnish history. By so doing it provided food for national thought. Although its eventual impact was to be immense, it had no immediate influence of consequence. Indeed, during the decade succeeding its publication, it only touched a narrow intellectual circle.

But the circle was that which gave rise to the Finnish Literary Society. This Society had its origins in 1831 in the modest little patriotic organisation known as the Saturday Society. It not only published Lönnrot's *Kalevala*, but in 1841 sponsored the journal *Suomi*, which was to lead the way in the promotion of Finnish studies. The archive of the Finnish Literary Society was to become the repository for the work of generations of scholars who were to comb the wildernesses of Finland and its neighbouring lands in their search for poetic fragments and ethnographic materials. The Society's work continues with unabated vigour. It is a long way from the carefully worked over manuscripts of Elias Lönnrot to the scientifically documented tape recordings of the last rune-singers; from the first gropings towards a Finnish grammar book to the highly sophisticated Language Bureau of the Academy of Finland which conceives as well as admits new Finnish words to fit new features and new situations. As a result, Finnish, although it remains an esoteric language in the Indo-European family, is a marvellously flexible and expressive language and one that is rich in growing points. Tongues of fire began to flicker in the Finnish Literary Society five generations ago. They continue to flame.

The pleasantly harmless patriotic feelings associated with language studies were given a new edge when philology became allied to politics. J. V. Snellman employed his talents as a political scientist in order to stimulate national feeling. He prosecuted his aim with vigour in his literary journal *Saima* and its publication was regularly proscribed by the government. From his chair in Helsinki after 1853, he rehearsed many of the political issues which formed the liberal state. Nor did he cease to proselytise the Finnish language. Together with a handful of disciples, he urged that Swedish-speaking Finns should discard their mother tongue and adopt that of the majority of their countrymen. Eventually Snellman became a member of the government where, by practical endeavour and personal persuasion, he helped to achieve the Language Decree of 1863. By it, Finnish was 'declared to be on a footing of complete equality with Swedish' in the business of the realm. The husk of the Swedish language was believed by some to have protected the Finnish kernel. But many metaphors were uttered that were wide of the mark. Swedish did not wither away as Finnish sprang to life.

The Rise of Education

Although Finland had a language of its own, the Finns only slowly became literate in it. Until a century ago, education was limited to a small minority of the inhabitants. School services in this thinly peopled country with its widely scattered settlements were a problem that awaited twentieth-century solutions. While contemporary international statistics indicate that present-day Finland is one of the most literate countries in the world, illiteracy was still widespread within living memory. Writing progressed more slowly than reading. Snellman printed his *Maamiehen ystäyä* (The Farmer's Friend) to spread agricultural ideas to the country folk of interior Finland. It even included a map to show them where Finland was in relation to Europe – and the place-names were appropriately fennicised. But the people of Savo and Kainu who received help through the Quakers at the time of the 1856 famine, and the workmen who helped to construct Saimaa canal, could only make their personal marks by way of signatures. As for arithmetic, its mysteries were more manifold in Finland than in most of northern Europe. It required familiarisation with two systems of measurement – the old Swedish (which still plays a role in the local market place) and the newly introduced Russian. And by the time that arithmetical tables had established themselves in school texts, Finland was following in the footsteps of its Scandinavian neighbours and adopting the metric system. The metric system was introduced in 1887. Money was also a problem. Swedish notes circulated side by side with Russian until the 1840s, when Finland began to have its own roubles.

At the time when Finland became a Grand Duchy of Russia, there was no organised education. There were a few Latin schools, a few local elementary schools, some Sunday School instruction. A system of apprenticeships was associated with the limited number of craftsmen who lived in the towns. The student's room, in Turku museum, with its wooden bedstead, heavy round leather travelling bag and copper chamber pot, may have been that of a watchmaker's apprentice or a saddler's apprentice. Merchants sent their sons abroad to acquire the methods of trading and of the counting house in Germany and Britain. Henrik Borgström, taking one of Bergsrådet Solitander's ships from Porvoo, established a personal association with merchant houses in Liverpool and with Lancashire industrialists. Out of his connections Forssa cotton mill was established. Otto Malm from Kokkola, Captain Backlund from Uusikaarlepyy, I. A. Grönberg from Vaasa and the Hackman family in Viipuri were others who despatched young members from their firms abroad for their education in practical commerce. To them, it was obvious that a knowledge of the languages of the trading nations of Europe was of no less importance than native Finnish.

It was not surprising that Finland's emerging captains of industry and trade should develop an early interest in schools. They had been anticipated by the clergy, who had worked hard to teach their parishioners to read. Here and there distinct success was achieved. On his Savo journey in 1819 John Paterson, then a representative of the British and Foreign Bible Society in St Petersburg, wrote that 'the people could all read'. The efforts of the clergy were paralleled by those of a variety of local dame schools. There was Fru Salmberg's Academy in Turku (where Fredrika Runeberg, wife of the poet, discovered Scott, Byron and Shakespeare) and Moster Stina's remarkable institution in Oulu. There was the Helsinki school of the 'Lapp woman', Sara Wacklin, and the *Mamselin koulu* for the children of millworkers in Tampere. Local businessmen helped to pay for the building of the school house in Kokkola in 1819 – and Liverpool merchants sent a subscription. But it was from the Lancaster Bell committee, established in Turku not long after the visit of the British educationalist William Allen in 1819, that new trends in education started. At Åminnefors estate, there are papers referring to 'the first Lankaster school in Finland . . . for Finnish-speaking children'. It was paid for by Johan Jacob von Julin and the local merchants willingly rallied support for its upkeep.

Independently of the need to cultivate Finnish, to retain Swedish and to add Russian, the significance of languages in general education grew as Finland's overseas contacts multiplied. Naturally, the fact was most evident in Helsinki. Here, Xavier Marmier commented in the 1840s, jokes from Tornio valley jostled with the latest news from the Neva, the poems of Lamartine mingled with the verse of Tegnér. Sara Wacklin's memoirs record the following conversation: 'Mother, I believe we are in Babylon,' commented a young girl at her first Russian ball in Helsinki, 'I have danced with eight partners. And they all speak a different language'. If the foreign books in the circulating libraries of the day are any guide, the precedence was French, German, English in the 1850s. French, indeed, was unexpectedly important – partly for Russian reasons. From his memories of Helsinki life in the mid-century, Anders Ramsay recalled how the 'crême de la crême' of this 'petit Paris' sought 'to mix the largest possible number of French phrases' in their conversation. Foreign-language teaching grew. The Helsinki press was liberally sprinkled with advertisements by teachers in the 1850s – from Herr Turnerelly's *séance specimen* for intending customers, through 'private instruction . . . for young ladies and children by a native of London' to the more advanced English course of P. T. Stolpe, lektor in English at the Emperor Alexander's University. Bookshops multiplied responsively. It was a paying proposition for Sederholm's bookshop in Helsinki to issue catalogues in the 1850s – and Tauschnitz editions claimed generous space in their columns. The English language was of especial importance for professional circles, such as the medical, and for technical groups, such as the navigational. Finnish medical practitioners were already collecting libraries of foreign texts in the early nineteenth century. The catalogue of Joseph Pippingskiöld for 1816 indicated a remarkable miscellany of medical literature. With the later nineteenth-century rise of navigation schools, English found an immediate place as a qualifying subject on mariners' certificates.

Once the significance of literacy began to penetrate Finland, education was speeded forward with determination. In 1843, the beginnings of school legislation were initiated: in 1869, a school board came into existence. Secondary schools were added to elementary; mixed and separate education were debated. But, more important, the language of instruction – whether Swedish or Finnish – divided opinion. Formal training for teachers was initiated in Jyväskylä in 1863 (Jyväskylä now has an institute of university standing). The institute was among the achievements of Uno Cygnaeus, who not only introduced the educational philosophies of Pestallozzi and Froebel to Finland, but also established *slöjd* (handicraft) as a basic principle in Finnish education.

Since nationality and literacy ran closely together, education was a vital key. A profusion of newspapers and journals emerged and a vigorous local press matched the national press. The local press has been persistent. It is one reason why the variety of publications to which the average Finnish family subscribes is impressive. But for many, the tradition of heavy and faithful subscription to the press is probably inseparable from the almost sacred character that the Finnish printed word assumed during the rise of nationhood.

The education of the nation meant a need for books. And the need was first and foremost for books about the nation. Among those who helped to fill the gap was Zachris Topelius. *Boken om vårt land* (A book about our country) described the essentials of the country in a simple and imaginative way for the schoolroom. Scores of editions later, it retains an honoured place as a virtual historical text. Children's games helped to convey the picture of Finland. The National Museum in Helsinki possesses a copy of an especially informative children's game, 'A pleasure journey to Aavasaksa'. Together with its accompanying text, it is a page from the social and economic history of Finland about 1865. Maps began to appear on the walls of schoolrooms. They brought home the size, shape and setting of the homeland. C. W. Gyldén's contoured map was a boon to Topelius who found it indispensable for his lectures on Finland's geography and history. By the mid-1870s a picture magazine, *Suomen Kuvalehti*, was circulating, and a decade later public libraries were initiated. By the end of the century Finland had its workers' educational organisation (with the first centre at Tampere in 1899), its schools of domestic science, and its folk high-schools in the Scandinavian manner.

There was also a complementary task in education – the enlightenment of the outside world about Finland and the Finns. For the small number of interested specialists literature was already being disseminated by the mid-nineteenth century. Karl Collan, Helsinki's university librarian, visiting the library of the British Museum in 1863, was glad that the catalogue included the names of Porthan, Tengström, Renvall, Lönnrot, Castrén, Wallén, Runeberg and Topelius. Even the journal *Suomi* was there. But Zachris Topelius was less than satisfied when visiting the London Exhibition in 1862 that Finland should have 'less representation than the Kalmucks and Khirgiz'. He would have rejoiced in the enterprise that promoted *Finland in the Nineteenth Century* or the first *Atlas of Finland*, and that sent them flying out like the sparks in Akseli Gallén-Kallela's cartoon 'Forging the Sampo' to the leading libraries of Europe.

The Discovery of Finland by the Finns

Education opened the eyes of Finns to Finland. In addition, it equipped them to deal with the resources and potentialities of the Grand Duchy. The realisation of the resources demanded a more scientific exploration and assessment of the land, new technical means of integrating the land, and new sources of capital to meet the cost of the equipment. For all of these purposes facts and figures were required. During its Swedish period, Finland had acquired experience in political arithmetic. A progressive Finland had to be numerate as well as literate.

Initial statistical surveys were begun by the Finnish Economic Society and pursued energetically by its secretary Carl Christian Böcker. Following pilot surveys in his home province of Vaasa, Böcker conceived a farm survey for the country at large. It was to be conducted on a parish basis and presumed the cooperation of the local clergy. The formula which he eventually produced exceeded eighty leading questions. The object of the exercise was a final statistical assessment which balanced agricultural resources and population. The arithmetic of the exercise was handled almost entirely by Böcker; but, as they were nearing completion, fire destroyed most of his calculations. He set about repeating the exercise, but was forced to admit his physical inability to complete it. Böcker had a broad and imaginative approach to the collection of facts and figures. He anticipated farm book-keeping and work programmes, and he gave practical encouragement to meteorological observations.

The two most vigorous protagonists of a statistical office were F. J. Rabbe and Gabriel Rein and, partly due to their efforts, a formal decision was made to found a central bureau in 1862. K. E. F. Ignatius became its first chief in 1865 and soon afterwards Finland set about the regular publication of statistical volumes about its population, manufactures and agriculture. They had a Finnish text with French sub-titles. Accordingly, from the dawn of its modern era, Finland has a broad statistical coverage. And the British consul in Helsinki, who in the late 1850s was complaining to Her Majesty's Foreign Office that he must pay a part of his personal salary to get commercial statistics from customs officials, had his grievance removed with the publication of the first bulky summary of *Finlands Sjöfart och Handel (1856–65)* in 1866. The trading figures even included Ladogan port traffic and winter movement through the seasonal customs stations along the land frontier.

This broadening approach to facts and figures was symptomatic of the discovery of Finland by the Finns, a discovery eased by the gradual introduction of new means of transport. They first appeared on the sea – and soon afterwards on the great lakes. The introduction of railways lagged a generation behind that of steamships.

Finland first saw the signs of steam when the tall-funnelled *Prince Menschikoff* and *Storfursten* took to the route between Stockholm, Turku, Helsinki, Tallinn and St Petersburg in 1837. Finnish entrepreneurs, such as Johan Jacob von Julin on his visit to London in 1815, had had their eyes on the auxiliary steam engine for some time before its introduction to Finland. The first steam engines came from England and they were powered by wood fuel. In 1870, the Finnish steamship company (*F.Å.A.*) was founded, with *Sirius* and *Orion* as the forerunners of its fleet. The steamship's potentiality on the lakes as well as at sea was rapidly appreciated. In 1846, parts for the first steam-boats to be used on Lake Saimaa were being carried over to

Siikaniemi for assembly: by 1875, over a hundred paddle steamers were operating on Finland's lakes.

Lake steamers were important for both commodity and passenger movement. 'Écurie à vapeur', the phrase used by Xavier Marmier for *Storfursten*, applied even more to them. Steamers became especially critical at ferry points. By the end of the Russian period, an effective integration had been achieved between railway and lake steamer in interior Finland. This traffic called for survey of the lakes. It was also facilitated by the opening of a series of canals. Chief among these was Saimaa canal. In 1856, figures of Neptune, Mercury and Väinömöinen presided over the opening of Saimaa canal, which provided a water link between Viipuri bay and Finland's largest lake. The realisation of the scheme, after fully two centuries of discussion, confirmed the growth of Viipuri into Finland's largest export harbour – and even led to the establishment of customs houses in lake ports such as Kuopio (in 1858).

Engineering and navigational equipment, which had to be imported, cost money, so that it was not until the last quarter of the nineteenth century that steam took precedence over sail in Finnish overseas trading. But as the use of steam gathered momentum, it caused a dramatic fall in freight rates – partly because of the increased speed of movement (which meant greater frequency of sailing) and partly because of the increased manoeuvrability of vessels (especially in the face of winter icing). By the 1870s the Finns were beginning to challenge winter by operating regular ferry routes from south-west Finland to Stockholm. In 1876, the steamer *Expressen* attempted to run a winter schedule; though winter postal services to most areas continued to use sleigh, ski and sled boat until the end of the century. Ekerö post museum in Åland still retains the transport equipment of the day. Winter movement in Finnish coastal waters remained a hazardous experience until the coming of the icebreaker. The first icebreaker acquired by Finland was *Murtaja*, launched at Finnboda wharf in Stockholm in 1890. At its time, it was the best in Europe. The attempt to guarantee winter shipping led in the 1890s to the decision to establish a winter harbour in Hanko (Hangö), in the extreme south-west of the country. The port became effective with the completion of a rail link to the Helsinki–Turku line, and for a short time Hanko became the leading winter harbour. For south Finland, at any rate, Thorsten Rudeen's late eighteenth-century lament no longer had meaning:

Isar, som min väg nu stängia,	Ice that now closes my way
Att iag ej min vän får see,	So that I cannot see my friend,
Ska sig snart i vatten mangia	Shall soon dissolve in water
Och mig farten öpen gee.	And give me open passage.

Railways were slow to make their impact upon the Finnish backwoods. In the late 1850s a few Finnish officials came to England to enquire about railway planning and construction. In 1862, the first locomotive, identified in charmingly naïve Finnish as *tulihevonen* (the steam horse), ran on a line from Helsinki to Hämeenlinna, with a miscellany of British rolling stock, 'snuggly and comfortably upholstered, without undue luxury'. Two Merseyside engine drivers, their wages £14 a month, came to instruct local crews. It was a state-owned line, and of the tracks which grew up, hardly any were privately owned. As the network gradually expanded, first along the St Petersburg–Turku axis, then up-country, businessmen and property-owners attempted to influence plans for the proposed routes. Others, in anticipation of railways moving through particular areas, bought tracts of woodland from unsuspecting country farmers. This was the case in the parishes north of Kuopio in Savo. It was in these same backwoods that the nineteenth-century novelist Juhani Aho wrote. His novelette *Rautatie* (The Railway) summed up the reactions of the north Savo people to the iron horse with its bulbous spark-catching chimney and cow-catcher front (for there was no cheap barbed wire to fence in the railway tracks until after the First World War). Finland's railway gauge was the same as that employed in Imperial Russia, so that a direct route ran from Viipuri to the Finland Station in St Petersburg. Today the rolling stock of the U.S.S.R. runs reciprocally to Eliel Saarinen's granite railway terminus in Helsinki – a monumental station which stands in complete contrast to the intimate railway architecture of the rest of Finland. Even some of the larger towns retain railway buildings of wooden clapboard and restrained fretwork, painted buff and white, curtained with icicles in winter and swinging with flower baskets in summer. Supervised by a civil service of red-capped station masters and mistresses, the buildings look out over the cobbled approaches to broad-gauged trackways, scythed lawns and summer flower-beds. Much remains unaltered, though earlier fears about the role of the railroad in Russia's broader strategy have evaporated.

Alongside the railways run the electric telegraphs which had already begun to play a part in Finnish affairs in the Crimean War. The 'seven-league boots' of the railways (as Topelius described them) transformed the postal service – a century ago it still took three weeks for a letter to travel from London to Kuopio. The telephone, which made its entry in Helsinki in 1882, was adopted by Finland with Scandinavian verve.

The coming of steam was coincident with shifts in the demand for Finland's products. First, what eighteenth-century encyclopaedists had called 'the English mart for tar' declined with the rise of alternate methods of distillation. In the early nineteenth century, Finland had several thousand tar pit sites. 'Parcels of pitch and tar', having been rafted in barrels a hundred a time on the smoother rivers or carried a couple of dozen a time down the rapid-ridden runs, moved to west European customers in cargoes to the value of £1,000 or more during open water. But the west European market for tar and pitch had disappeared completely by the First World War. And Finland began to import coal and coke from the coal-tar producing countries that had formerly consumed its tar.

Simultaneously the demand for charcoal fell away. The slow combustion of the charcoal burners' pyres disappeared before the changing methods of iron and steel production. The size of operations made possible by the Bessemer process and the new large-scale sources of ore supply rendered available by the Gilchrist Thomas process left little room for small-scale plants such as those which characterised Finland. The change came about within two generations. In the Marquis of Londonderry's *Recollections of a Tour in Northern Europe, in 1836–7*, reference was made to 'immense beds of iron ore . . . along the shores of lakes and at the bottom of marshes'. He listed a considerable number of small forges and smelting houses, including thirteen 'wrought iron' making centres. Some of these were operated by foreign technicians: some were owned by foreign companies. The churchyard of Joroinen in Savo has the graves of Lancashire puddlemasters and their families from the 1860s; while as late as 1872, British interests paid £100,000 for the *Finland Charcoal Iron Works* near Oulu, which was based on lake ore. The company only lasted five years before going into liquidation.

A handful of old-established iron mines in south-west Finland continued to produce modest quantities of ore until such time as import became cheaper. The guest book at Fiskars recorded visitors' impressions of the mineral workings. On 8 October 1839 D. Pennefather referred to its mine as 'more sublime and interesting than Dannemora' (in Sweden). Miners knew no compulsory safety precautions. Joseph Travers visited 'this mine and sincerely wish(ed) that none of his friends (might) break their necks there'! The picturesque caverns from the early mining days in Finland's little Bergslagen may still be seen.

Geologists were thin on the ground in nineteenth-century Finland, but they were convinced that ore bodies of economic value must exist. New deposits were sought out on 'geognostic journeyings' through Finland by Russians and Germans as well as Finns. Among Finns, Nils Nordenskiöld introduced many geological ideas to Finland. He was active at the British Association for the Advancement of Science and earned himself the title of 'father of Finnish geology'. It was copper that was to make the chief contribution for Finland's future. The deposits at Outokumpu, now one of Europe's principal producing centres, were first exploited in 1912.

Quarrymen also opened up their holes in the ground with greater ease as new explosives and methods of trimming stone became available. The land of granites was too distant from markets to be able to benefit from its resources of stone, though the Petalahti quarries supplied considerable quantities of ornamental stone to St Petersburg. Around Helsinki spacious quarries still recall the days when kerb stones, paving stones, road setts, doorsteps, foundations, basements and stairways were commonly blasted and trimmed from this material. Helsinki went through an extended phase of granite construction before it began to look to brick and reinforced concrete. A durable legacy remains, announcing itself through the sole of the shoe as well as in the Kalevalan motifs which decorate the solid façades of pre-World War I buildings.

But the declining pursuits were more than offset by the immense growth in demand for forest products in the west European market after 1860. The rapid increase in European population and the associated large-scale building programmes opened new Finnish export possibilities. Initially quality restricted demand for Finnish deals, which were inferior partly because of primitive sawing methods. When Finland became a Russian Grand Duchy, water sawmills were still at a premium. Improved saw blades were speedily disseminated, but the application of steam to saw-milling was delayed until the 1860s. Meanwhile, as a London merchant house wrote to Malm's trading company, 'English capital is working large numbers of steam sawmills in Sweden and Norway and pouring into this market immense quantities of well-manufactured and sound deals and boards'.

The expansion of coal mining in western Europe intensified demand for pitprops; the rise of 'Electric telegraph companies' called for 'redwood poles'; international shipment of goods required crating and packaging (and Finland was well equipped to support a plywood industry); the pressing need for paper forced on the development of mechanical and, later, chemical pulp.

The effects of all of these developments were transferred speedily to forest owners and forest utilisation. In response, a group of far-sighted Finns urged the more careful management of forestry. The need to conserve timber had already been stressed by late eighteenth-century husbandmen. Pedagogues quoted traditional proverbs – 'Honour the spruce tree under which you live': a handful of patriots built their homes of plaster and stone – St Maaria vicarage bears a plaque inscribed 'To conserve the woodlands, the country's wealth'. But the result of generations of selective felling for building and construction, for fuel and for the tar pit, of rotational burning for agriculture, of forest grazing and of general neglect, meant that already by the time of the revaluation, the more accessible (and therefore more valuable) woodlands no longer carried merchantable trees. In 1851, a law was passed which restrained forest burning, set limits to cutting programmes for local sawmills and prohibited bark stripping (for tanning). But positive steps were taken simultaneously. Two examples must suffice. First, C. W. Gyldén, like so many of his contemporary Finns a man of many parts, took the initiative in 1853, with a practical handbook of forestry. The book instructed readers in the art of assessing the height and growth of standing timber, provided tables for estimating long-term yields of sample blocks, advised on the selection of seed and on planting, outlined forest taxation and made proposals for the establishment of experimental plots. Gyldén was in a strong position to influence forest policy, because he was both director of the Land Survey Office and sometime chairman of the national committee for improving communications. In order to indicate the distribution of timber stands of different quality, Gyldén also produced the first qualitative forest map of Finland. It is an historic document in its own right.

Secondly, the first institution for the study of forestry was established at Evo, 20 km. north of Helsinki, in 1862. It thrived under the devoted leadership of A. G. Blomquist and, on eventual transfer to the University of Helsinki, became the department of forestry. Partly because of the early appreciation of the need for restraint, excessive exploitation of Finland's woodlands was prevented. But late nineteenth-century Finland – harvesting its timber crop with lumberjack and hardy horse, sleigh and ski, river and timber sorter; breaking the forest's winter silence with the blows of axes (varied sufficiently in design to cover a wall in the present-day museum of forestry) – had a glimpse of softwood opportunities ahead. At their best, in the words of John Kolehmainen, these were the 'flush and boisterous logging years, when the horses of the lumber barons drank champagne and the nabobs themselves lit their cigars with banknotes'. At their worst, they were the years when Finland was about to realise that it was exchanging a subsistence but independent rural economy for a trading but dependent international economy. And trade cycles began to extend their effect.

Most of the woodlands affected by the changing demand were privately owned. The units of ownership varied greatly, though the excessive fragmentation in areas such as Ostrobothnia had been partly reduced through extensive land reorganisation. The agrarian background against which Finland was to receive the impulses of change from the outer world may have been dominated by the independent owner-farmers, but many farms were so small that they only supported a marginal existence. In addition, there were large numbers of tenant farmers owing labour dues to their landlords and of landless labourers who were employed on the bigger estates. These elements of the community constituted an incipient rural proletariat.

Farming conditions lagged behind those of much of western Europe both socially and economically. By comparison with what Finnish visitors such as Anders Ramsay called the trim garden of the west European farm scene, the general impression of west European visitors to the Finnish countryside was the reverse. The primitive implements and methods which Gösta Grotenfelt gleaned with ethnographic eagerness at the end of the century were viewed in a different light by foreign visitors. The wooden ploughs, spades and harrows that were used in fields around which split-rail fences sometimes formed veritable thickets were not even regarded as picturesque. 'The farming is very slovenly', reported two members of the Society of Friends in 1856.

But if agricultural practices were old-fashioned, domestic arts and crafts were lively. In the log-built farmhouses, home-made wooden furnishings not far removed from those of the Middle Ages might prevail; but local schools of carpenters and cabinet-makers often displayed craftsmanship of a high level. They painted as well as carved furniture, excelling themselves in the colourful 'rose' designs that distinguished the Vaasa skerries. Wood was worked into spinning wheels, barrels, casks, platters, buttermoulds and cheese presses: it was manipulated into traps for hunting. It assumed more elaborate designs in courting gifts such as distaffs, winding pins, weaving shuttles and swingles. Cartwrights and wheelwrights stuck to utilitarian forms, but sleigh-makers let their imaginations play in colourful horsebows and panellings. At the same time bark was carefully stripped from birch trees and plaited into products as diverse as cradles and satchels, hats and shoes, fishermen's salt pots and ropes. And, in the calendars that the rural craftsmen used, the old names of the months remained – the Harvest Month instead of August; the Month of Slaughter instead of October.

Nevertheless, the seeds of change were being scattered at an early date. Re-appraisal of the traditional methods of cultivation was already the object of pamphleteering in the 1830s – for example, C. C. Böcker's tract dated 1831 against the burning-and-paring of mossland (F. *kydönpoltta*: Sw. *kyttning*). Interest in technical equipment spread slowly but surely. The relative merits of the Scottish, Hampshire and American ploughs were being debated at a meeting of Finnish farmers in Turku in 1847. The press began to advertise equipment. *Suometar* printed a sketch of Taylor's patented harrow in 1852. A smallholder's churn came into use in the 1850s. The need for improved cattle stock was discussed among progressive farmers. Johan Jacob von Julin bought a Hereford bull from the Coke estate in Norfolk for £35 in 1827; though the performance of the breed was disappointing in Finnish conditions. The Senate set aside a sum of money in 1845 to buy animal stock in England and the choice fell upon Ayrshire and Pembroke cattle. In the ensuing five years, sixty-six of the former and nine of the latter were obtained. Within a century, over a thousand Ayrshire pedigree animals were imported to Finland against the background of this early decision. The

Ayrshire breed was to become the principal foreign constituent in the Finnish dairy herd and the wheel came full circle when three Ayrshire bulls and two heifers were sold back to Scottish dealers in 1950.

Technical training and technical literature were slowly diffused. By the 1860s, agricultural experimental schools were developing – at Mustiala, Viipuri and Tampere. Advisers were being paid by the government to go the rounds of farms – among them was a Scot, Henry Gibson. *The Report of the Committee for the Relief of Famine in Finland* (1858) resulted in 'an agricultural teacher' going into Kainuu to instruct 'the farmers to ditch their fields, the cattle-breeding and so on'. The reclamation of peatlands proceeded with especial vigour, so that great new areas of grassland (in Muhos, for example) were added for fodder. Swedish, German and British farming publications had found an established place in the libraries of the Finnish estate-owners by the middle of the century. The rich technical library of Johan Jacob von Julin at Fiskars included many of them: so did that of Baron Nikolai at *Mon Repos* near Viipuri. A garden culture was also fostered and an impressive hothouse was built in Helsinki University botanical garden in 1832. English and German seeds, shrubs and fruit trees were advertised in Finnish newspapers. It was a reflection of the gardening practices of merchants' families that Marie Hackman, wife of the Viipuri businessman, should have been nicknamed 'The Duchess of Sparragras, Artichoke and Colliflower'. By 1860–70, industrialists such as the Frenckells in Tampere and Nikolai Synebrychoff in Helsinki had gardens and greenhouses built beside their factories. Greenhouse cultivation, developing on a larger scale after 1900 and illustrated by M. G. Stenius's extensive premises in Leppäsvuolle, was especially significant for Finland. Today Finland has acres under glass.

The diffusion of farming techniques was paralleled by a more scientifically organised series of phenological observations. Two hundred and eleven contributors added to the wealth of material assembled by Adolf Moberg for the series *Bidrag till Finlands Naturkännedom* (Åbo, 1860). These observations on dates of flowering and of ripening, of the arrival and departure of birds, of the appearance of insects and the behaviour of animals complemented the meteorological records of the day. Little by little, they helped the agricultural possibilities of the land to be construed.

While farming was a widely distributed pursuit and the forest industries took absolute precedence in the limited manufacturing scene, workshop activities steadily multiplied. Some workshops, such as those producing the rag-and-straw paper, withered as new methods of production entered the picture; others have grown into pillars of contemporary Finland's industrial structure. Several examples must suffice. The Turku merchant Johan Hjelmerius had a drawing made of his tobacco factory and plantation at nearby Cuppis and eulogised it in a little rhyme:

Se detta fält och detta tempel	Gaze upon this plot and temple
Där fordom Ceres dyrkad blev	Where Ceres was worshipped in former times.

Tobacco plants may still be cajoled to heights of six feet in Turku gardens and Rettig's multi-storied tobacco factory occupies a commanding position in the old sector of the town along the left bank of the Aura. A scatter of textile mills evolved against the background of the old-established domestic tradition of spinning and weaving; though they turned from the limited supplies of domestic flax and wool to imported cotton. The Tampere mill of the Glaswegian James Finlayson, established with privileges granted by Tsar Alexander for custom-free import of machinery, came into being in 1820. It was taken over from its Scottish founder in 1835 by William Wheeler and a German, Ferdinand Uhle. The Lancastrian John Barker, also one of its technicians, left to establish his own factory in Turku. It occupies a dominant site on the seaward approaches of the city and still bears his name. Lancashire and Liverpool were closely linked with all the cotton mills, those of Vaasa and Forssa continuing the association. There were also old-established manufactories – Noutajärvi, with its candy-striped glassware, and Berga with its green glass. In the magic crystals blown by their workmen seers might have read the signs of a world-renowned industry. In 1874, Sweden's Rörstrand company decided to establish a small ceramic factory outside Helsinki. The site chosen was that of a villa named Arabia, the exotic name having been given in 1763 to the field where it stood. In the mid-twentieth century, the name was to stand for the largest and, in some respects, the most artistically productive ceramic factory in the whole of Scandinavia.

Above all, the bases of Finland's giant softwood industries were being established. Some such as that of W. Gutzeit and Co., the progenitor of the present-day Kaukopää plant, were located along Kymi river: others grew up at the head of the Gulf of Bothnia (with the brothers Åström establishing plants on Oulu river). Antti Ahlström pressed steam into his service, bought Noormarkku and Strömfors, founded a softwood empire oriented to Kumo river, and built up a network of international trading. Juhani Aho called him *Pirkkalan poika* and suggested that the blood of the Birkala traders ran in his veins. New towns to accommodate new timber industries emerged – Kemi in 1869, Kotka in 1874. By the mid-1880s, Finns were rivalling the more advanced industrial nations in the detail of their first census of industry and manufacturing. One hundred and forty categories of activity were listed.

The sea continued to foster shipyards which were of varying size and fairly evenly spaced around most of the coast. But as steel plate replaced wood in shipbuilding there was a decline in Finnish activity. The wharves at the estuary of the Aura river, which had been fostered for several generations by engineers, persisted. Those of Hietalahti (Sandviken) at Helsinki were added by 1890. But it was not until the mid-twentieth century that Finland was restored to the status of a significant shipbuilding country.

Meanwhile, the small mercantile marine both developed in size and engaged in more varied enterprises. By the 1860s, for example, Åland trading vessels were beginning to acquire a European reputation as carriers. The vessels were generally owned and operated cooperatively by local smallholders (*bönder*). The period when they dominated the Åland economy yielded much local wealth, great expertise in the management of sea-going vessels, and a tradition out of which was to grow the almost legendary Åland sailing fleet. Another aspect of the commercial revolution was the growth of long-distance trading – not only winter journeys in the North Sea and Mediterranean when the Baltic was closed by ice, but tramping through the seven seas. Malm's merchant fleet, based on Kokkola, was sailing regularly to the West Indies and south-east Asia in the 1860s, and was covering the Pacific in the 1880s.

Helsinki, primarily concerned with administration, developed as a haven of trade and a hearth of industry. In 1878, a correspondent of *Hufvudstadsbladet* complained of the cacophony of its whistles and hooters. They sounded a new stage in the growth of the city and the need for civic control. In 1887 and again in 1892, areas for factory development were allocated in the environs of the city. The demand for labour which grew simultaneously was met principally by immigration. Proletarian districts began to emerge in the city with their associated problems. From 1905 onwards its inner differentiation can be detected in the statistics of its social, economic and spiritual life that were published annually.

Those who were engaged in this gradual transformation became increasingly conscious of social conditions. Finland was slowly lifted out of the rut of rural poverty, but disease and high mortality remained. They were largely the results of serious and widespread deficiencies in the diet of the majority of the people. Undernourishment remained a problem over much of rural Finland until the twentieth century. The number of beggars requiring parish assistance was a depressing statistical feature of C. C. Böcker's rural surveys. A letter dated 1832 from James Finlayson in Tampere to Daniel Wheeler reported 'vast crowds of poor starving women, children and men, daily wandering, begging'. In 1857 as a token of recompense for the actions of the British fleet around the Finnish coast during the Crimean War, the Society of Friends organised famine relief to interior Finland. The same summer John Good reported distressed and hungry people pouring into Raahe. A decade later Herman Lorentz wrote to *The Times* of starvation in eastern Finland, while A. Meurman published an entire book on *The Famine Years of the 1860's*.

There was no effective medical service to deal with health problems until the twentieth century. Provincial hospitals with restricted facilities had existed in south-west Finland from the end of the eighteenth century, but they were inaccessible save for a handful of people. Helsinki's university hospital, a pleasant courtyarded feature of the present city, came into being in 1828 and a Board of Health was established two years later. Lacking the service and advice of the doctors who practised in the towns, country people looked to three principal antidotes to illness – alcohol, tar and the sauna. A few sophisticated Finns took the water of mineral springs, though they have left Finland no legacy of a spa. Pharmacies were slowly established in the market towns – and one has been preserved as a museum on the right bank of the Aura at Turku. They were to acquire a status very different from that of the shop of the dispensing chemist in Britain or the drug store of the U.S.A. The first census of industry listed factories and workshops with hospital and medical facilities.

Finland began to absorb the more advanced ideas of western Europe rapidly in the last quarter of the nineteenth century.

Preventative medicine was preached beside curative. The Finnish Red Cross came into existence in 1877. As early as 1897 a Mental Health Society was established, while thanks to the enlightened leadership of Baron von Wrede and his wife Mathilda a more humane approach was encouraged in the treatment of the under-privileged and of criminals. In 1889, the Salvation Army initiated its work in the working-class districts of the capital; though by this time poor-law relief had been established on a commune basis.

Public assistance and other welfare measures had to be paid for. In the process Finland began to exchange its system of indirect taxation for one in which direct taxation predominated. Early attempts to introduce direct taxation in the 1860s failed, but a succession of laws after 1910 initiated income and property taxes.

Side by side with the elaborate statistical records kept of these developments there evolved specialist surveys of particular problems. The central administration, for whom J. C. Frenckell had printed the first comprehensive list of laws in 1855, published an annual volume of legislative enactments from 1860 onwards under the title *Suomen asutus kokous*. A steady stream of committee reports or 'white papers' had been added by 1900. In 1901, the survey into farming structure and production was carried through under the leadership of Hannes Gebhard. The report and its two accompanying atlases illustrated the changing approach to Finland's economy and society.

The elected representatives who came to debate the increased legislation and the surveyors who went into rural Finland to collect their data witnessed steady changes in the countryside by the end of the century. It was a countryside where a whole armature of oil lamps began to illumine the winter darkness (though their fuel had to be imported); where the cast-iron stove that could burn firewood billets provided new opportunities for heating and cooking; where the manufactured pan competed increasingly with the traditional earthenware pot; where factory-made clothing and footwear began to take precedence over the custom-made suits of the itinerant tailor and the boots from the village cobbler's last. In this setting, seasonal and regional games were still played by adults as well as by children – from the rough-and-tumble of the Christmastide *Karhun kaato* and the masque of *Tähtipojat*, through a variety of ring dances to the *naurisleikki* or turnip game of east Finland. Here, too, the strange fusions of old and new fashions that a later generation was to

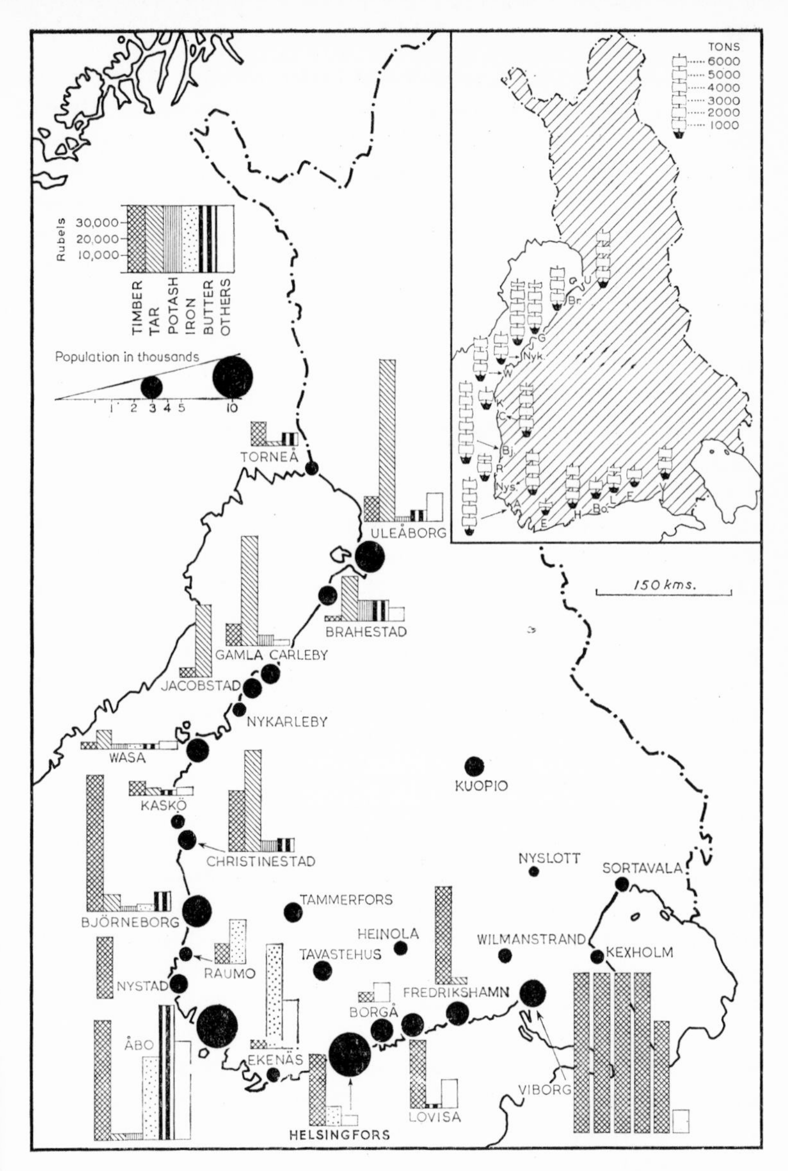

3. The Principal Trading Centres of Finland c. *1840*

The diagram is based on the information assembled by one of Finland's first statisticians, C. Gyldén in *Historisk och statistiska anteckingar om städerna i Finland* (Helsingfors, 1845). Urban population and shipping tonnage are for 1842: exports are given in roubles for 1843.

revive as 'folk costumes' were passing away – the embroidered bonnets and fichus, the shawls and full-pleated skirts. Glass had already cheapened to multiply windows, where curtains began to appear; rag mats on the floor complemented the woven rugs on the wall, sheets began to enter the box-shaped beds, matches had driven out the tinder box. And the surveys were conducted by investigators who were transported along unsteady railway tracks to the excited whistle of wood-burning locomotives, who had already experienced Helsinki's electric tramway in 1900, who were to encounter in 1903 the first 3 or 4 h.p. combustion engines in the streets of Helsinki, the first motor-boats in its coastal waters, and to see the first flimsy aircraft take off from Töölö in 1912.

The Nourishment of the Economy

While deficiency of food sapped the energy and resistance of the Finns, shortage of capital hampered their more progressive leaders. The motto, 'Time is Money', might be painted on the frieze of *Societetshuset* in Rauma, but most Finns had all the time in the world and no source of money to make it tick. Money had to be found and to be made to work. It had to be accumulated and acquired through banks, through corporate institutions and co-operative societies.

Among the first to realise the need for capital accumulation was Johan Jacob von Julin, who founded the first savings bank in Finland in 1822. A generation later there were over twenty. In 1837, he was pressing for the establishment of private banks. The Bank of Finland, which had been founded in Turku in 1811 and shifted to Helsinki in 1819, was given new powers in 1840. It was joined in the capital by the Finnish United Bank in 1862, the United Northern Bank in 1872 and Kansallis Osake Pankki in 1892. Post Office savings banks belong to the 1880s. The Grand Duchy acquired its own unit of currency in 1865 and began to quote its transactions in the silver *markka* instead of the silver rouble. In 1878, Finland was brought into line with most west European countries when it adopted the gold standard.

Shareholding companies developed slowly. They had their modest beginnings in Helsingfors theatre in 1825, Brunnsparken in 1834 and Åbo Theatre in 1836. There were over sixty shareholding companies in existence when the law of 1864 formally established the joint stock position. In the ensuing fifty years over 900 came into being, 200 of which were in Helsinki. Since the 1890s a Register of Trade has been kept.

It was not enough that Finland should accumulate capital domestically and acquire foreign exchange by trading. Investment was also sought from abroad. Finland was slowly becoming known in European commercial circles. Xavier Marmier, visiting Turku in 1843, wrote somewhat fulsomely of Finland as 'a Newfoundland discovered by the genius of commerce', in the hotels of which the commercial jargon of Dutch, Belgian, German and English stirred the air 'from one end of the table to the other'. Map 3, based on C. W. Gyldén's statistical appreciation of Finland's towns, provides a picture of its external trading circumstances on the eve of technical change. By the 1860s, officials of the Bank of Finland were negotiating their first international loans, in offices dark with mahogany and ponderous with furniture of the Biedemeier style. In 1861–62, they conducted their first business with the House of Rothschild. From N. M. Rothschild and Son in London, they extended their contacts to C. J. Hambro and Son and to Baring Brothers. Messrs Hambros and Barings remain the principal British bankers associated with the Scandinavian market today.

It was natural that financiers in Britain, the world's leading exporter of capital in the nineteenth century, should be courted. Meanwhile, others courted the Finns. The number of visiting agents multiplied. Their names can be discovered from the columns of local newspapers which recorded the arrival and departure of hotel guests. Some came to establish their own organisations in Finland. G. F. Stockmann came from Germany in 1862 to lay the foundations of Helsinki's largest department store. Advertisements in the Finnish press sought business. They included those of foreign insurance companies (such as Phoenix Fire, Pelican Life, and the North British and Mercantile), which anticipated domestic companies such as Kaleva (1874), Patria (1888) and Suomi (1890).

Capital was also accumulated through the cooperative societies. The societies came into existence for other purposes, but speedily acquired wealth in their own right. Denmark led the way in adopting the principles of the Rochdale pioneers and in applying them to the agricultural sphere. It was natural that rural Finland, with its tradition of *talkoot* (of collective house- and barn-building, harvesting and fishing), should follow the Danish example. Its progress was sufficiently powerful that after a generation a Norwegian observer proclaimed Finland a veritable 'nation of cooperators'. Among the protagonists who urged cooperation none was more persistent than Hannes Gebhard. He was a moving spirit behind the Pellervo Society, which laid the foundations of present-day Finnish co-operation in 1899. Cooperative dairies had already been established in the 1880s, but it was the liberalising law of 1901 that encouraged cooperation to forge ahead. Names now familiar to every Finn began to enter the scene – S.O.K. (*Suomen Osuuskauppojen Keskusosuus-kunta*), the Finnish Cooperative Wholesale Society, in 1904; *Elanto*, originally a cooperative bakery, and the *Valio* Butter Exporting Cooperative in 1905. Cooperatives for meat processing, egg collecting, grain milling and fish marketing came speedily into being. Purchasing cooperatives sprang up beside marketing cooperatives; credit and mortgage societies followed. Eventually, cooperation organisations were integrated across national boundaries with the systems of the Scandinavian countries. Within fifty years of their foundation, the major Finnish cooperative societies were to be included among the wealthiest and most influential institutions in the country. They not only brought financial nourishment and managerial stimulus to the Finnish economy, they brought them through self-help.

The new capital resources might purchase new engines and bring increasing security, but they also introduced a new discipline to daily life. Technical equipment called for a technical élite. Polytechnics which claimed less than 200 pupils in the early 1870s were not enough and Finland's Technical High School (now the Technical University at Otaniemi) came into being as an institution of university standing in 1908. The machines demanded uninterrupted supplies of energy and continuous attention. At the beginning of the twentieth century only a tenth of Finland's working population was employed in factories, but the rhythm of their working day was transmitted to the service and transport activities, and indirectly to the countryside. Moreover, the new disciplines imposed by management and machines were international as well as national. To the extent that Finland was integrated with the European economy it was exposed to secular changes in international trading. It seemed that domestic insecurities had been exchanged for international insecurities.

The new pressures and uncertainties bred protest, and as in other countries prompted the rise of trade unions. The first Finnish unions date from the late 1880s, though the printers had banded together earlier. The gathering strength of the trade unions was first felt in the general strike of 1906: their first conference was held in Tampere in 1907. Trade unionism was inseparable from political developments. Socialism had entered Finland in the 1880s, though it was not until 1899 in Turku that a workers' party came into being. It acquired its own educational organisation in the workers' institutes, founded in 1899. It assumed a social democratic title in 1903. In 1907 the pressure of the machines was somewhat controlled when a ten-hour working day was established.

The Panacea of Emigration

One consequence of domestic insecurity has been the flight from the land – the famine land. By the 1860s it was finding expression in emigration as well as migration. 'Nature seems to cry out to our people "Emigrate or die" ', Topelius told his university students in 1867. 'The heart pleaded no, but the stomach commanded yes', Axeli Järnefelt-Ravanheimo repeated in his emigrant novel *Amerikkaan*. The first of the new stream of Finnish emigrants went west (some as Norwegians, some as Russians) in the later 1860s. *Helsingfors Tidningar* (No. 207) carried a letter in 1866 from a countryman bound for Hull who had encountered emigrants setting off for America, 'some with a psalm book, others with bottles of beer'.

Many factors prompted emigration. The system of land ownership was among them. Although large numbers of Finns owned family farms, rural Finland had over 50,000 small tenant farmers who as well as paying rent were required to perform labour duties – both so-called 'horse days' and 'foot days'. Tenants rarely had any form of written agreement with their landlords, were unlikely to receive compensation for improvements and had no right of passing on their tenancies to their sons. In addition, there was a landless rural proletariat of some 200,000 at the turn of the century. It is ironical that at the same time as Finnish intellectuals were cultivating such an affecting and affectionate approach to their land and its national institutions, this substantial army of country people should wish to shake off their native soil. 'No land, no fatherland', was the cry of many who left for the New World. Far more were motivated by social and economic facts than were moved by the worsening political relationship with Russia.

The peak movement across the Atlantic came during the twenty years before the First World War. Between 1901 and 1905, emigrants totalled 81,056: in 1913, the figure again exceeded 20,000. By comparison with the other Scandinavian countries, American fever was delayed in Finland. In time, it paralleled more closely the movement from eastern Europe. From 1893 onwards, Finland kept emigration statistics. They indicate that, while emigrants hailed from all parts of the country, Ostrobothnia was the principal source and Vaasa province provided nearly half of the total. The butter ships from Hanko speedily became a principal emigrant route: Ernest Young saw them in 1906 with emigrants 'loaded like animals'. Emigrant parties even had group photographs taken on the quayside. Emigrant streams commonly passed through the great passenger ports of western Europe. In such Atlantic harbours as Hamburg, Liverpool and Rotterdam, the Finnish Seamen's Mission discovered that its services were as much needed by emigrants as by regular seamen. Handfuls of more adventurous Finns sought more distant pastures. Some moved to Australia, where they helped to construct the Queensland railway. On 20 May 1899 a group headed by Matti Kurikka petitioned 'the Manager of the Colonial Department . . . of the government of England (to open) up its part of New Guinea' to Finnish emigrants.

Because of their tardy participation in the immigrant stream, Finnish settlers in the New World either moved directly to the cities or to the less favoured margins of the occupied land. The American frontier was ostensibly 'closed' by the 1890s, though there were still gaps to be filled. The interstices between established settlement, usually on the poorer soils or in the 'cut-over' land, offered possibilities. The softwood fringes of the northern Middle West received the principal concentrations of Finnish immigrants. Up-state Michigan, Wisconsin and Minnesota became their *Uusi Savo* (new Savo) or 'havens in the wood' (as John Kolehmainen has called them). Here, they trimmed timber, quarried rock, mined ore (iron after copper gave out), fished the lakes, cultivated their smallholdings, christened them with Finnish names, created their cooperatives and faithfully lit their Saturday night *sauna*. They retreated from rather than embraced the modes and manners of their adopted land, reluctantly gave up their native tongue and were correspondingly slow to be assimilated. As at home, they ran to philosophical extremes, the pious Lutheran and the strict Laestadian standing in

1 THE SOUTH-WEST FACE OF FINLAND

The clay plains of Uusimaa, south-west Finland, display an old-established agricultural landscape: Scale 1:22,000

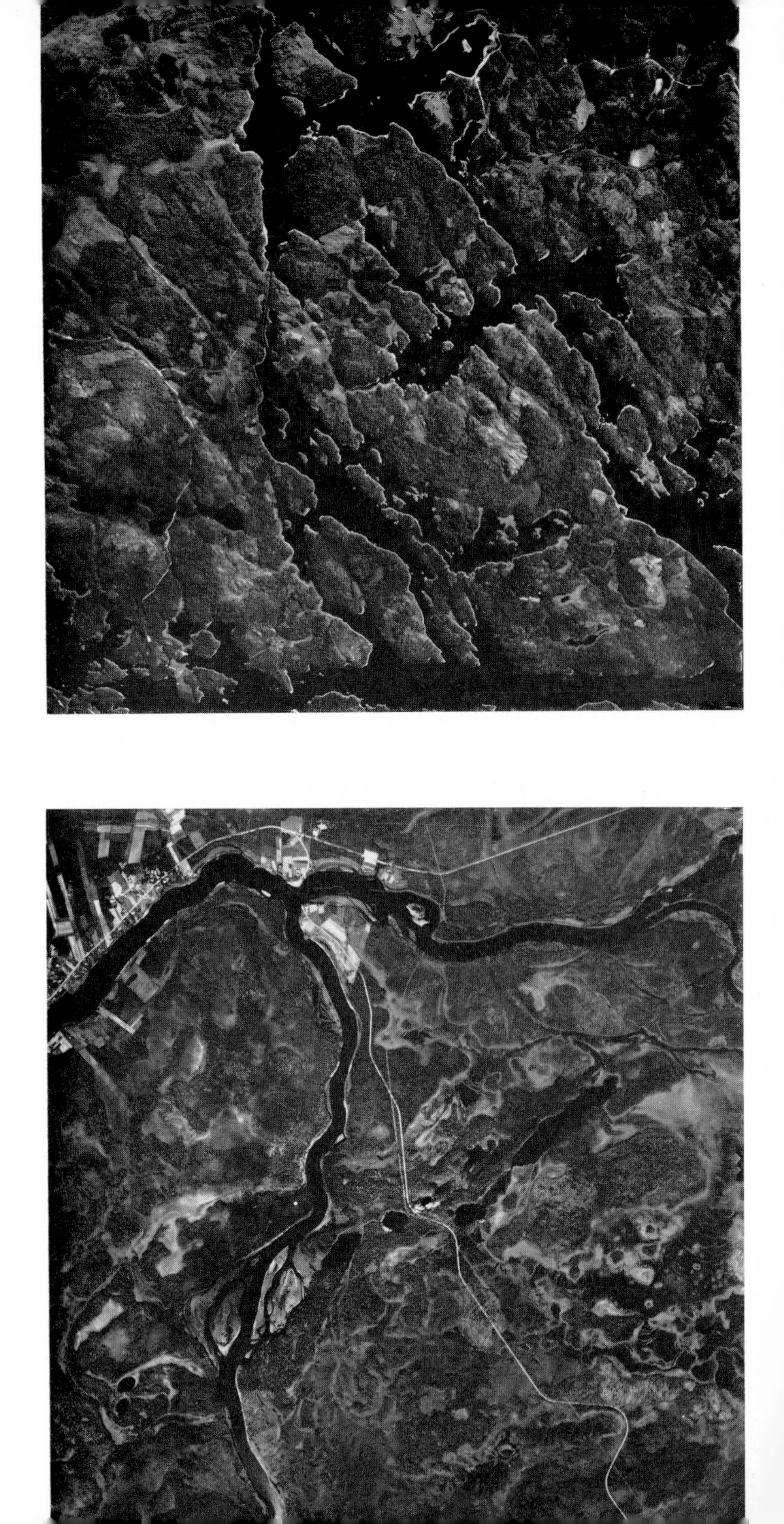

4 THE WINTER APPROACHES TO FINLAND Shipping being escorted to south-coast harbours through channels kept open by icebreakers in winter

[*Opposite*] 2 THE SOUTH-EAST FACE OF FINLAND This is a tract from Puumala parish in the south-eastern Lake District. The intricate pattern of waterways is a part of the great Saimaa lake system. It is a predominantly wooded landscape with islands of cultivation. Scale 1:30,000

3 THE NORTHERN FACE OF FINLAND Swamplands and rivers play a much more important role in northern Finland. The rivers were the historical routes of entry and their valleys are still followed by the principal lines of communication. The illustration is from Pelkosenniemi, in Lappi province. Scale 1:30,000

5 PORTRAITS FROM FINLAND

Above: Täti (1898) by Hugo Simberg and Ukko Istolainen (1897) by Juho Rissanen

Below: Hauta-Heikin mummo (1897) by Juho Rissanen and Aks (1897) by Hugo Simberg

6 PORTRAITS FROM FINLAND

Four sketches by A. Gallén-Kallela, 1887–91

7 FINLAND IN OLAUS MAGNUS'S 'GOTHIC MAP', the *Carta Marina* of 1539

England. Ivinghoe uti Buckinghamshire.

d. 5 April. [illegible]

Wäderleken, [illegible] solsken och [illegible] hela dagen: [illegible] så [illegible] at [illegible] på [illegible]. efter [illegible] begynte blåsa och [illegible]. — NW. 1.

Th. [illegible] 5½ [illegible] 0.
[illegible]

Om morgonen togo wi en liten Farmer, som war boende en [illegible] af Landthushållning, med oss, och begåfwo oss på vägen til Ivinghoe, hwilket låg uti Buckinghamshire 4. Engelska mil härifrån: Little Gaddesden, hwarest wi hade wårt logement, låg uti Hertfordshire, men just ytterst på gränsen mot Buckinghamshire, så at man kunde [illegible] wid somliga gårdar uti Little Gaddesden i portarne, och med en steen kasta in uti Buckinghamshire. [illegible] med denna [illegible] war [illegible] Ivinghoe, [illegible] Mr. Ellis berättade, at utsigten och landet och jordmån war aldeles skild ifrån hwad det är här wid Little Gaddesden, ty här är Chiltern land, men der Vale land.

Agrifolium ansenlig stor. — wid en [illegible] ifrån en gård sågo wi at träd af Agrifolium Raj. syn. 466. som war en af de största [illegible] här i England: [illegible] war [illegible] 14. alnar, [illegible]; [illegible] peripherien af [illegible] 9. [illegible]: [illegible] til 2. alnars längd [illegible] at [illegible] som [illegible]; de [illegible] communication med [illegible]. [illegible] Bokar. Karlen, som följde oss, [illegible] af detta träd, at [illegible] til bränsle.

[illegible] på [illegible]. — Wid en [illegible] gård sågo wi [illegible] som tilförene p. 283. är beskrefwen, [illegible] på [illegible]: [illegible] med [illegible] a Wheat-frame.

[illegible]. — En [illegible] med [illegible] bränsle, [illegible] [illegible] på ordinaire [illegible].

8 A PAGE FROM THE MANUSCRIPT NOTEBOOK OF THE MID-EIGHTEENTH-CENTURY NATURAL HUSBANDMAN PEHR KALM

It is from April 1748 and refers to his sojourn in Hertfordshire at Little Gaddesden on his way to North America

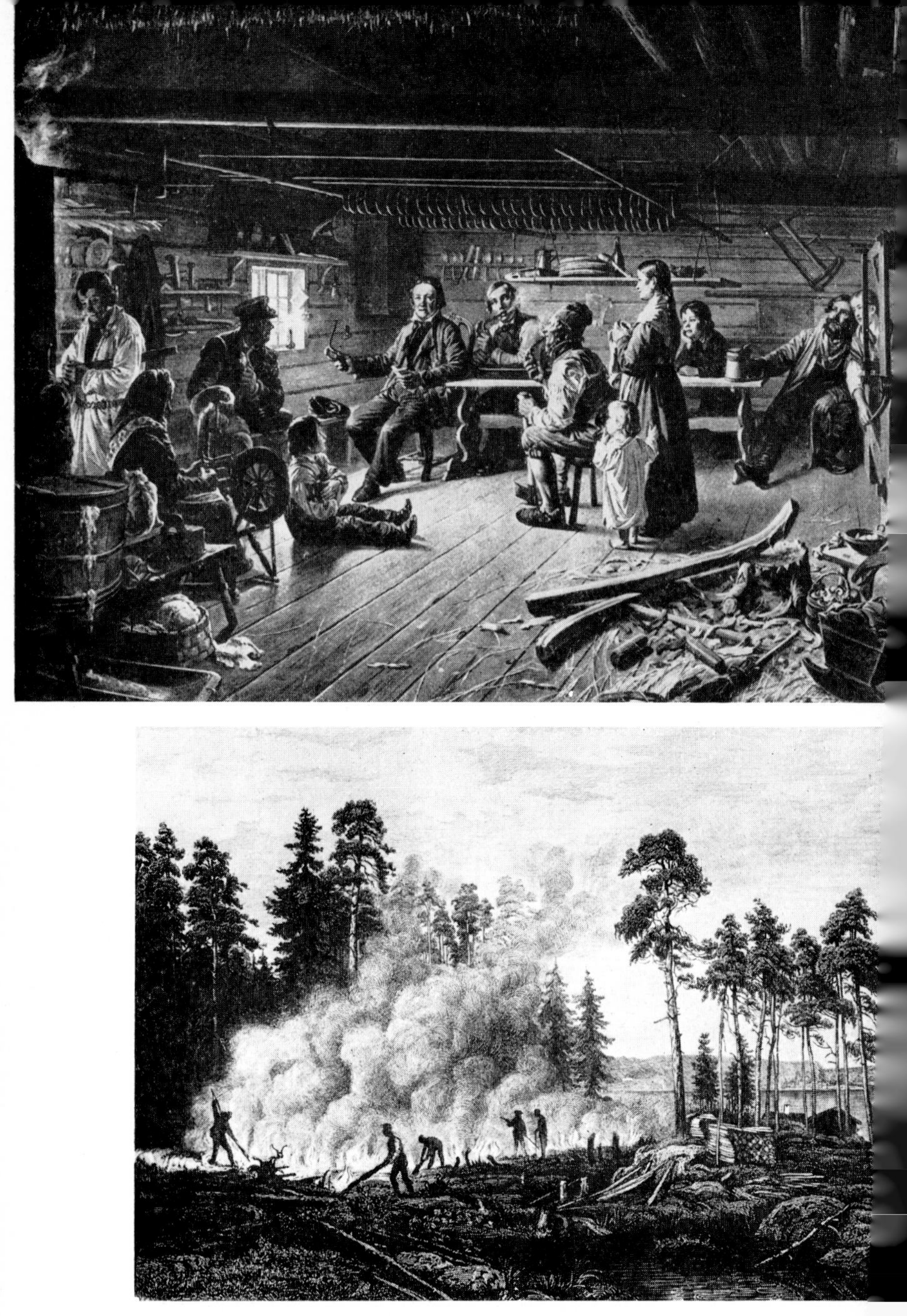

9 AN INTERIOR BY R. W. EKMAN, 1848

The painting depicts Pentti Lyytinen reading in the living room of a Savo farmhouse. It illustrates something of the arts, crafts, and costumes of the day

10 LAND CLEARANCE BY FIRING IN IISALMI, NORTHERN SAVO

A mid-nineteenth-century engraving by Berndt Lindholm included in Z. Topelius, *En resa i Finland*, Helsingfors, 1872–3

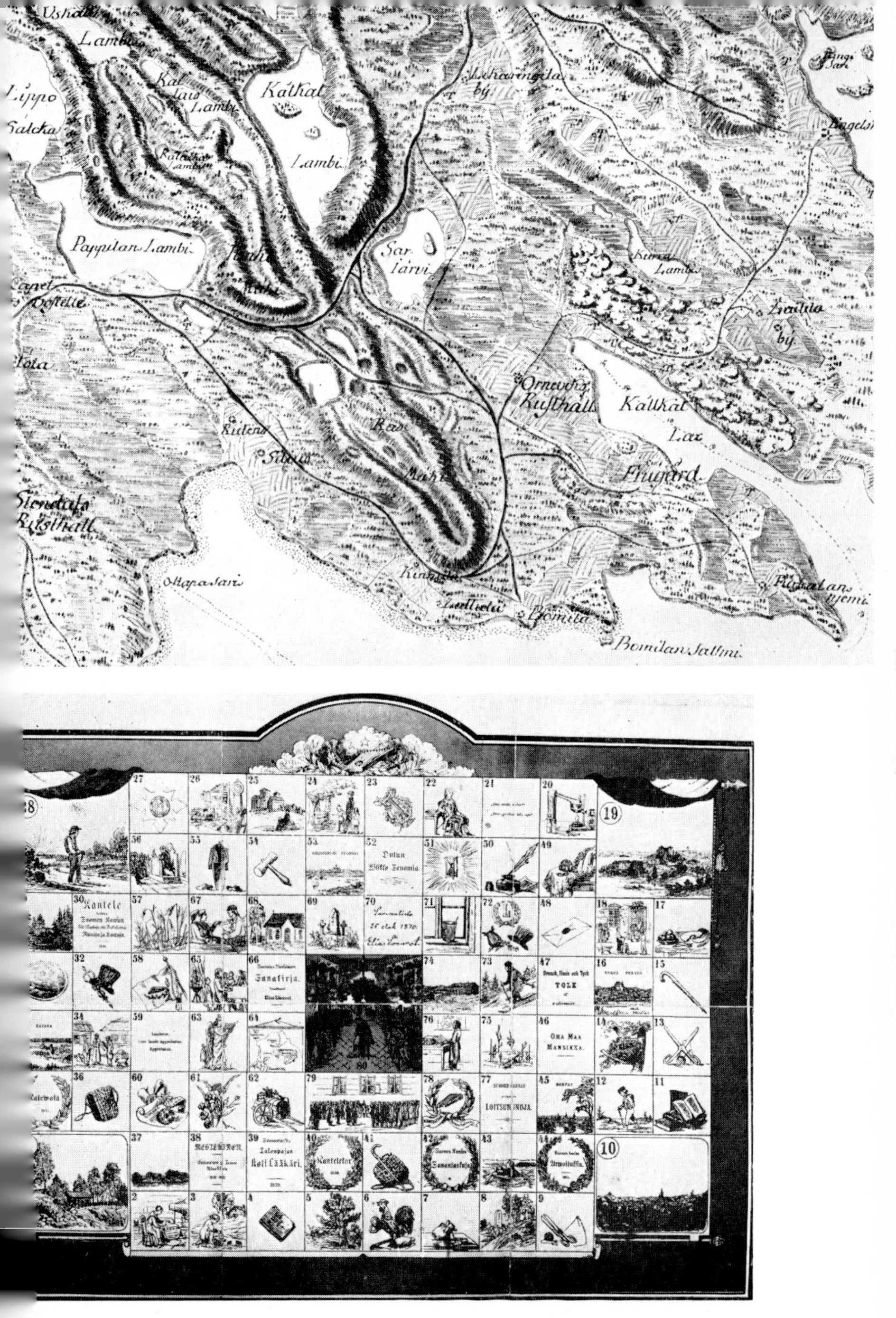

11 THE MILITARY RECONNAISSANCE OF FINLAND A sample map from the reconnaissance in the parish of Joroinen, Mikkeli province, *c.* 1780

12 A NINETEENTH-CENTURY GAME BASED ON THE LIFE OF ELIAS LÖNNROT A number of card games of a geographical and historical character were introduced to Finland in the last century with a view to fostering knowledge about the country and its great men

13 A CARTOON FROM THE TIME OF THE CONSTITUTIONAL STRUGGLE

The cartoon illustrates the proscribed newspapers and the stamps withdrawn by Russian decree

14 THE DECLARATION OF INDEPENDENCE [*Opposite*]

(*a*) The Senate, under the Chairmanship of P. E. Svinhufvud, that declared independence on 6 December 1917
(*b*) The Constitutional Document addressed to the Finnish People (*Suomen kansalle*) on 4 December 1917

Samalla kuin Hallitus on tahtonut saattaa nämä sanat kaikkien Suomen kansalaisten tietoon, kääntyy Hallitus kansalaisten, sekä yksityisten että viranomaisten puoleen, hartaasti kehoittaen kutakin kohdastansa, järkähtämättömästi noudattamalla järjestystä ja täyttämällä isänmaallisen velvollisuutensa, ponnistamaan kaikki voimansa kansakunnan yhteisen päämäärän saavuttamiseksi tänä ajankohtana, jota tärkeämpää ja ratkaisevampaa ei tähän asti ole Suomen kansan elämässä ollut. Helsingissä 4 päivänä joulukuuta 1917.

Suomen Senaatti:

15 MARSHAL CARL GUSTAF MANNERHEIM (1867–1951)

16 PRESIDENT JUHO KUSTI PAASIKIVI (1870–1956)

17 CROWD SCENE

Soldiers, sailors, and members of the Social Democratic party on their way to the Senate Square, 17 April 1917

18 THE FINNS AT WAR UNDER WINTER CONDITIONS, FEBRUARY 1940

19 A STATUE OF THE POET, EINO LEINO, BY J. LEPPÄNEN, 1953

20 INTERIOR OF HYVINKÄA CHURCH, BY ARMO RUUSUVUORI

21 INTERIOR OF KALEVA CHURCH, TAMPERE, BY REIMÄ PIETILÄ, 1966

22 SAIMAA CANAL A view of the reconstructed waterway that links Lake Saimaa with the Finnish Gulf in Vyborg (F. Viipuri) Bay. The canal was reopened in 1968

23 THE SIBELIUS MEMORIAL IN HELSINKI, A PRIZE-WINNING DESIGN BY EILA HILTUNEN

antithesis to the vocal supporters of the Socialist Commonwealth. Such organs as *Työmies* and *Red Star*, produced by Finnish radicals, were calculated to have a powerful effect upon conformist Americans. Under these circumstances, it was not surprising that the desirability of Finnish immigrants was occasionally questioned.

The law had ample means for excluding unwanted aliens. One ground for restraint was relaxed when a case was successfully brought by John Svan, a very Swedish Ostrobothnian, before a judge of the District Office Court of Duluth, Minnesota. On 17 January 1908 Svan was selected in order to provide physical testimony that Finns were not Mongolians and that they conformed to the definition of 'white person' within the meaning of the American citizenship acts. Canadians in the forest-mining areas of north-central Ontario had their own uncertainties about Finnish immigrants, though their experiences sprang out of the radical elements who left for North America following the Finnish Civil War in 1918.

Blood-letting by emigration has had several results for Finland. First, it has given rise to ethnic groups of Finnish descent in overseas countries – about half a million altogether. Secondly, it established a tradition of emigration similar to that in the other Scandinavian countries. Thirdly, short-period migration was added to permanent migration, with the object of accumulating capital to pay off mortgages or to establish new enterprises at home. The saga of emigration has now been repeated, with variations on its themes, for four generations. It has its own literature – printed and unprinted. Emigration has become a part of the mentality of the Finns.

Fin du Siècle

Viewed from the year 1900, Finland's 2.7 million inhabitants constituted a nation still on the edge of the modern era. They were allying industry to agriculture, enjoying an expanding international market, experiencing a new integration through improved communications and sharing in the benefits of cooperation. But political stress and strain were already entrenched in the domestic scene and the miracle is that so much was achieved in the midst of so much division. One cause of domestic differences has already been identified – the existence of a large propertyless minority in a country traditionally dominated by free-holding farmers. The problem was partly eased by immigration; partly by the land laws which bear the title *Lex Kallio* (after President Kallio) that followed the Civil War.

There were other issues no less sensitive in character, though they took their origins principally in intellectual circles. They were rooted in Finland's dichotomy of languages and cultures. The romantic enthusiasm which sought to create a Finnish Finland not only encountered bureaucratic obstruction but gave rise to a powerful academic reaction among young Swedish-speaking Finns. Fennoman consequently became ranged against Svecoman: *Finskhet* (eventually *Suomalaisuus*) against *Svenskhet* (*Ruotsalaisuus*). Leadership of the young Swedes was assumed by A. O. Freudenthal and considerable bitterness sprang out of the doctrine of racial distinction between Swede and Finn propagated by the Swedish journalist and publicist A. Sohlman. The Swedish case was both strengthened and complicated by the simultaneous development of Pan-Scandinavianism – a movement which reached a climax after 1860. While the Fennoman and Svecoman factions tended to attract extremists, the more liberal element had another programme. Its objects were to strengthen the position of the Grand Duchy in the Russian Empire and to urge progressive policies that would bring Finland into line with the countries of western Europe. There were modest concessions from Imperial Russia – a certain liberalising of the Diet in 1869, the establishment of a Finnish army in 1878, the introduction of an income qualification for election to the House of Burghers in 1879.

The three groups gathered strength as political parties and by the 1880s were ranged in an uneasy triangle in the Houses of the Diet. The Svecomen were headed by a number of academics and estate-owners whose families had provided Finland's leadership for many centuries and who were adding commercial to administrative leadership. The Fennomen party's late nineteenth-century leader was Georg Z. Forsman, who subsequently changed his name to Yrjö-Koskinen. Forsman was among the intellectuals of his day who wrote history as well as making it. As with Zachris Topelius, he was intensely interested in producing a formal history of Finland. Although the liberal party had in Leo Mechelin a patriot who was to play a leading role during Finland's Russian crisis, the intensity of the cultural conflict was too great to be absorbed by the liberals. As emotion triumphed over reason the liberal party was slowly absorbed by the other two groups. The struggle was conducted in the Houses of the Diet in the 1880s; it was simultaneously pushed with vigour into local government, into secondary education and into the

University of Helsinki. The modern era was foreshadowed in the last decade of the nineteenth century when Finnish-speaking secondary schools claimed as many pupils as Swedish-speaking, when Yrjö-Koskinen addressed the House of Nobles in Finnish for the first time, and when E. N. Setälä first used Finnish formally in the university consistorium.

The problem of the rural proletariat and the emotions generated by Swedish-Finnish differences were bedevilling influences in Finnish domestic politics. They still cast occasional shadows. Yet in spite of them, *mieli* (the common mind) prevailed over *kieli* (language) and Finland contrived to push forward the liberalisation of its political life. Even after Russian restraints in the 1890s, Finland speeded the emancipation of women. It was the second country after New Zealand to admit women to Parliament. The victory was the more significant because the first substantial volume of Finnish election statistics, published in 1907, indicated that there were more women electors than men. In 1908 *The Illustrated London News* carried a photograph of thirteen formidable lady members. Since 1894, they had fostered their cause through a suffragette journal *Nutid*, which in 1906 was able to declare 'Segern vunnen' ('The victory is won'). Finland had its first woman cabinet Minister in Mina Sillanpää in 1926–27.

Mirrors of Nationality

Social and economic changes were shot through with powerful artistic and spiritual forces. As early as 1817, the Finnish ethnographer C. A. Gottlund was writing of poetry as 'the crystal in which nationality is mirrored'. Before he died a heritage of narrative verse and lyrics was being accumulated. No one contributed more generously than Johan Ludvig Runeberg. In poems as contrasted as the affecting *Lily of the Valley* and the long narrative work *The Elk Hunters* he captured the detailed personal experiences of many Finns. Runeberg wrote exclusively in Swedish and he was a poet appreciated throughout Scandinavia. In his *Tales of Ensign Stål* (1848) he created for the Finns a minor portrait gallery of historical characters. This collection of narrative poems, put into the mouth of a Ruovesi veteran, romanticised a series of episodes in the war of 1808–09. It was conceived on a broad canvas, created an image of a resilient and resistant people, suffused an heroic atmosphere of 'old, forgotten far-off things and battles long ago' and was rich in the symbols of nationhood. Runeberg's home in Porvoo remains a national shrine and his birthday in February is a festive occasion when the townsfolk light commemorative candles in their windows. A frock-coated statue of the Finnish laureate stands on Helsinki's Esplanade. On its granite plinth are scrolled the words of the national anthem, *Vårt Land*. Runeberg's work, which claimed the early attention of the Howitts and Edmund Gosse, retains a continuing place in the life and thought of the modern nation.

Among Runeberg's gifted contemporaries, none was more productive than Zachris Topelius. Although his father had bidden him learn Finnish, he too employed Swedish for his written work. Topelius differed greatly from Runeberg. He was less of a poet – though he was sensitive to the mood of the moment no less than his contemporary. For example *Islössning i Uleå elf* (The thaw on Ule river) employed with great effect a natural phenomenon to symbolise a national feeling. Topelius was a gifted and fluent author of historical romance. *Fänriks Berättelser* (Tales of a Field Surgeon) have romanticised the spacious days of Swedish Finland as *Fänrik Ståls Sägner* have immortalised its eclipse in 1808–09. Above all, Topelius spoke to and for the world of children. There was a spark of the universal in him. It is fitting that the memorial in Helsinki of this quizzical little man should include a trio of children attentive upon 'Uncle Topelius'. Both Runeberg and Topelius had international reputations. Many of their works were translated into the world languages in their lifetimes. As a result, Topelius's Canute Whistlewinks was introduced to the young of Great Britain and the U.S.A., while Runeberg's *King Fjälar* and *Nadesha* were adapted as libretti for operas. Reciprocally, the two authors were influenced by British and European literature. Runeberg, in particular, had the services of a linguistically gifted wife to help with his interpretations of Scott, Byron, Dickens, Bulwer Lytton and others. Topelius, who was also editor of *Helsingfors Tidningar*, played the part of political pamphleteer as occasion demanded. After the 'Affair at Hanko' in 1854, his poem *The First Drop of Blood* was translated and circulated by the peace party in the British House of Commons.

While they were still at the height of their powers, Runeberg and Topelius were overtaken by authors who began to write in the Finnish language. The coastlands yielded their lyricists, who sang in Swedish, but many of the new generation of authors had their roots in interior Finland and their homes in the Finnish equivalent of the

American log cabin. Alexis Kivi, the most brilliant of the vanguard of Finnish-language authors, came of humble rural stock, as did the artist Juho Rissanen. While many of the characters created by Runeberg and Topelius have a Swedish air, those of Kivi are essentially from the backwoods of Suomi. Moreover, his fictional country-folk in behaviour and appearance remain readily identifiable in present-day Finland. Partly for this reason, few books are dearer to the Finn than *Seven Brothers*, which was first serialised in 1870. It is a saga rich in incident and homespun character, leaning heavily upon autobiographical experience and drawing its local colour from Kivi's home area of Nurmijärvi. *Seven Brothers* is allegory as well as fiction, for in the taming of the animal spirits in the brothers is seen the civilising of Finland itself. Kivi was a dramatist and a poet, too. *The Heath Cobblers* (1864), full of incident and quotable comment, remains a favourite piece inside and outside the theatre. The pensive sculpture of Kivi in Helsinki's Railway Square, the work of Väinö Aaltonen, captures the sense and sensibility of a man who (like all too many Finnish men of letters) died young from the killing disease of his undernourished times.

The linden trees on Helsinki's Esplanade also shade the proud statue of the vigorous non-conformist Eino Leino. The climax of his restless but prolific life coincided with the latter years of Russian suzerainty. His work is verbally rich (in classical allusion and metaphor as well as in vocabulary), rhythmically experimental and intellectually profound. It was, moreover, cast into the mould of an increasingly supple Finnish language, in which (as Leino saw it) 'Spartan qualities were transformed through a new Atticism'. The poems balance the stresses and strains of the mind against those of the natural world – the hardships of his childhood country of Kainu with its frost in summer, darkness in winter and unrewarding soil. Leino was a poet of international stature but of minority appeal. He was a Lucifer, a prince of darkness, baptised with the tongues of flame of *Whitsuntide* (the symbolic title of a collection of his poems), learning his *Lesson from the Sun* and composing his *Hymn to Fire*. 'He who is fire, let him serve the fire.' He was like William Blake's tiger, 'burning bright in the forests of the night' – and as untranslatable into English as Blake would be into Finnish.

These were some of the authors who invaded the burgeoning capital first with their romanticism and then with their realism – a capital which only had about 100,000 inhabitants at the turn of the century. But there were others who throve on capturing scenes from provincial life. They included Juhani Siljo, a poet of the wasteland who lamented the restlessness in a seemingly peaceful nature; and Johannes Linnankoski, whose *Song of the Blood Red Flower* romanticised the life of the summer loggers and whose *Fugitives* is the apotheosis of the sacredness of the Finnish soil. Kuopio nursed Finland's first woman playwright Minna Canth – and the store that she founded over a century ago still operates in the bustling provincial capital of Savo today. Gustav von Numers's plays *Behind Kuopio* and *The Vicars Family*, as well as K. A. Tavastjerna's *Uramo torppa*, are of the same genre as the social dramas of Minna Canth. Juhani Aho also belongs to Savo. The hamlets and villages of interior Finland retain many of the features caught in the vignettes of his short stories, which he chose to call *Lastuja* ('wooden chips'). The bosky churchyard of Iisalmi parish church and its nearby vicarage have altered little since Aho frequented them.

Art was delayed in its response to the awakening nation. Partly, perhaps, this was because the demand for pictures was less than that for books; partly because the schooling and upbringing of the artist was different from that of the author. Finnish art only assumed a significant national expression when it was disciplined by training abroad and infected by international influences.

A sprinkling of amateur artists caricatured early nineteenth-century Finnish society in empire gown and hussar regimentals and left a legacy of rather impersonal portraits. It was Alexander Laureus and R. W. Ekman who first presented scenes that were distinctively Finnish. Ekman's peasant interiors and rural scenes from the 1830s and 1840s resembled those of Norwegian and Swedish artists of the day, while his illustrations for the poems of Runeberg and for the incidents of *Kalevala* had similar Scandinavian parallels. He and his contemporaries were encouraged by authors such as Zachris Topelius who emphasised the importance of book illustration. *Finland framställdt i teckningar* (Helsingfors, 1845–52) attempted through its 120 lithographs to perform an educational as well as aesthetic function. Ekman's work had a second phase of significance when the Board of Education printed his pictures for propaganda purposes in the early twentieth century. His well-known illustration of the Tsar Alexander I proclaiming Finland's rights at the Diet of Porvoo in 1809 enjoyed a popular revival.

Ekman's work was complemented by the art of the brothers

Magnus, Ferdinand and Wilhelm von Wright. Reproduction of their faithful records of local scenes and colourful bird paintings have a wide appeal. The almost photographic likenesses of Annegatan in Helsinki and Skatudden by Magnus von Wright are near historical documents. In their day a more powerful impact was made by the rural idylls of Werner Holmberg and Hjalmar Munsterhjelm, whose heavy woodlands of Häme and lowering lakescapes of Näsijärvi began to spread their canvases across the wall of spacious town drawing-rooms.

These pioneers anticipated an imaginative group of skilled artists whose work bore the distinct stamp of a new Finland. Principal among them were Aleksi Gallén-Kallela (his adopted Finnish name), Albert Edelfeldt, Juhani Rissanen and Hugo Simberg. All combined national fervour with artistic ability. All realised the importance of international association. Gallén-Kallela gave visual form to *Kalevala*, so that most Finns (as well as most foreigners) see the mythical characters and incidents of the national epic in his highly personal terms. But he did much else beside, capturing the limbs and lineaments of the northern firs, filling his sketch books with the portraits of country folk, enshrining life and death in the frescoes of Juselius's mausoleum. Albert Edelfeldt has perhaps done most to fix the country scene in Finnish imagination. Many of his best known paintings are pastorals, though the glint of naturalism breaks through the romance. His smoke-blackened pioneers and summer milking scenes still find echoes in Finland's rural depths. Naturalism in life and labour are repeated in the work of Eero Järnefelt and in the Tuusela landscapes of Pekka Halonen. Juhani Rissanen introduced to the more sober company of the naturalists a broad humour which is as alive today as when he painted. His men and women are all slightly larger than life and, although they are usually primitive in representation, they are immediately recognisable Finnish rustics. Hugo Simberg, painting at the end of the Russian period, added satire, symbolism and a preoccupation with death. The genius of Helena Schjerfbeck was less rapidly absorbed into the national consciousness, but her distinctive approach was swiftly recognised in Sweden. By the turn of the century, efforts were also being made to bring art into the open spaces of the towns. At the same time as the restrained profiles of the Munich-named *Jugend* style slowly won their architectural victory, sculptures began to take up their sites – Ville Vallgren's *Havis Amanda* with her circle of seals on the quayside market place of Helsinki, E. Wickström's *Elias Lönnrot*, Robert Stignell's *Shipwreck* on Observatory Hill.

The civic conscience was also pricked at an early stage by the other arts. Eino Leino had been an early protagonist of *leipä ja laula* (literally bread and song, though perhaps justifiably translated as bread and circuses). Music and the theatre were felt to be natural media for national expression. Music developed against a choral background, though the tradition was lay rather than ecclesiastical, and the *cantor* continues to lead the singing in the Finnish church. University glee societies in the eighteenth century were supplemented by an academic music society in 1834. Against this background, Fredrik Pacius emerged as Finland's first noteworthy composer. Although he was followed by others, such as Johan Filip von Schantz, Finland made no international musical impact until the works of Robert Kajanus, who was associated with the Helsinki City Orchestra from its foundation in 1882, appeared at the end of the century. In the meantime, the enthusiasms of Kaarlo Bergbom had introduced opera to Finland, though no permanent opera was founded until 1911. By then Jean Sibelius was launching his major symphonies and Finnish music was sailing on the flood tide of Kalevalan romanticism. His near contemporaries – Erkki Melartin, Armas Järnefelt, Leevi Madetoja, Aare Merikanto, Toivo Kuula and Yrjö Kilpinen – were moved by the common impulse of national feeling. Their lyrical compositions carried emotional overtones in their titles; their songs entered the repertoires of the *lieder* singers. In such artists as Aino Akté and Ida Aalberg, Finland established its own international tradition. At the same time, folk-song and folk-music were slowly put in their international context by the musicologist, Ilmari Krohn.

The theatre was no less active in the Russian period. The atmosphere of earlier days may still be recaptured in the Swedish theatre at Turku, built in 1838 and a museum piece worthy of the care bestowed upon the Opera House and *Svenska Teatret* of Helsinki. The Finnish National Theatre, born in 1872, acquired its own sturdy granite home in 1902.

And to indoor entertainment was added an interest in open-air sports and gymnastics. A central physical education and sports league had been proscribed as politically subversive until 1906. With its support, Finnish teams made their Olympic debut – in London in 1908 and Paris in 1912. Records began to be kept as a challenge for succeeding generations. Winter sports acquired an especial popularity. The essentials of Finland's sporting organisations were established in the latter days of the Grand Duchy. They had a most important effect upon physical fitness as well as upon national morale.

While these various artistic and athletic manifestations absorbed the spiritual energies of many people, the less sophisticated found their outlet in vigorous revivalist movements. These were partly a protest against traditional church authority, and the not infrequent social cleavage between priest and parishioner, though they were also inseparable from the new literacy and new attitudes that penetrated Finland. The pietist movement, gathering its strength from the lake district and from Ostrobothnia, from women as well as from men, was summed up in the name of Paavo Routsalainen. In its strong Puritan tradition are rooted many of the attitudes of the modern nation, not least among them the state policy on the sale of alcohol. Pietism, which expressed itself in different ways in different areas, was complemented by the evangelical movement of F. G. Hedberg in the south-west and the extremist movement associated with L. L. Laestadius in the north. Sects such as the *Hihhulit* tried to foster ecstatic experiences which in some of their manifestations bordered on the frenzies of the ancestral shamans.

Although there were schisms in the Church, its development proceeded uninterruptedly. Many of its familiar features today derive from the Tsarist period. Parishes multiplied, impressive new buildings raised their wooden porticos in homage to Engel or their fretted spires in sympathy with Europe's neo-Gothic revival. The new hymnal that came into being, incorporating songs of praise by some of the new Finnish poets, is still used. Church boats, rowed by half a dozen pairs of oars and carrying two dozen or more people, operated well into the railway age. An overseas mission was established in 1859 and a Seamen's Mission in 1875. The Bible Society, founded in 1812, maintained its association with the parent organisation in London. A Sunday School movement acquired formal organisation in the 1880s; while, at the other end of the ecclesiastical spectrum, a school of academic theologians gave a new impetus to doctrinal debate and biblical research. The state Church, supported by a direct tax in which the Orthodox Church shared, experienced little rivalry from the free Churches. It was the Church of the Establishment and the nation was of the Establishment.

During the last generation of Russian rule the works of Finnish authors and artists, the sermons of preachers and the feats of athletes became a part of the *légende* or a nation hungry to become a state. They were as significant for the thoughts and conversations of most people as the actions of the activists were to the politically committed minority. They were the more significant because of the limited size of the community which experienced them. Finland was not only a country of established professional integration, but of increasing social integration. Above all, there was an intimate communion between the arts: sometimes, a virtual family communion.

The circle of the Järnefelt family was a prime example. It consisted of Arvid, the Tolstoyan and author of idealistic fiction; Eero, the painter; Armas, the composer; Aino, the wife of Jean Sibelius (Ainola, the name of their Järvenpää villa). *Atelier* and *salon* were somewhat pretentious words to fit the studios and workshops of the rough-hewn land where they worked. But the clientele which sought the plush and gilt of the Hotel Kämp was Finland's counterpart to that of the Café Royal. If their conversations have vanished with the cigar smoke and the brandy fumes their correspondence remains. For the artists of the day were irrepressible diarists and letter writers – and, moreover, unbelievable hoarders of the written word. Among those around whom webs of correspondence knotted was Eino Leino. His correspondents included poets of such contrasting personalities as 'His Majesty' Otto Manninen (the epithet applied to this writer of sensitive lyrics by Leino) and '*Malmtorparen och backstugusittaren Bertilius Gripenbergius*'. He turned his pen, as a natural laureate, on the death of public figures to write odes on Leo Mechelin and P. Svinhufvud. At the same time, in a country where thanks for past entertainment are liberally strewn, Leino delivered poems instead of flowers. Ladies vied for the diverse favours of his genius. Real or imagined, their memoirs of days that were politically dark but artistically bright have matured in the mid-twentieth century to give a new gloss to the Grand Duchy's gilded age.

Russian Retrospect

The image of the Tsarist interlude is largely drawn in terms of the conflicts that characterised Fenno-Russian relations from 1899 onwards. But until that time discords between Finland and Russia were restricted in their effects. Contrastingly, for a variety of Finns, the value of the Russian association was considerable.

In the first place, educated Finns were able to gain experience – even renown – in the Russian civil and military services, qualifying for pensions and acquiring the ribbons of lesser orders of chivalry. Some of them served in distant places. Arvid Etholén reached high rank in the Russian naval service, helped in the administration of the Russian-American company, and bequeathed collections to Helsinki University from his Alaskan years. C. H. F. Furuhjelm served in Pacific Russia and had an island and peninsula named after him; Uno Cygnaeus occupied the chaplaincy in Sitka for five years after 1839; while Turku shipping men even organised a Finnish-Alaskan whaling enterprise. University men were able to broaden their experience in St Petersburg. A. J. Sjögren was representative – and his status entitled him to the uniform of a major-general as well as the designation Excellency. For those attracted by exploration or ethnographic research, the link with Russia meant that a largely unknown sixth of the land surface of the globe was potentially available. Using this opportunity Castrén and Europaeus penetrated into the western Finnic areas, Kai Donner to Mongolia, J. G. Granö to Altai and, eventually, Carl Gustaf Emil Mannerheim embarked on his memorable journey to China. Another consequence of this freedom of access was observed by Sjögren in 1821: 'Our union with Russia will give us freer communications with people of our own stock who live there.'

Secondly, the association favoured businessmen. They found in Russia an ample market of a not especially exacting character, where their manufactures were less exposed to competition than in the more demanding west European market. They also experienced more favourable tariff treatment. Again, the mills and homes of St Petersburg provided an outlet for the surplus labour of a considerable number of Karelian artisans. Indeed, local church records indicate that for the Grand Duchy at large a variety of Finns migrated to St Petersburg. Summer steamers and, after the 1870s, the railway also carried Finnish visitors to savour the splendours (if to suffer some of the miseries) of the city on the Neva.

Reciprocally, Finland received a summer stream of Russian visitors. Alexander III's rustic fishing lodge on the Kymi river at Langinkoski recalls the escape that the royal family intermittently sought from the formality of the court. Villas in eastern Finland were already popular among St Petersburgers before the coming of the railway. The Vuoksi valley, in particular, had its admirers.

Hangö became a favourite Russian resort at a later stage, and the fretwork whimsies of its seaside villas remain.

For at least half of the Russian interlude, the attitude of Finns was coloured by the gesture of respect for their constitution made by the Tsar Alexander I in 1809. Some even applied the adjective 'great' to Alexander's name. The gilded throne that he imported for use on his visit is still an impressive feature of the National Museum. The meeting at Porvoo cathedral at which Alexander received homage is a not unfamiliar illustration in Finnish school texts: but it is complemented by Edvard Isto's more forceful propaganda piece – *Hyökkays* – which illustrates Finland as a sturdy maiden endeavouring to protect the book of laws from the talons of a Russian eagle. Tsardom retained its positive image in Finland for a long time. Nicholas I, whose autocratic behaviour afflicted other parts of his realm, maintained peaceable relations with Finland. The great church in Helsinki that is now the cathedral was dedicated by him to St Nicholas. The statue of the liberal Alexander II still occupies the centre of Senate Square, the most prominent position of any in the Finnish capital: nor are plaster busts of benign tsars lacking in older Finnish homes. While other countries were rising in revolt against absolutist governments, the Finns were largely unmoved. The only event that caused a ripple in the Year of Revolutions was the first performance of Runeberg's *Vårt Land*, sung to music in Helsinki on Flora Day, 1848. Meanwhile, the university library was enjoying the privilege of Russian copyright editions and a remarkable collection of books was being accumulated for future generations of scholars. Meanwhile, too, neo-classical Orthodox churches, sometimes built to meet the needs of garrisons, accumulated their rich furnishings of candlesticks and ikons – St Nicholas, the worker of miracles, St Alexander of Svir, Our Lady of Kazan.

For Finland, the association with Russia was marked by a general absence of military involvement. Accordingly, a country which had suffered generations of war experienced a respite of more than a century. The only episode that disturbed Finland's foreign relations was the Crimean War. It was a war which largely isolated Finland from Sweden-Norway, with whom Britain and France had a secret understanding. Under different circumstances Finland's position might have been serious. Throughout, Finland remained loyal to Russia.

The Crimean War impinged directly upon the coasts of Finland.

During the summer engagements of 1854, the British and French fleets attacked and destroyed the fortress erected by the Russians at Bomarsund in the Åland islands in the 1830s. In 1855, they followed up with a direct attack on Suomenlinna. In retrospect, both incidents have a Gilbert-and-Sullivan flavour. The assaults took place with flags flying and bands playing. In the words of an Ostrobothnian observer, the ships came in 'dressed like brides'. Midshipman Francis Edwards, aged eleven, wrote of the bombardment of Suomenlinna taking place to the tune of 'Willikins and his Dinah'. War artists, such as E. T. Dolby and O. W. Brierley, drew sketches of camp life and naval manoeuvrings; cartoonists, such as Sweden's Fritz von Dandels, satirised the family Tuting that came to have a grandstand view of the naval encounters. At a later stage more spacious canvases, such as those of Z. W. Schulman, commemorated the war and Liewendal's lithographs began to decorate Finnish homes. Nor were the experiences of Finnish prisoners-of-war brought from Bomarsund to Britain and France without their lighter sides.

A score of Finnish coastal settlements suffered intrusion by marauding fleets because one of the functions of the navies was to destroy stocks of pitch and tar. In some harbours, as at Kokkola, a British military burial place recalls the event. Elsewhere, as in the dialect of the district around Rauma, an incident has given rise to a continuing simile – 'to laugh like an Englishman who set fire to the harbour'. Primitive Finnish paintings, tucked away in the corners of local museums, recall other incidents. Popular songs from the period are still sung. Johan Rännäri of Liminko is usually regarded as the most prolific composer commemorating the naval encounters. But by far the most memorable chorus is *Oolanin sota* (Åland's War), sung to the tune of the stirring *Björneborgers' March*. It tells how a handful of Finns put to flight no less than three hundred vessels of the British navy –

> Kun kolmella satalla laivalla
> Seilas enkelsmanni Suomenemme rannoilla.

Meanwhile, Finnish ships on the high seas were intercepted and taken as prizes of war. Yet, if it destroyed some personal friendships, the war strengthened others. Letters passed between the belligerents throughout the hostilities. Merchants in Liverpool and Hull looked after their beleaguered Finnish friends, buying their ships, freezing their currency, shipping products to them in 'neutral bottoms'. 'The

Reason Why' Finland became involved in these complications is as deserving of a monograph as that which moved Cecil Woodham Smith to cast an eye on the Crimean theatre.

In the broader European context, the war gave considerable publicity to Finland. In Britain, the press devoted columns to the campaign in the Baltic (where the first Victoria Cross was won at Bomarsund). *The Illustrated London News* provided imaginative pictures and *Punch* its occasional cartoons. The implication of Finland also provided Britain's anti-war faction with powerful parliamentary argument.

The Peace of Vienna which concluded hostilities was of lasting consequence for Finland. By it, the Åland islands were neutralised and demilitarised. During both World Wars the neutrality of Åland was subjected to certain infringements. But following the affirmation of demilitarisation in 1921, the islanders have remained free of military service.

Changes in the European balance of power were to alter Russia's external relationships in the last generation of Finland's Russian association. The Grand Duchy remained aloof from the Balkan War of 1877–78, though Finns in the Russian army were implicated. The Russo-Japanese War occurred at a critical stage in Russo-Finnish domestic relations – and there were moments when limited Finnish circles sought to connive against Russia. The swift rise of Germany, with which country Finland rapidly developed strong technical and commercial associations, transformed the earlier discords of France, Britain and Russia into harmonious understanding. As Finland's domestic relations with Russia were strained to breaking point, the Grand Duchy found itself in a situation where those who professed to uphold liberty had to withdraw their support in the face of more compelling circumstances.

The Birth of a Nation

The period of Finland's constitutional association with Imperial Russia is a well-defined chapter in its story. The association began in defeat and ended in transfiguration. In the earlier nineteenth century, to the outside world, the Finns appeared to be turned in upon themselves and curiously changeless in a changing Europe. Bishop Heber at the beginning of the Russian period thought Finland 'looked as if age after age had passed over the heads of the people without their attempting any improvement in the arts of civil life'.

Léouzon le Duc, writing in the 1840s, commented of the Finns, 'Leur vie est presque toute intérieure, qu'elle a peu ou point de retentissement au dehors'. It was a far cry from the seemingly withdrawn land upon the edge of western Europe to the challenged duchy whose state roused the passions of liberal Europe after 1899.

The attitude of Russia to Finland changed in response to a changing international situation, but it was inseparable from the spirit of the age. Russian chauvinism was partly an expression of forces similar to those that stirred Finnish nationalism. At the same time Slavophils regarded Russia as superior to the countries of western Europe. Since Finland had associated itself with west European ideas and fashions, it was natural that the Pan-Slavists should denigrate it. Independently of the rise of nationalism, Russia was increasingly afflicted with insecurity. Any related territory with more liberal attitudes than Russia was a natural object of suspicion. Finland was subject to limited Russian interference in the early 1890s. There had been a measure of infiltration into its civil service and an intrusion upon the control of its Post Office. But the storm broke when in 1899 the Tsar reduced the law-making powers of the Finnish Estates to a nullity. A nation-wide petition, supported by more than half a million signatures, many gathered by skiers and some by reindeer sleigh, was brushed aside when five hundred leading Finnish citizens attempted to present it to Nicholas II in St Petersburg. The protest was taken up at the international level. A document, now bearing the title *Pro Finlandia* and pleading the cause of the Finns, was signed by over a thousand eminent Europeans. It was received with no greater courtesy than the Finnish petition; but was eventually to be deposited as one of the more remarkable documents in the Finnish State Archives. Russian interference was felt at all levels of society. The Russian-controlled Post Office discontinued the sale of stamps bearing the familiar Finnish lion-escutcheon in 1901. Censorship of the press was introduced (and accompanied by a rash of underground publications); a third language was added to street names (the *Russian* palimpsest can occasionally be seen to this day). There was infiltration – 'mole-work', the British lawyer Joseph Fisher called it. There was pressure to teach more Russian in secondary schools, though this merely served to make Russian an undesirable language to learn.

Much more serious was the introduction of new conscription laws. An attempt to conscript recruits to serve under Russian instead of

Finnish army regulations resulted in widespread refusal to report for service. As a direct result, a resistance society, bearing the name Kagal (F. *Kagaali*), came into being. It spelt the beginning of yet another division in Finnish society. Although there was universal opposition to Russian intrusion, opinion was divided over the form that resistance should take. The more extreme members of the constitutionalist group stood ranged against the compliance party. But officials continued to be removed from office, voluntary and enforced exile mounted, and, as Consul-General Mitchell wrote, the 'ladies of Helsingfors, now wear deep mourning' as a sign of public protest. Tension reached a climax in 1904, when the Governor-General Bobrikov, a powerful protagonist of Russification, was assassinated in the capital by Eugen Schauman.

The climax coincided with the ill-conceived Russo-Japanese War of 1904–05. The war, in turn, was accompanied by exceptional domestic stresses in Russia; they were reflected in Finland in a general strike in 1905. In the face of both external and internal pressures, Russia's tightening grip on Finland was relaxed. During the break in the Finnish clouds the February Manifesto was rescinded and Russia acquiesced in considerable constitutional reforms. The bases of the present-day governmental structure were laid with the replacement of the outmoded Four Estates by a single chamber in 1906. In the accompanying system of universal suffrage, with secret voting for all over twenty-four, women were accorded equal voting rights with men. The first elections resulted in the emergence of a powerful Social Democratic group – a feature to continue in the Finnish electoral scene. Among those to be returned was Väinö Tanner, a figure who was to play a leading role in Finnish politics for over fifty years. In the same year, Finland was represented for the first time at a meeting of the Inter-Parliamentary Union held in London. Side by side with this apparent triumph and in order to underline Finnish consolidation, many people changed their family names from the original Swedish stem into Finnish. The process of *nimenmuuttoja* as it was called was legally conducted through the official Finnish publication *Finlands Allmänna Tidning*. Supplement no. 111 for 1906 announced thousands of changes. Some of the conversions for Nådendal (Naantali) parish illustrate the nature of the change – Ahlman to Aalto, Forsman to Koskela, Grönberg to Vihervuori, Jern to Rautakari, Lindfors to Lohikoski, Rosenberg to Ruusuvaara, Sjöstedt to Merenlinna. It is one of the ironies of Finnish history that during this constitutional and personal ferment the key figure of Finland's twentieth century – C. G. Mannerheim, an aristocrat of Swedish lineage and holding high office in the Russian army – was undertaking a superhuman ride from Tashkent to China.

But the constitutional respite was temporary and by 1908 a new period of restraint was under way. The cry of *Finis Finlandiae*, voiced by M. Pentunkevitch in 1910, was taken up in Russian political circles; Finland was represented as a threat to the security of the realm at the gates of St Petersburg and arguments against the dissident duchy foreshadowed those of the 1930s. The outbreak of the First World War only served to strengthen Russia's excuse for subordinating Finland. 'Ukko Pehka' Svinhufvud, later President of Finland, was among the politicians despatched to Siberia. A granite obelisk at Luumäki railway station commemorates his point of departure to the Eurasian wilderness from the intimacies of his home at nearby Kotkaniemi. And Hjalmar Procopé, finding poetic images in the Old Testament in general and in Babylon in particular, voiced the burning hatred of oppression. It would take more than 'two words of Latin' and the Tashkent corps to efface Finland from the map.

In the pre-war international scene, Finland in duress made a disproportionately wide impact. It claimed attention in part because it had already caught both the eye and the ear. For example, at the Paris Exhibition of 1900, the Finnish contribution outshone the Russian. Jean Sibelius's *Finlandia* began to acquire the reputation as a second national anthem in the same year. International literature about Finland began to multiply simultaneously. The English-speaking world enjoyed the redoubtable Mrs Alec Tweedie's *Through Finland in Carts.* (Mrs Tweedie was a staunch feminist and her London drawing-room continued to attract Finnish company for forty years.) Rosalind Travers instructed her readers on an oppressed country in a series of well-informed *Letters from Finland* and, having become *persona non grata* in Finland, returned to London where she became one of the first joint honorary secretaries of the Anglo-Finnish Society. Harry de Windt wrote with American jauntiness of the Grand Duchy and J. E. Fisher traced the constitutional relationship of *Finland and the Tsars*. The Everyman Library printed William Kirby's translation of *Kalevala*. Kirby was a lepidopterist at the Natural History Museum and he was spurred on to complete his translation by Aino Malmberg, a Finnish suffragette and activist who was much in London during the difficult years. Politicians and publicists in western Europe were carefully cultivated by patriotic Finnish émigrés. Liberally-minded editors, such as William Stead of the *Manchester Guardian*, maintained a lively interest in Finnish affairs.

But it was not easy for west European countries to support the Finnish cause, sympathetic though many of their citizens might be. All had foreign policies which at some point might run counter to Finnish attitudes. For example, it was difficult for Britain to show public sympathy for the Finns at the time when it was engaged in the Boer War and itself conducting an apparently oppressive campaign in Ireland. Realists such as A. V. Dicey knew that there was no prospect of Britain offering direct assistance. There were other tangled threads in the Finnish skein. It was all too easy for patriots to become allied with revolutionaries and anarchists. In 1905, the episode of the *John Grafton* – a vessel chartered to carry arms to Russian radicals, paid for by the Japanese but wrecked on the Ostrobothnian coast – illustrated the lunatic fringe of these endeavours. Indeed, because Finland provided a springboard for underground activity, it was to become a setting for adventures rivalling those in cloak-and-dagger fiction. Lenin's use of Finland in 1905, 1906, 1907 and 1917 is commemorated in the Lenin Museum in Tampere and illustrates the degree of connivance between subversive elements in Finland and Russian revolutionaries. In a letter to Julius Reuter, J. E. Fisher spoke of the need for emulating Italy's Cavour, who 'never allowed the revolutionaries to make use of him or involve him in revolutionary movements'.

By the time the First World War was under way, Finnish patriots were not only courting potential Russian revolutionaries, but also turning to the enemies of Russia as their logical allies. Finland had already established firm German commercial and academic connections before the outbreak of war. In early 1915 the plan to train a corps of potential Finnish officers became a reality. Out of it grew the Jaeger battalion that was to play a critical role in the establishment of the modern state of Finland in 1918. About 2,000 men received training in it. The Jaegers remain a vivid memory. At Porosalmi, near the site of a memorable engagement which took place in the war of 1808–09, is a manor which houses their pensioners. It is a lesser Finnish counterpart to Chelsea Hospital though the number of its occupants dwindles. A latter-day Runeberg might well use the Jaeger experiences for a twentieth-century counterpart of *The Tales of Ensign Stål.*

The year 1917 was to be most critical in the history of Finland. Internationally developments in the Grand Duchy were completely obscured by more far-reaching events in the European arena. In the face of the bloody engagements on the western front and the collapse of Russia on the eastern front the fate of the Finns was largely forgotten. For a brief while it seemed as if the two events that could help Finland to throw off the Russian yoke were happening simultaneously – a victory for Germany and the elimination of the Tsarist régime. But Finnish anticipations were not realised. And the bitter disappointment had to be absorbed by a Finland that was divided against itself. The shock, even the brutality, of many of Tykö Sallinen's expressionist paintings anticipated artistically the discords that were to rend the nation.

The steps to independence were conducted against a background of changing governments and the break-up of the old order in Russia. The March Parliament of 1917 was dominated by the Social Democrat Party (the strong radical tendencies of which have been long since dissipated). It was led by Oskari Tokoi. During the period of its government, the Tsar Nicholas II abdicated and the Finnish legislature sought to abrogate his powers. The provisional Russian government demurred, dissolved the Finnish Parliament and awaited new elections. When Parliament reassembled in November, the Social Democrats found themselves without their majority. Simultaneously the Bolshevik revolution in Russia left the Finnish government free to make its own legislative decisions. On 15 November it took over the powers of the Tsar 'for the time being' and a government was set up under P. E. Svinhufvud, in which the Social Democrats declined to share. On 27 November a majority agreement was reached on independence. The new constitution and declaration of independence, drafted by the future President J. C. Ståhlberg, were ratified by 100 votes to 88 on 6 December. On the last day of 1917, Finnish independence was recognised on behalf of the Bolshevik government by V. I. Lenin – an act which was probably not inseparable from genuine feeling for Finland. France and the central powers followed suit with immediate recognition.

These seemingly clear-cut constitutional steps were taken in a disturbed domestic setting. A national strike was declared on 12 November and, paralleling the situation in Russia, a national revolutionary council was set up. Although there were divisions of opinion on the use of force among the Social Democrats, party discipline was strong enough to maintain unity. Disaffected Russian soldiery totalling some 40,000, independent of Russian sailors, were scattered in a variety of localities and especially concentrated in southern Finland. Their presence and their pressures also influenced the decisions of the Finnish radicals.

In 1917 Finland disposed of the Tsar, but it was unable to dispose of Russia – and Russia was to remain an enigmatic and unpredictable neighbour. The Finns acquired constitutional freedom, but were faced with revolution. The common experience of unity in the face of external pressure that had contributed so fully to the forging of the nation was replaced by domestic disunity. Modern Finland suffered a civil war which continues to colour its thinking and its action. It was a conflict written in domestic terms. Yet, in its causes it was inseparable from the radical thinking and action of Russia, and in its consequences it was to play a continuing role in Russian relations. 'Independent Finland is a child of the revolution' was the conclusion of the post-war envoy, Lord Acton. Leaders of the Soviet Union have not ceased to echo his words.

Chapter 6

The Trials of Independence

FINLAND'S FORMAL declaration of independence was followed by the most disruptive phase in its history. In the short-term problems that followed and in the solutions that Finland adopted for them were born its larger and longer-term difficulties. The Civil War was short-lived but it left deep wounds in society. As a consequence of it party politics tended to run to extremes. The extreme right and the extreme left were to become more pronounced features of Finnish politics than in any of the Scandinavian countries. A second consequence of the Civil War was that Finland implicated itself with Germany, thereby delaying its recognition by the western powers and engendering future Russian suspicions. It had to establish its position in a divided Europe and to maintain its position in a continent where the balance of power might shift but the divisions remained. In addition the Civil War left its mark in detail and at large upon the economy of a country which had already been badly strained by the disruptions of the First World War.

The Civil War

Social tension had already been given expression in the strong left-wing vote registered in the democratically elected government of 1906. Dissatisfaction was rooted in widespread poverty, especially rural poverty, rather than in a pronounced maldistribution of wealth. The pathetic condition of casual labour in Kotka, for example, emerges clearly from the childhood memories of the novelist Toivo Pekkanen; while the lot of the poor was underlined in the poems of the radical aristocrat, Hjalmar Procopé. The result was the swift rise of socialism, but a socialism which was pragmatic rather than doctrinaire. The example of the Russian revolution, the presence of Russian revolutionaries in Finland and the refusal of the Socialist element to compromise with the non-Socialist element in the Parliament gave rise to the head-on collision in 1918. The two factions rapidly lined up as 'the workers' and 'the bourgeoisie', with their Red and the White Guards respectively.

Civil unrest assumed a critical form in January. Gustaf Mannerheim, whose adventurous return to Finland from Russia seemed almost to anticipate the predicament of the country, was invited by the government to accept the post of Commander-in-Chief. He left for Vaasa in the middle of January with a view to organising a national army in the calmer atmosphere of Ostrobothnia. The legally elected government also shifted to Vaasa. The revolutionary government that came into being in Helsinki in late January anticipated insurrection. Both sides took to arms on 28 January. Mannerheim's army of 40,000 troops, eventually increased to about 70,000, was pitched against a revolutionary army which with Russian troops mustered about the same number.

The conflict was well-identified geographically. The Red forces were entrenched in the south – especially in the southern third of Finland with its bigger towns, industries, administrative offices and larger rural properties. The White forces drew their strength from the heart of the countryside. Population was about evenly divided on either side of the 'front line'. Ostrobothnia was the first area to be cleared. In the march south, an especially bloody engagement took place around Tampere. A week later, on 12–13 April, the White Guard entered Helsinki.

While the Red forces drew limited strength from the east, the legally constituted government found itself privately hoping for German aid, but publicly disclaiming it. The German-trained Finnish Jaegers, the crowned lion of their flag supported by four crowned eagles, came to Vaasa in February to form a cadre of officers. About 12,000 German troops, commanded by General Rudiger von der Goltz, eventually landed on the south coast to join the White troops in April. Karelia was not brought under the control of Mannerheim's forces until mid-May; a victory parade was held in Helsinki on 16 May. It was a hollow victory following upon five months of pitched battles and public slaughter, of local feuds and private torture. The 70,000 prisoners-of-war might be slowly rehabilitated. The 400 industrial establishments directly affected might be restored to operational effectiveness. The damage, robbery and theft of equipment might be made good and the broken contracts mended. The near famine might be withstood. The great statistical enquiry organised by Einar Böök might assess the crude mathematics of the disaster. But only time – and much of that – could begin to make good the spiritual disruption. Personal and private tragedies that set family against family and group against group were to poison social relations for two generations. The legacy of bitterness was also to remain a powerful influence in voting patterns.

The defeated Red forces were dispersed in many directions. Some were shot. Some, including members of the revolutionary government such as Kullervo Manner, Edvard Gylling and Otto Kuusinen, sought asylum in Russia. Some escaped to join the British Expeditionary Force in Murmansk as a motley Finnish legion. Here the strange fortunes of war dressed them in British uniforms and eventually restored them to Finland, some with pardons, others to await investigation. Some crossed to the sanctuary of Sweden. Some, such as Oskari Tokoi, left by way of England for Canada and the U.S.A., where their political philosophies were tolerated if not encouraged, and where their memoirs eventually accorded to them a new respectability. Thousands died in prison camps through disease and starvation. But following conviction, prison and pardon, most had to return to the community that they had unsuccessfully sought to change. None was allowed to forget the interlude of violence. Wayside tombstones and memorials to about 20,000 dead recorded it for posterity. Those commemorating the Red Guards and their sympathisers were only slowly accepted by the new society.

Violence ended but stability was only slowly restored. The impossibility of policing the eastern border made it difficult to control the movements of activists who transferred their centre of operations to Russia where they established the Finnish Communist Party in August 1918. Both personal differences and ideological schisms slowly reduced their ranks, but the zealots that peer from the activist photographs of the day pursued their agitations well into the 1920s. A few survived to attain varying forms of notoriety at later stages in their political careers. Among them were Arvo Tuominen, Niilo Wälläri and Otto Kuusinen. Tuominen, sometime secretary of the Finnish Communist Party, eventually withdrew his allegiance. His memoirs are rich in the symbolism of the faith that he discarded. His mother, carrying the sickle as a day labourer into the harvest field, and his father, holding the hammer of his trade as a carpenter, provide powerful images: so do the Kremlin bells within the sound of which he lived for five years. Wälläri slowly moved away from the extreme left wing to a more moderate position and ended his days in 1967 while still engaged upon the second volume of his autobiography. He was a giant among Finnish trade unionists, constantly at odds with Moscow because of his independent attitude, in and out of prison for his intransigence. Although he has been affectionately caricatured as an almost avuncular figure, in his prime he held in his sway the union of seamen and dock labourers and could command the ports of Finland from Tornio to Hamina. Kuusinen, who during his earlier days held to the opinion that revolution in Finland could only spring out of Finland, was the only leader among the Reds successfully to seek his fortunes in the inner circle of the Russian Communist Party. In the years immediately after the Civil War Kuusinen moved in and out of Finland in a manner which Tuominen described as resembling that of Kilroy. The cat-and-mouse game played between the Central Criminal Department of Finland and Otto Kuusinen was also emulated by others. Others, too, engaged in illegal journeys across the isthmian boundary of the Systerbeck (Rajajoki) river to join the miscellany of international delegates who attended the party congresses. They were days of strange intrigues the purport of which has been forgotten, conducted in the bourgeois salons of Stockholm as well as of Helsinki with alert and attractive women playing the role of party messengers.

While security officials had to contend with these underground agencies, the emerging state of Finland also engaged in a measure of connivance with the interventionists who were operating around Russia's margins. For example Admiral Sir Walter Cowan, conducting his own 'private' war in the Baltic from 1918 to 1920, deployed units of the British fleet in Finnish waters. It was from bases in the Karelian isthmus that Augustus Agar won a Victoria Cross for his leadership in a daring motor torpedo-boat raid on the Russian fleet off Krondstadt. But by this time Gustaf Mannerheim, who had opposed collaboration with German forces, had retired from his command of the army; while Väinö Tanner, who was to be another stalwart in the difficult years of independence, was searching for a formula for a reconstituted Social Democratic Party. Finnish society needed a stabilising force moderately left of centre in the political scene: he was the architect of it.

The Identification of the New State

The new Finland had to establish itself diplomatically, territorially, commercially and socially. It had come into being in a world at war and it had associated itself with the losing side. Its eastern borders marched beside those of a neighbour whose frontiers were fluid and whose territory contained a possible irredentism. At the same time it was urgent that trading relations should be restored and that the country should present to the commercial world at least the semblance of stability. And only reluctantly was literature sympathetic to the losing side tolerated. Väinö Linna's *Täällä pohjontähden alla* (Under the north star), which revealed the problems of a tenant family in the fictional west Finnish village of Pentinkulma, was the first popular presentation of another point of view. It appeared forty years later.

The first step was to organise a stable government. Almost immediately, its form was the subject of dispute. Although the majority of Finns undoubtedly favoured a republic, there was a strong feeling that a constitutional monarchy in the Scandinavian tradition might be more expedient. Germany had available candidates and approaches were made to Prince Frederik Karl of Hesse. But the victory of the allied powers eliminated the suitability of the German royal house and prevented a King of Finland from joining the monarchies of Europe, so that Finland became the first 'Scandinavian' republic. Temporarily Finland lacked a titular head of state, though P. E. Svinhufvud and later C. G. Mannerheim acted as its Chief Executive. New elections were held in March 1919, a republican constitution was formulated in the same year and K. J. Ståhlberg, a member of the Progressive Party, was elected as the first President.

Between 1919 and 1939 Finland held nine elections. Five principal parties contended for the 200 seats and their candidates were elected by a system of proportional representation. They were the Social Democrats, Agrarians or Farmers' Party, the National Union or Conservative Party, the National Progressive Party and the Swedish-Finnish Party. From 1922 to 1929 and under the guise of a succession of names, the Communists held about a tenth of the seats. The People's Patriotic Party, a right-wing organisation, mustered a handful of seats between 1933 and 1939. Probably the most interesting political development of the inter-war years was the speedy rehabilitation of the Social Democratic Party. It remained the largest single party at each election. By 1927 faith in it was sufficient for Finland to accept its first Social Democratic government under Väinö Tanner.

From the outset, the number of political parties has resulted in government by coalition. Since a Prime Minister can rarely maintain a coalition which commands a majority for more than a short period, Finnish governments tend to convey an impression of domestic instability. Yet, although Finland's political representatives group and regroup themselves, there is more continuity in their operations than appears to the outsider. In the absence of a second chamber, the cabinet of fifteen members tends to play a more critical role than in many countries. Familiar faces have a habit of reappearing in successive governments.

Finland's written constitution outlines the essential structure of government from the central to the local authority. The President is elected by a college of presidential electors, the 300 members of which are appointed by a system of proportional representation. The voting is oral and consequently is a long procedure. The President holds office for six years, but is eligible for re-election. His powers are extensive, ranging from the direct conduct of foreign relations to the appointment of senior civil servants – including university professors. The constitution makes provision for an *Ombudsman*, whose powers closely resemble those of the British Lord Chancellor. The essential rights of citizens are codified in the Constitution Act. They have been subject to intermittent modification.

At the head of local government stand the provincial boards, which are the counterparts of British County Councils. They are presided over by provincial governors, who are the local officers representing the head of state. From 1865 onward local civil government developed on the basis of communes. Fifty years of powerful change have led to considerable modification in the boundaries and functions. In 1920, there were 38 towns, five urban districts (F. *Kaupala*: Sw. *Köping*) and 499 rural communes: in 1965, the figures were 46, 24 and 477 respectively.

The organisation of a firm and acceptable government was critical because Finland had to establish diplomatic relations with the outer world. Until the cessation of European hostilities, this was almost impossible. Throughout 1918 the German orientation of Finnish policy implied Allied suspicion of every move. Even when the purchase of 50,000 tons of wheat were negotiated with the U.S.A., British foreign office reports were supplemented with sceptical notes on the ultimate market for the grain. The possibility of open conflict was never far removed – the more so since the territorial objective of Finnish activists in the Baltic–White Sea arena conflicted with British policy. Thus the expeditionary force of General Maynard which was centred on Murmansk had to contemplate the possibility of encounter with Finnish White army forces in both the Petsamo area and east Karelia.

Only reluctantly in October 1918 did Finland begin to adjust itself to a situation in which the defeat of Germany was imminent. In the process of adjustment Mannerheim assumed the Regency and J. Paasikivi the presidency. The change of face was slowly succeeded by a change of heart.

Meanwhile Britain had despatched a Consul-General to Helsinki. He was a personable businessman of Scottish extraction, Henry MacCready Bell, and he helped to pave the way for formal recognition. The miscellany of signatures from his visitors' book, published in his memoirs, indicates the kind of society that was circulating around the British political representative of the day. But the scanty references to Finland in British official papers from the time reflect the limited attention paid to the emerging new state during the critical months of its infancy. It was this situation which prompted Finland to send emissaries to Atlantic Europe.

As a Grand Duchy Finland had had no separate diplomatic and consular representation. There had been discussions with Russia about the establishment of Finnish consulates – or even Finnish- or Swedish-speaking interpreters in Russian consular offices. In fact a special appointment of this character was established in London in 1890. But, for a variety of reasons, Finland found itself forced to build up a system of commercial agents overseas who worked through the Finnish Export Association, founded in 1891. Naturally, the agents had no official status, but they were helpful in succouring the little group of what Juhani Paasivirta has called Finland's 'pioneer diplomats'. This company of negotiators, who were familiar with the countries that they sought to inform and to persuade, were already known for the part that they had played in Finland's constitutional struggle with Russia. They included L. Kihlman, E. Wolff, J. N. Reuter, Kaarlo Ignatius and Rudolf Holsti. The nature of their task, as may be gleaned from the correspondence of J. N. Reuter, was to speed Finland's passage through the period of quarantine to which the country was subjected by the western powers.

Although Finland's aspirations to recognition as an independent state chimed with those of the principle of self-determination, they were not entirely in accord with the hopes of the Allies for the settlement of eastern Europe.

Vi vänta att höra det lösande ord Som visar vår plats vid nationernas bord	We wait to hear the inviting word That will show us our place at the nations' board

wrote Procopé, but the western powers were slow to extend a welcome to the new nation. Their attitude towards Finland only became more understanding after it was clear that the restoration of Russia to its Imperial status within its pre-war frame was no longer a reality. British restraint and French vacillation continued until the March elections of 1919: in May, France ratified its decision of 1918 while Great Britain and the U.S.A. accorded recognition. In due course west Europeans came to regard Finland as a part of their eastern *cordon sanitaire*.

The problem of definition lay partly in the territorial delineation of Finland's boundaries. At the same time as the country tried to resolve an anarchical domestic situation, its leaders were engaged in attempts to clarify their external relations. The confines of Finland had to be agreed in the east, in the north and in the south-west. In the south-west, the Swedish-speaking minority group of Ålanders actively sought a revision of the Grand Duchy's maritime boundaries in favour of Sweden. This was resisted by Finland. In the east, the south-east in particular, Finnish activists sought an expansion of territory. Until the defeat of the central powers, Finland's Karelian policies were linked with German objectives, including the destruction of the recently completed Murmansk railway. Subsequently, Finland sought to foster the closest possible relations with the Finnic peoples of eastern Karelia, of whom there were probably 130,000.

Readers of the Finnish periodical *Aika* were reminded in 1918 of Per Brahe's concept of *Suur Suomi* – a greater Finland stretching to the shores of the White Sea. Nineteenth-century romanticists had laid firmer foundations for the idea, with extremists such as Emil von Quanten and more moderate enthusiasts such as Zachris Topelius proclaiming alike the reasons for a more broadly based Finnish realm. By the early twentieth century the east Karelian community had become an irredentism with the *Vienan Karjalan Liitto*, a small body of émigrés, aiming at union with Finland. Against the background of Russia's political disintegration, the possibility of boundary revision became a live issue. Both military and political solutions were sought in 1918. Germany was not unsympathetic to the creation of a 'Nordic bridge' or transit land to serve its own purposes between the Baltic and the outer ocean. There was also a phase when Swedish circles balanced a change in sovereignty of the Åland islands against support for Finnish expansion into east Karelia.

There were a series of Finnish assaults into east Karelia. In late March 1918, for example, members of Finland's White Protective Corps moved to Uhtua, the northern centre of Karelian activism. Later, although the entire question of territorial adjustment was cast into a new mould with the defeat of Germany and although the central Finnish government attempted to disassociate itself officially from 'adventurous policies' in east Karelia, a volunteer force of several thousand took action into their own hands in the spring of 1919. An expedition was mounted into the Olonetz area, between Lakes Ladoga and Onega and called by Finns Aunus. Its primary object was to capture Petroskoi (Petrosavodsk). In the broader European panorama this independent action into Oloniia conflicted with the policies of the interventionists and non-interventionists alike. Suffice to say that the east Karelian episode found a lowly place on the agenda of the Peace Conference and that opinion favoured postponement of a settlement until Russia was able to negotiate the matter. As in all of Finland's immediate post-war negotiations with the Allies, the pervading influence of the 'White Russians' delayed a clear-cut decision and it was difficult for Finland to avoid implication in interventionist activities. The east Karelian issue was eventually settled as a part of the direct negotiations with the Russian government leading to the Peace Settlement of Dorpat (Tartu) in 1920. It was here that 'the borders of the Grand Duchy' were formally recognised as those of independent Finland, though a corridor of land through to Petsamo on the Arctic Coast was conceded in accordance with a Russian promise in 1864. As a result, Finland acquired a new shape in its northlands; while its 1914 boundaries in the south-east were confirmed. The confirmation, agreed by a delegation led by J. Paasikivi, had both immediate and long-term consequences.

An immediate consequence was the withdrawal of Finland from the coveted border parishes of Repola and Porajärvi and their incorporation in the new autonomous Russian Karelia. Withdrawal was accompanied by acts of martyrdom, which were among the factors helping to give birth to the revisionist Academic Karelian

Society (I.K.L.) – a society which was to play a powerful intellectual as well as a political role for the next generation. The fate of the Karelians was to be as the Finns feared. In spite of official protests sovietisation proceeded apace. It was difficult to control the extended frontier, where bands of partisans began to take up arms against the Russian authorities. A full-blown insurrection manifested itself in the winter of 1921–22 and Fenno-Russian relations were again in danger of disruption. In 1923, an Autonomous Soviet Socialist Republic came into being.

But the Karelian situation was much more involved than appeared from the Finnish side of the border. While the government of the newly-fledged Finnish state were in negotiation with Russia, Finnish émigrés including Edvard Gylling were formulating their own plans for the creation of a Karelian workers' republic. Almost immediately, they encountered a language problem. In the first stages, it was decided that the Karelian language should be rejected in favour of the joint official use of Finnish and Russian. After 1924 a programme of 'Karelisation' was initiated, while Finnish administrators such as Gylling and Kustaa Rovio urged forward the territory's economic development. The swift emergence of a revisionist attitude to nationalities after 1935 resulted in the removal of the Finns. By 1938, Finnish-language publications had been banned in Soviet Karelia though Karelian was permitted as a minority language. To all intents and purposes, Russian became the only language of consequence. In the Russification of Karelia many of the Old Guard of the Finnish Communist Party were finally liquidated. Karelia as understood by Finnish romanticists and realists alike virtually disappeared – as was to be discovered when a Finnish army next entered into 'Greater Finland' in 1941.

Throughout the period that Finland was seeking a solution to its aspirations in the east, it was confronted with a separatist movement in the west. A solution to the problem, reached on an international level, was delayed for three years while deliberations on the political allegiance of the Åland islands disturbed the Baltic situation in general and Swedo-Finnish relations in particular. The Åland islands had been saved from the full impact of the Civil War and from German intrusion by Swedish intervention in 1918. For a variety of reasons the Åland community (22,000 in all) voiced a desire to change its allegiance and expressed it in a convincing plebiscite. In order to settle the matter at an acceptable international level it was raised at the Peace Conference in 1919 and subsequently by Sweden at the League of Nations. The League pronounced in favour of Finnish sovereignty with stipulations which converted Åland into a self-governing province. Finnish legislation to this effect was formally introduced in 1921 and simultaneously the neutralisation and demilitarisation of the archipelago were confirmed internationally.

The first international trial of independent Finland was over with the definition of its borders. In the world made safe for democracy, presided over by a benevolent League of Nations, it seemed as though a policy of neutrality might be a possibility. Finland's second international trial was to face the consequences of this illusion. Meanwhile it had to wrestle with problems of economic solvency and social friction.

The Struggle for Economic Viability

The early days of Finnish independence were hungry times. During the immediate pre-war years, Finland had imported over half of the rye and nine-tenths of the wheat needed for the daily bread. In 1918–19, it was impossible to obtain bread grains from its traditional sources of supply. Many were reduced to the harsh substitute of bark bread. Hunger gnawed its way into politics. John Hodgson considers Finnish communism to have one of its roots in hunger, while Oskari Tokoi believes that the shortage of food and its unsatisfactory distribution were prime causes of the left-wing revolt and the Civil War. The situation was exaggerated because the value of money was uncertain. In addition to disturbing the mechanism of daily trading, inflation reduced the external purchasing power of the Finnish mark. As with the rest of exhausted Europe, Finland turned to the U.S.A. Echoes of this action remain. *Elää hooverille*, which may be roughly translated as 'to live on the parish', is a colloquialism attributable to the release of American grain to Finland by President Hoover during the time of starvation.

While individual citizens were in need of daily bread, the country was hungry for capital goods. The speedy restoration of domestic production and of international trading were critical for the provision of both. By 1922 it was estimated that domestic production had returned to its pre-war figure. The powerful fluctuations in Finland's international exchange rate were slowly smoothed out, so that by the mid-1920s the Finnish mark had stabilised at about 200 or more to the pound sterling. As if to announce the achievement of stability, brave new commercial and public buildings began to grace the streets of the capital, while new spires added variety to its skyline.

When it became an independent trading country, Finland had to consider its situation in new perspectives. Formal trading agreements were negotiated in the 1920s with most European countries, but they served to underline the inherent difficulties of Finland's physical situation. Its resources were limited in variety and yielded a one-sided export structure. In addition, Finland was essentially a producer of raw materials and value was commonly added to them by manufacturers in other countries. These characteristics placed Finland in a sensitive situation for foreign trading. In the years immediately following the Civil War, its problems were exaggerated by the disruption of overseas markets. The entire commercial situation was modified with the virtual closure of Finland's eastern frontier, where the 'iron curtain' came down economically as well as politically. As a result the timber-deficient lands of western Europe assumed a critical importance: among them, the markets of Germany and Great Britain took precedence. In the trading triangle which developed, Finland balanced a positive trading balance with Britain against a negative balance with Germany. Viipuri blossomed as Finland's principal export harbour and traffic on the supply line of the Saimaa canal reached a maximum. The structure of its commerce and the character of its domestic economy rendered Finland especially vulnerable to cyclical trading disturbances. Finland's link with the British money market caused it to leave the gold standard in the wake of Britain in 1931.

For most Finns neither gold standard nor large-scale capital investment meant very much. But most Finns had a stake in the land and the years of depression meant a decline in the market for their farm and forest products, a corresponding increase in indebtedness and a rise in the rate of bankruptcy. During the first generation of its independence Finland not only remained a country with an essentially rural emphasis, but the number of personal stakes in landed property multiplied considerably. In the years following the Civil War attempts were made to reduce the rural proletariat and to broaden the basis of land ownership. Conditions of land purchase and colonisation were eased in 1922 by a law providing land for settlement initiated by Kyösti Kallio, the Minister of Agriculture of the day. During the inter-war years, and partly owing to *Lex*

Kallio, farmed land expanded by a third. More important, there were all-round improvements in field and animal husbandry, with consequent increases in crop and stock yields. The effects of investment in farming and forestry were slow to gather momentum, but they were increasingly apparent. At the time of the 1930 census most of the working population of Finland was engaged directly or indirectly in agriculture and forestry. The growth in investment and the changing character of farm enterprise had their complement in signs of rural over-population.

Max Weber's distinction between the rational and the traditional modes of behaviour continued to be illustrated in many parts of Finland. The inter-war years witnessed a blending of the old and the new. Circles wider than academic realised that there was a new urgency to record or to save something of the traditional for posterity. The flail no longer beat the threshing floor, but sickle and scythe still had a place in harvesting. Agricultural machinery began to increase and to be diffused with greater speed; but the tractor was still only numbered by the hundred in contrast to the tens of thousands of farm horses. Stock was still widely open-ranged (to the detriment of timber growth) and kept out of cultivated lands by Finnish-spun barbed wire. Bygones were increasingly collected for local museums which, after the Scandinavian fashion, frequently took on an open-air character. Barns and boathouses, galleried storehouses and windmills were assembled to illustrate the regional characteristics that were soon to disappear in the face of prefabrication. The Martha League (*Marttaliitto*), which celebrated its silver jubilee in 1924 and sought to promote higher standards of Finnish home-craft, fostered the making of a dozen different kinds of bread, of a variety of different milk cultures and types of cheese, the salting and smoking of fish. It encouraged the preparation of regional and seasonal dishes – from the *munajuusto* (egg cheese) and *mämmi* (malt dessert) of Uusimaa, the *rieskä* (rusks) and *suolimakkara* (salt sausage) of central Pohjanmaa to the *kalakukko* (fish pie) of Savo and the *piirat* (savoury pies) of Karelia. The Martha League also urged the principles of domestic cleanliness – and godliness. But it was to take a long time to eliminate pockets of rural squalor – near, if not quite, Zolaesque in their earthiness. The reverse of the Martha's shining coin was manifest in the Häme setting of F. E. Sillanpää's *Meek Heritage* and Joel Lehtonen's squalid tale from Sääminki parish, *Potkinotko*.

In keeping with a rural economy in which the products of farm and forest exceeded in value those of factory until the 1930s, most Finns were not seriously exposed to urban life until after the Second World War. Even a large proportion of those employed in factories lived and worked in rural areas (as they still do). Social legislation was pushed on apace in the inter-war years, so that by 1939 conditions of work conformed to those of the most advanced countries in the world. The foundations of the modern system of social insurance were laid and growing attention was paid to housing. No less important in the evolution of social services was the intensification of the network of communications. In due course this was to help the concentration of medical and educational facilities though the widespread dispersal of settlement remained a continuing administrative problem. Among the consequences of economic and social development two were outstanding. The first was the general improvement in the health of the nation and especially the decline in infant mortality. The second was the increase in population mobility. New opportunities for movement and the need to look for new jobs intensified internal migration. Even so the drift from the land and the complementary increase in urban population were retarded in Finland in comparison with its Scandinavian neighbours.

At the same time Finland began to enter the orbit of ordinary European visitors. Curiosity about the country was aroused principally by a handful of Finns. Among them Jean Sibelius took pride of place, though by the time that his seven symphonies and score of tone poems had become a regular part of the repertoires of world orchestras the composer had entered his thirty years of silence. Nevertheless, the legendary figure at Järvenpää, hazy in 'sun dust and cigar smoke', provided an image which Finns were happy to cultivate. Sibelius was at once a national and an international figure, a romantic and a realist. His stern head, sculptured by Väinö Aaltonen, stands for the realism: his preface to *Tapiola* for the romance. Small countries need big men. For half a century Sibelius was a symbol of Finland, speaking to much of the world for it and, reciprocally, drawing people to it.

Other Finns also aroused curiosity. Sportsmen were fascinated by the international successes of Finnish athletes in general and of the sprinter Paavo Nurmi in particular. War denied them the privilege of holding the Olympic Games in Finland in 1940 and it was 1952 before Helsinki was able to play host to the Olympiad. By then the

Finns had attained a rare standard in track events. Architects had also begun to hear of Finland. Eliel Saarinen had left for the U.S.A. in 1923; but he bequeathed a tradition and an inspiration to the succeeding generation of Finnish architects. His successors were men who were concerned with combining utility with beauty: functionalism was the style that they helped to create. Their contributions are summed up in such structures as Paimo sanatorium (1933) and Sunila pulp mill (1939), both the work of Alvar Aalto. They turned to concrete as a material in which to experiment. In response to the demand for this raw material the old-established lime and cement works at Parainen (Pargas) took on a new lease of life and set up daughter plants, such as that at Lappeenranta, where pockets of limestone were to be found. The applied arts of Finland began to make an impact, with glass and ceramics already attracting a discerning few: others admired (but could scarcely emulate) the wall hangings or *ryjyy* and the hand-woven linen products with their simple traditional designs. In addition, Finland appealed to a handful of visitors as one of the 'quiet' corners of Europe. It was a cheap corner, too. Even in 1939 the equivalent of ten pounds sterling provided west Europeans with the return fare to one of Europe's least sophisticated lands. For the French, Georges Duhamel recorded his reactions to Finnish enchantments in *Le Chant du Nord*. For the British, J. Hampden Jackson dismissed the 'vacant' description of Finland as a land of ten thousand lakes, and urged its example in finding a middle way between communism and fascism, capitalism and socialism. German youth found in inter-war Finland a sympathetic holiday country, where their own language took precedence over other foreign tongues.

Almost everybody came to Finland by sea and this was an attraction in its own right. Travellers on the age-old shipping route from the North Sea to Finnish landfalls might still see the full canvases of an Åland fourmaster. They might even sail on one of the last clipper ships that carried passengers to Finland, imagining as they rounded the windy Skaw that they were participating in the grain race round the Horn. The Ericsson fleet reached a climax of interest in the 1930s. Echoes of it are found in Ellis Carlsson's saga *Mother Sea*, in Pamela Ericsson's memoir of the ill-fated *Herzogin Cecilia* and in the finely imaginative maritime museum in Mariehamn. Few were aware that Finland's air age had its humble beginning when Aero Ltd. – later Finnair – was born in 1923.

Most of those who travelled to Finland in the inter-war years were unaware of the heritage of literature that was being created in the new nation. They might have encountered translations such as those of J. Linnankoski's *Song of the Blood Red Flower* and Jarl Hemmer's *Fool of Faith*: the former romanticising the life of the timber-floater – Casanova and circus actor rolled into one; the latter revealing the personal perplexities of prison life in the fortress of Suomelinna. But for the Finnish bibliophiles the infant years of the independent state were rich. They were a compound of the homely short stories of Maria Jotuni and of the *Niskavuori* plays of Hella Wuolijoki, of the youthful narrative poems of P. A. Mustapää (whose pen name concealed the enthnographer and folklorist Martti Haavio), of the contemplative lyrics of Edith Södergren (anticipating her brief life even in the titles of her poems – *The Shadow of the Future*, *The Country that is Not*), of Uuno Kailas's apotheosis of children (even lean and hungry ones), of the song of the imperious machine as interpreted by Elmer Diktonius, of a dash of Dadaism from Gunnar Burling, of the 'pagan smell of the skin of the earth' as it was sensed by Katri Vala and of 'the Holy light' of spring upon the tree tops as it was seen by Lauri Viljanen. They included the Estonian tales of the Finnish authoress, Aino Kallas, for the sister republic across the southern gulf was held in especial affection by the Finns. They relished the imaginative approach of Yrjö Hirn to the literature of the western hemisphere; they enjoyed the theatrical dash and sparkle (in person and pen, in classics and economics) of Amos Anderson. They witnessed the trickle of print turning to a torrent – in doctoral dissertations by the hundred, in journals and newspapers by the thousand. They displayed them on the shelves of some of the largest bookshops in the world.

The minor literary florescence with its focus on Finnish themes had its counterpart in artistic circles. The best work of a number of competent artists coincided with the crises of independence. There was plenty of sombre realism in the air – the dark, lowering canvases of Tykö Sallinen, the grey mood of winter as seen by Alwar Cawén, the sober landscapes of Ragnar Eklund. But Wilho Sjöström could reflect the radiance of March sun, Marcus Collin could bring summer warmth to his Ålandic scenes, and the whole world could filter through in gayer shades to Ellen Thesleff. Nor were the fashions of the outer world slow to penetrate Finland. In the swirl of his design and the brilliant dappling of his colours, Werner Thomé recalled Edvard Munch; while the suggestion of Modigliani in some of Eero Nelimarkka's portraits made his Finns appear even more Finnish. The age of the cocktail (officially denied to the Finns by prohibition) had its mixture of art forms – surrealist, cubist, abstract, non-figurative, eclectic; but it was in the field of sculpture rather than painting that genius flowered. No one had previously chiselled the native granite of Finland with greater feeling than Väinö Aaltonen and few had treated bronze with greater effect. Aaltonen grew up on the outskirts of Turku and the city has done him the signal honour of gathering together a large collection of his works in a gallery on the banks of the Aura. Yet it is in public places that Aaltonen's work is best appreciated. Paavo Nurmi sprints for posterity under the shadow of Helsinki's stadium and his toes scarcely touch the plinth on which they rest.

Problems of Society

While the economics of day-to-day living in the years between the wars probably stir relatively few memories, other features of the social scene have left deeper imprints. They remain the subject of reminiscence in *sauna* and by log fire, though they are largely drained of passion today. Each was rooted in historical circumstance and each makes its contribution to the thinking and feeling of the modern state. Oldest among the features that made an imprint was the friction between Swedish-speaking and Finnish-speaking Finns: most intense was the renewed conflict between Communist and other elements in the political sphere. Both issues encouraged extreme reactions: both were acutely felt by the rising generation of Finns. In contrast to the common European experience inter-war student opinion in Finland was predominantly right-wing, largely nationalistic and often curiously intolerant. A third division of opinion was registered over prohibition; though this was on a different plane.

The language issue sharpened with the establishment of independence. Finndom had fulfilled itself in achieving the new state and the Swedish-speaking minority group was sensitive about its rights. A formal extension of the constitutional guarantees was urged by the Swedish People's Party. In 1919 and 1922 legislation was introduced to define unilingual and bilingual administrative districts, with an understanding that they should be reviewed decennially. Simultaneously the situation in legal matters was strengthened by the acceptance of the right of a defendant to use Swedish in ordinary courts and the classification of all superior courts as bilingual. In a variety of different contexts, Finnish activists and Swedish activists adopted extreme postures so that it was frequently impossible to achieve a rationally balanced view. The proportion between Finnish-speaking Finns and Swedish-speaking Finns in most administrative sectors was a continual source of friction. The disproportionate number of Swedish-speaking Finns in the executive structure of industry and commerce was also a frequent subject of comment. Although church circles were more conciliatory, a special bishopric to serve the Swedish-speaking parishes was created in Borgå (Porvoo) in 1923. Helsinki and Turku became the centres of pressure, though both were officially recognised as bilingual cities regardless of percentage clauses. In Turku the opposing factions established two distinctive universities. *Åbo Akademi*, founded in 1921, was in a way a university *redivivus*, restoring to the city an institution the original of which had been transferred to the capital as the national university after the fire of 1827. The Finnish-speaking foundation of *Turun yliopiston* occupied a corner of the market square for forty years before it was transferred to a hilltop site in this city of hump-backed hills. The University of Helsinki was declared bilingual in 1923. A climax of language dissension was accordingly reached when the demand to make it Finnish-speaking came to a head in the middle 1930s. A compromise was attained in 1937, when a restriction was placed upon the number of 'Swedish-speaking' chairs and competency in Finnish was required of their occupants for examination purposes. In the interval the number of 'Swedish-speaking' chairs has kept pace proportionate to the growth of the student population. In keeping with developments in the other Scandinavian countries, high schools of economics were also established in the capital during the inter-war years: they, too, divided along language lines. The conflict gave rise to literary apologists, among whom Arvid Morne wrote eloquently and evocatively for the minority element.

Tensions of a different character were generated by the attempts of the Communists to reassert themselves in the late 1920s. Popular reaction to their constitutional manoeuvres and public gatherings reached a critical point in the Ostrobothnian church village of Lapua in November 1929. A provocative meeting of the so-called Young Workers' Educational Association was broken up with a fair amount of violence. On the rebound, and within a week, an anti-Communist front took its origin in Lapua. The movement gathered momentum swiftly and within six months the demand for the suppression of communism had found wide support. The failure of Parliament to deal with the wishes of a large and vocal element of the electorate led to direct action by Lapua supporters. Destruction of Communist property and kidnapping of party members was supplemented by attacks on prominent parliamentarians of liberal persuasion who had adopted ameliorating positions. One of the largest demonstrations witnessed in the history of Helsinki took place in the summer of 1930, when 12,000 farmers converged upon the city to demand the implementation of their programme. In November 1930 the constitution was amended to prevent the representation of any party the object of which was to overthrow the republic. The Finnish Trade Union Organisation was also proscribed and replaced by a new body initiated by the Social Democrats called the Finnish Confederation of Trade Unions. Even when the agitators had achieved their objective and Communists were excluded from the Diet for the next fifteen years, many remained uneasy. In 1933, they established a new party, the People's Patriotic Party (*Isänmaallinen kansanliike*), which adopted a neo-Fascist line. Although the I.K.L. never succeeded in mustering more than a handful of seats, it attracted surprisingly powerful support from intellectual circles, not least in the Church and universities. Both the extreme right and extreme left wings in Finnish politics ultimately committed themselves to violence if need be. The record of the right has been exposed, but it is unlikely that that of the extreme left will ever be available for a dispassionate comparison to be written.

Temperance issues cut across both ethnographic and political divisions. The Friends of Temperance, who had come into existence in 1877, persuaded the government to contribute substantial subsidies for the furtherance of their work from 1886 to 1908. The dramatic 'Drinkers' Strikes', which helped towards fuller legal restraints on the manufacture and sale of alcohol in the parliamentary bills of 1907 and 1909, achieved the fulfilment of their objective in the Prohibition Act of 1919. The considerable success of their campaign for abstinence was rapidly succeeded by an apparent increase in the consumption of alcohol and a definite increase in drunkenness. The experiment foundered on the impracticability of any widespread and effective system of control and a commission of enquiry into the difficulties was already appointed in 1922. For the successful supervision of medical and veterinary prescriptions to the prevention of rum running and illicit distillation an army of excise men would have been required. For example, more than four million prescriptions passed annually through the office of the Comptroller of Apothecaries of the Temperance Department between 1926 and 1928. The conflict between Konsta Kurtti and the Revenue Man in Laryn Kyösti's grim story of *The Smugglers* describes the hazards of the trade in the archipelagos; the Railway Museum in Helsinki has exhibits – from false oil-cans to fitted body canisters – which display the lengths to which operatives and passengers alike went to conceal smuggled liquor. It is estimated that six million litres were illegally imported in 1928 alone. At the same time, the Irishman's distillation of poteen or the Hill Billy's moonshine had nothing over the Finn's *pontikka.* John Wuorinen has concluded that prohibition failed in Finland because it could not prohibit. Address and counter-address were delivered to the President of the Republic and, at the end of 1931, a special parliamentary bill arranged for a consultative referendum. The Prohibition Act was rescinded in 1932 following a powerful vote against it in the plebiscite. At the same time a state monopoly for the manufacture, purchase and distribution of alcohol came into existence. *Oy. Alkoholiliike Ab.*, as it is called, has retail distribution centres far enough apart from each other to discourage many from making more than infrequent visits to them, aims at low price fixing to offset smuggling, encourages the consumption of wines rather than spirits, and employs a percentage of its profit for social works and public projects. It represents a compromise similar to those of Sweden and Norway and may lay claim to a fair measure of success.

All three of these sources of stress in the independent state had been indulged in an atmosphere depressed by a slump in world trade, bemused by the concept of peaceful coexistence, and under the quietly confident presidency of Relander. The tussle with resurgent communism and the debate over prohibition reached a peak during the worst years of the economic depression. The sharpening of the differences between Swedish-speaking and Finnish-speaking Finns coincided with the deterioration of the international situation. A battle of books accompanied the running debates in the *Eduskunta* and the occasional scuffles in the market place. Such journals as *Nya Argus* championed the Swedish-Finnish cause: *Suomalainen Suomi*, the Fennomen. *Ajan Suunta* waved the banner for the extreme right: *Suomen Työmies* for the extreme left. It would have required a Jonathan Swift to satirise acceptably these sensitive areas of the social scene. The leading sociologist of the day, Edvard Westermark (who, like the aesthetician Tancred Borenius, held a chair in London), turned his attention to the social customs of Morocco.

But there was no escape from involvement in the Second World War. As an independent state Finland had become a member of the League of Nations and had leaned towards the countries of Norden and their policy of neutrality. Once external pressures began to assert themselves domestic affairs were speedily subordinated. As public need took precedence over private differences even Communists found that they could be Finns first.

The Winter War

Superficially Finland continued to be a quiet corner of Europe, but from the spring of 1938 there were attempts on the part of the U.S.S.R. to adjust Fenno-Soviet relations to the changing European scene. In particular, discussion centred on a revision of the border along the Karelian isthmus. The negotiations only came into the open after the outbreak of the Second World War in September 1939 – even then in ignorance of the division of spheres of influence outlined in the secret protocols of the Russo-German non-aggression pact of 1939. Arguments for the adjustment echoed strangely the resolutions passed after a lecture given by N. N. Kovero before the united nobility of the Russian Empire at St Petersburg in March 1910 – 'The province of Viborg, if left in its present condition with a frontier not more than 20 miles distant from the capital and not subjected to the supervision of the Russian authorities, is a menace to the political and strategic interests of the Empire . . . the state can no longer tolerate at the gates of the capital an independently governed territory.' In October 1939 Molotov was formulating Russia's 'minimal' adjustments – 'a naval base at the western end of the Gulf of Finland . . . and a small area of a few dozen square kilometres north-west of Leningrad, in return for which we are willing to give them an area twice that size'. A mutual assistance pact similar to those signed by the Baltic republics in September and early October was also proposed. Finland rejected the Russian overtures – having issued a declaration of neutrality in common with the other countries of Scandinavia on the outbreak of war.

Following the rejection Russia intensified its war of nerves; but, since this made no impact, declared the Finns as aggressors on 29 November, a frontier incident having been reported in the isthmus three days earlier. The full-scale assault launched by the U.S.S.R. the next day seemed in its externals not far different from that of the Germans on Poland in September. The attack was resisted in a four-month struggle now known as the Winter War. Finland was ill-equipped for the encounter in all but spirit. It was challenged by a display of power politics of the crudest kind and reacted with a unanimity unequalled in its history. The apparent innocence of Finland and the contrasting guilt of Russia enabled the episode to be described in black and white. It was a clear-cut issue which immediately engaged international attention.

While the war in the west stagnated, events along Finland's eastern front provided a hungry press with a harvest of stories. So many people had never written so much about Finland before – and in all the languages of the world. To add to the drama, the struggle took place during one of the coldest winters on record. Temperatures of −30°C played havoc with mechanical equipment, and effectively immobilised the Russian navy by ice. The skilful deployment of Finland's limited troops and scanty equipment, coupled with extraordinary miscalculations on the part of the Russian High Command, made it seem temporarily that the Finns might succeed in the impossible. The most humble among them were translated into white-hooded heroes in a snow-clad landscape confronting the dark forces of Muscovy. Immaculate in a conspicuous white fur hat, their Commander-in-Chief became the subject of endless anecdotes, both true and apocryphal. Regardless of the publicity that it received and the flood of military metaphors released, the Finnish campaign of resistance was phenomenal. But in the final analysis it was a fight for existence: this, above all, endowed it with epic strength. Once the new cabinet presided over by Risto Ryti had been rebuffed in its final attempt to persuade Russia to let Sweden mediate, the alternatives to resistance could not be countenanced. In this context, the puppet government set up by the Russians under Otto Kuusinen in the Isthmian seaside resort of Terijoki three days after the outbreak of hostilities, could only demonstrate how much Kuusinen had forgotten about his native land during his years in Soviet corridors of power.

In spite of infinite goodwill no country provided Finland with direct military aid. The last act of the expiring League of Nations was to expel the U.S.S.R. for its aggression. Thereafter Finland was left to fight alone. Up to 400,000 men and women found their way into the armed forces by the end of the Winter War and they were supplemented by a small international brigade of sympathisers and idealists which included 8,000 Swedes. In the final place no Finnish army was capable of stemming Russia's limitless reserves. By the middle of February 1940 Russian troops had begun to penetrate the series of strongpoints and pillboxes known as the Mannerheim Line. Within a fortnight they had passed through the narrows of the isthmus to the gates of Viipuri – *Hannibal ante portas*. Throughout the latter part of the campaign, as Georg Gripenberg indicated in the memoirs from his diplomatic interlude in London, hopes were held high that help might come from Britain and France. Troops ultimately embarked from Scotland at the end of February with their sights bent upon entry into Finland by way of northern Scandinavia. Three days from catastrophe, to employ the title of Douglas Clark's record of the event, they returned. Once again Finns were mindful of the words inscribed nearly 200 years earlier on the wall of Gustav's bastion at the fortress of Suomenlinna – *Efterverd! Stå här på egen holten och lita ej på främmande hjelp.* ('You who follow us, stand here in your own strength and wait not upon foreign aid'.)

It was the task of Väinö Tanner, Foreign Minister in the wartime cabinet, to lead the negotiations that ended the Winter War. Contact was struck with the Soviet government through Madame Kollontai, the Russian ambassador in Stockholm. On 4 March Marshal Mannerheim informed the Finnish cabinet that his army was no longer capable of resisting the Russians. It is generally believed that no commander other than Mannerheim could have appealed to the discipline of Finnish troops so effectively at this critical moment. His order of the day at the conclusion of hostilities remains a much-quoted document. The shock of defeat was the harder because the will of the people was unbroken. The armistice of 12 March 1940 had only one positive side: it ensured that Finland was not occupied by Russian troops. By the terms of the peace settlement Finland lost about a tenth of its territory. The principal losses were in the south-east where a boundary roughly following that of the Uusikaupunki peace of 1721 was drawn. It was a territory which Peter the Great had once described as 'a cushion . . . upon which St Petersburg may rest secure' and it included Viipuri,

Finland's third largest city. In the north the Russians advanced into the Rybachi peninsula on the coast of Petsamo and took over the eastern half of the Salla area. A thirty-year lease on the winter harbour and summer watering place of Hanko gave Russia the effective power to seal off the Gulf of Finland. In addition the Finns were required to construct a railway line to link Tornio on the Swedish border with the Russian boundary to the east of Kemijärvi.

Territorial losses resulted in an urgent refugee problem. Fully 420,000 displaced people trekked out of the ceded territories with such personal belongings as could be gathered together and such farm stock as could be moved in the sunny but bitterly cold conditions of the spring-winter. Reception areas were matched to evacuation areas. The costs of accommodating displaced people and of compensating property losses in the ceded areas were offset by a capital levy. Long-term plans for settlement were also defined. At the same time Finland had to suffer the problems springing from 25,000 war dead and nearly twice as many injured.

And then, almost as suddenly as Finland entered world headlines, it left them. Only a few weeks after the Moscow peace treaty the 'phoney war' in the west ended with the German invasion of Denmark and Norway. The Atlantic front took precedence in world affairs. But Finland, largely forgotten in western Europe, continued to be the object of Russian pressures. There is no doubt that the U.S.S.R. planned to reduce it to a satellite as swiftly as possible. In this atmosphere of insecurity confusion was added to depression and the nadir in the fortune of independent Finland was reached. The only large power capable of providing any form of succour was Germany – Germany which had isolated Finland and which was allied to Russia. The autumn of 1940 provided an opportunity to restore the German connection. If Russia claimed transit rights through beleaguered Finland, it could scarcely object if the same privileges were extended to its German ally. Accordingly German troops and materials began to pass in and out of north Norway through Finland.

The Continuation War

On 22 June 1941 Germany set in motion 'Operation Barbarossa' and the eastern front was opened. The action, which immediately changed Finland's situation, marked the second stage of its experiences during the Second World War. It is unlikely that it will ever be known what was the precise *casus belli* of Finland's second war with Russia. In the electric atmosphere of the time a volley of shots into no-man's-land was sufficient to precipitate action. At any rate border incidents were claimed by both sides and in the face of Soviet land and air attack, the Finns mounted defensive actions out of which grew the Continuation War. The war was to last for more than three years.

There were essential differences between it and the Winter War. In the Winter War Finland was a victim of great power politics: in the Continuation War it played its own game around the margins of great power politics. The Winter War was entirely a war of resistance for national survival: the Continuation War was not. The former commanded the general support of world opinion: the latter was supported by few other than the Axis powers. During the Winter War Finland's neighbours in Norden were united in their support of the fifth member of their fraternity: the Continuation War and its consequences divided the Scandinavian countries. The Winter War was fought by a united nation: the Continuation War was conducted in the face of variable domestic opposition. It was initially a popular campaign because the desire to reoccupy the territories taken by Russia was strongly and widely felt. But the war was a gamble. Both wars had one common feature – they were lost to the same enemy.

A sovereign state has the freedom to choose which road it shall take. Regardless of the attitude of others, it is the function of an independent state to take any steps necessary for the maintenance of national sovereignty. In 1941, Finland had little room for manoeuvre. None of the western Allies could guarantee Finland against the mounting pressure of the U.S.S.R. The experiences of the neighbouring Baltic republics provided a depressing example of the likely Finnish prospect. Germany was the only straw at which it seemed possible to grasp. The argument in favour of the choice was that of the victim who is attacked by ruffians and who wisely chooses to ignore the reputation of the man who comes to his aid. Although it provided a base for German troops, Finland was never formally allied to Germany as, for example, Britain was allied to the U.S.S.R.; but it joined the Anti-Comintern Pact and, *in extremis* during the critical days of June 1944, President Ryti committed the country to fight by the side of Germany to the end. Throughout the war Finland accepted that it was a co-belligerent with Germany but asserted that it was engaged in an entirely separate war. In part testimony of this Mannerheim and the Finnish army leaders regularly asserted their independence of action. Inside Finland, opinion ranged from those who accepted the Hitlerite doctrine to others (including some otherwise eminent and respected citizens) who were imprisoned for 'calculating on a Soviet conquest of Finland', as John Hodgson describes their action. The outer world may have regarded Finland as a satellite of Germany but the Finnish press remained remarkably untrammelled. It was ironical that Britain, which nearly came into the war as an ally of Finland against Russia, should have declared war on Finland in 1943 and, of all days, on 6 December, the anniversary of Finnish independence. There was never any direct action between Britain and Finland; but, as a belligerent and together with a miscellany of other nations, Britain had a place at the peace table. The U.S.A., although it withdrew its diplomatic representation from Helsinki in June 1944, never declared war on Finland. Neither did France.

Finland had reoccupied its ceded territories by December 1941 and the great majority of the displaced people flocked back to their homeland. There were temptations to join the German *putsch* on Leningrad – even the projected assault on Murmansk – but these were resisted. But in one area there was a deep penetration into Soviet territory. The historic tracts of Finnish settlement between Lakes Ladoga and Onega which had stirred so much emotion immediately after independence, were now occupied by Finnish troops virtually to the line of the Svir river. The local population registered little more than indifference to their intrusive kith and kin; but for the Finnish ethnographers who recorded their relics of folk life and language the occupation of Aunus was a memorable experience.

With the stabilisation of the fronts action stagnated. As 1942 yielded to 1943 there developed not only a certain *malaise* but also uneasiness over the course of events in the international scene. For some, Olavi Paavolainen struck the mood in his war diary, *Synkkä yksinpuhelu*, a monologue in a minor key from Ladogan Karelia. Peace feelers were first extended to Moscow by way of Stockholm in February 1943; but it took Finland over a year and a half to extricate itself from the Continuation War. A succession of attempts to arrange a settlement were directed through the intermediacy of both Sweden and the U.S.A., but either Finnish overtures were rebuffed by Russia or Russian proposals were rejected by Finland. The longer the deliberations were dragged out the worse the German situation grew – and the more exacting its consequences for Finland. Since Finland was virtually imprisoned in the Baltic, it was – save for limited supplies from neutral Sweden – absolutely dependent on Germany for vital economic as well as military needs. Some strategists have gone so far as to argue that if Finland had contrived to remain out of the war in 1941, shortages of essential food and supplies alone would eventually have forced it into the German camp. While the Finnish minister in Stockholm went from confidential rendezvous to confidential rendezvous and messages were transmitted from chancery to cabinet room, it seemed as though a settlement might be fatally delayed in the quicksands of consultation. The crisis came in June 1944, when a major Russian assault in the isthmus ruptured the Finnish defences and Viipuri was captured.

The situation was sufficiently serious for Germany to send its Foreign Minister Ribbentrop to Helsinki. In exchange for promised aid, President Ryti agreed not to 'make peace with the Soviet Union except in agreement with the German Reich'. His letter prompted the withdrawal of American diplomatic representation from Finland; while within the space of a month cabinet disapproval led to his resignation, to the appointment of a new government and to the election of Marshal C. G. E. Mannerheim as President. Events moved swiftly forward. At the end of August discussions with Moscow were initiated, the conditions of peace were accepted in a Russian ultimatum dated 2 September, a cease-fire was arranged for 4 September and a final armistice agreed on 19 September. For Finland it amounted to all but capitulation. The Treaty of Peace was formally signed in Paris in 1947.

The settlement was harsh with a forceable turn of the screw on the 1940 terms. Territorially the adjustments were the same in the south-east and north-east; but in the north, Finland was shorn of its Arctic outlet of Petsamo. Russian occupation of Hanko was given up in favour of a fifty-year lease of the Porkkala peninsula, immediately to the west of Helsinki. Rights of transit between the Soviet border and Porkkala were also stipulated. Precise dates were set for the evacuation of all ceded areas. More immediately critical was the demand for the expulsion of German troops from Finland. Although no time limit was set on this operation, it was made clear that failure to achieve the object would be remedied by the despatch of Russian troops. All German property in Finland was taken over by the Russians. Finnish forces were to be reduced to their pre-war footing within six months of the armistice. Para-military organisations, such as the celebrated women's army auxiliary, *Lotta Svärd*, had to be disbanded; so had any political organisations, such as the I.K.L., which had near Fascist leanings. A reparations bill totalling 300,000,000 gold dollars defined in terms of rigid deliveries in kind and payable over eight years was imposed. A group of 'war criminals' was arraigned: they included the former President Risto Ryti, the minister to Germany Kivimäki and a group of wartime cabinet Ministers. Reciprocally the Communist Party re-entered the political arena.

Post Mortem

Post mortems on the war years were luxuries in which Finns could not immediately indulge. That they should lose the wars fought against the U.S.S.R. is understandable: that they should contrive to win the ensuing peace is less readily explained. Of all the countries of mainland Europe involved in the Second World War, Finland was the only one that did not suffer extensive occupation. In the long run it was the only east European country to remain a democracy in the west European sense. There is no simple explanation why Russia did not occupy Finland in the same way as it occupied the Baltic republics to the south. Bearing in mind Russia's gigantic task of domestic reconstruction, perhaps Finland disciplined by reparations was to be preferred to Finland occupied and undisciplined. Geography, independently of that unscientific factor called national character, would have made Finland a difficult country to subdue. Perhaps it was believed that failure to fulfil the severe programme of reparations would provide an eventual excuse for interference in Finland's internal affairs. Perhaps it was assumed that domestic anarchy would result from the superhuman task of trying to resettle – for the second time – a tenth of the Finnish population at the same time as the country's industrial structure was being changed to meet the reparation requirements. In such a situation it might be postulated that the resuscitated Communist Party together with the fellow travellers would be able to effect a political *coup* within. Perhaps, having achieved the territorial ambitions to which it aspired in 1939, the U.S.S.R. really had no further demands in the north. Perhaps there remained a residue of respect among the Russians for the Finns.

Meanwhile the Finnish generals (and their German counterparts) have refought their wars in print and the politicians have conducted their negotiations for a second time in their memoirs. The war of the man in the front line has also been revealed. It has been recorded in both fact and fiction – in Väinö Linna's highly successful *Unknown Soldier*, the saga of a platoon's experiences during the Continuation War written in the style of Erich Maria Remarque – filmed, dramatised and ultimately converted into an opera. It has been viewed from other angles in Veijo Meri's wartime stories strung together in his book *The Cord*, in Pentti Häänpää's grimly humorous war reports, in Paavo Rintala's adventures and Unto Seppänen's Kanneljärvi trilogy epitomising life and death in the Karelian isthmus. Nor have the poets been silent. V. A. Koskenniemi was in many ways the laureate of the war years, commemorating in simple lyrics and odes the popular feelings about the people and places involved in the eastern campaigns. The soldiery and their Marshal, the *Lottas* (the Women's Army Corps), the border people and Karelia were all subjects which moved him to heroic and elegiac expression in a collection called *Latuja lumessa* (Tracks in the Snow). Yet, despite these varied and many-sided revelations, there remain critical gaps which prevent the full explanation of Finland's wartime role. Access to German foreign office and military archives has shed light from one angle. Finnish sources are not without their lacunae. The dark side of the moon is Russia.

As a part of the European 'shatter belt' between east and west with frontiers agreed by a weak Russian government, it was not surprising that Finland should be subject to pressures resulting from inter-war shifts in power. In different ways these were appreciated by Finns as varied in their political outlook as Mannerheim, Paasikivi, Tanner and Wiik. Social Democrat opinion, as expressed by its leader Väinö Tanner and the main member of the opposition K. H. Wiik, favoured concessions on the basis of negotiation with the U.S.S.R. in 1939. It was the manner in which the U.S.S.R. sought to achieve its objectives that ultimately brought about the open conflict. Perhaps the war could have been avoided if the Finns had accepted Russian demands: perhaps the outcome would have been better if they had acquiesced. Certainly most Finns still believe that their own way of making post-war Finland safe for democracy was more effective than any of the methods advised by well-meaning foreign diplomats and propagandists. Perhaps the ultimate justification for the policies adopted by Finland is the status and condition of the modern state.

The second military struggle for the survival of an independent Finland ended bleakly. It has had universal implications for the Finns – from the descendants of the Swedish-speaking aristocracy in their manor houses and entailed estates of the deep south to the humblest Skolt Lapp, whose reindeer were slaughtered to feed the retreating German armies in the high north. Scarcely a family was untouched by tragedy – the churchyards with their uniform ranks of granite headstones, their trim summer flower-beds and their mid-winter candles testify to that. The citizens of the south coast had new sounds to contend with as well. The spry whistle of the Finnish steam locomotive was accompanied by the hollow wail of the Russian engines as they trundled through to Porkkala, while from the naval base sounded the reverberations of gunfire – target practice into the open sea.

Yet the physical sufferings and mental discomfitures only served to create more fully and freely a new fatherland out of the old homeland. There may have been divided opinions during the Continuation War, but the memories of the shared experiences of the Winter War were never forgotten. And there were father figures in whom there reposed ultimate confidence. Marshal Mannerheim might appear perennial, but he was seventy-seven at the time of the armistice. It was natural that there should be new faces in high offices. When Mannerheim resigned the presidency, however, he was replaced by the familiar J. K. Paasikivi. Paasikivi had served the independent republic in a number of offices for thirty years. To him was ascribed a particular understanding of the Russians. In any case, as a member of the minority group who had not been averse to frontier revisions in 1939, he was *persona grata* to the Soviet government. His presidency anticipated new orientations and carried Finland through the twilight years of its rehabilitation.

Chapter 7

The Consequences of the Peace

The Twilight Years

The ordeal of the war was succeeded by the ordeal of the peace. Ironically, one of the stipulations of the peace – that the Finns expel the German armies from their country – sounded the trumpet for the beginning of a short but bitter resumption of hostilities. The heaviest concentrations of German troops were in north Finland and, retreating through the winter twilight to Arctic Norway, they scorched the earth in their wake. The northern third of Finland, as with its Norwegian counterpart, was left a *tabula rasa*. Every building, every bridge, even individual telegraph poles, were blasted or fired. Mines and explosives littered the routes of retreat. Most of the nightmares with which Lemminkäinen and Väinömöinen were confronted in the land of Pohja were reincarnated in the north-country campaign of the Finnish troops. As a result, of all the parts of post-war Finland, it was the province of Lappi which displayed the most widespread and fundamental ravages of war. Most of the other battlegrounds had been in the territories ceded to Russia. Yet there were scars in urban areas and, because of building priorities, reconstruction was not speedy. Eventually the badly damaged castle in Turku was resplendently restored. Elsewhere, as in Oulu, it was deemed more important to create new residential precincts than to reconstruct the older bombed areas.

The years of peace were an ordeal because the entire fabric of Finland's society and economy had to be stretched and strained in order to comply with the twin problems of rehabilitation and reparations. At the same time, Finland was forced to adjust itself to the new political circumstances in Europe. Yet at the personal level the post-war anxieties of international insecurity and domestic uncertainty frequently weighed less heavily than the insistence upon unremitting labour and universal shortages. They were the days of rationed living space as well as rationed food, of empty shop windows and of black markets. Occasionally civic genius outwitted those who profited around the shady margins of trading. For example the state set up its own 'black market' in unrationed coffee and sold at a price which competed with those of the black marketeers. Some of the profits were used to build impressive hospitals. It was one way in which Finland contrived to extract some fortune from its misfortune. There was more important and longer-term recompense. The shadows cast by the costs of resettlement and reparations were long, but not long enough to obscure for some the opportunities for development that lay beyond them. In the very tasks of meeting the reparations programme and organising new homes for displaced people, Finland had to experiment with new methods of production and exercise to the full its ingenuity.

Internationally Finland had to work out a new *modus vivendi* with the U.S.S.R. This was the government's most important single post-war task. The exercise both sharpened Finland's national identity and threw it into new perspective. For example, the more closely the words of treaties and the deeds of trade integrated Finland and Russia, the more internationally assertive Finland became. Again, the more intensive the cooperative and administrative links became with the countries of Norden, the more divided official opinion became as to whether Finland should call itself a Scandinavian country.

The twilight years lasted until 1952. In the summer the Olympic flame was kindled in Helsinki's stadium: in the autumn Finns were able to celebrate the last reparations deliveries. It seemed as though the era of servitude was over. Gradually, the Finns began to realise that they had come into possession of their land more fully than ever before. The loss of a tithe of the country to Russia had forced on the more intensive use of the remainder; while the rehabilitation of Lapland was initiated at the highest scientific and technical level. The neglected northland was slowly brought into the *oecumene* in the process. Gradually, too, the technical advances of the war years became more abundantly available for peaceful uses. Because of its physical environment alone the technological advances meant proportionately more to Finland than to many countries. And they meant the more because Finland emerged from the aftermath of the war as a predominantly industrial state instead of an agricultural land; a nation of town-dwellers rather than of countryfolk.

The Resettlement of Displaced People

In September 1944 the great trek of displaced people from the ceded territories began all over again. It was swollen by the addition of those who left the 152 sq. km. of the Porkkala peninsula and by the several thousand inhabitants of the Petsamo Corridor. Three main principles were adopted in defining reception areas. First, communities were kept together as much as possible. For example those from the parishes to the east of Lake Ladoga were moved to parishes in Savo. Secondly, the northern third of the country was excluded from the reception programme, partly because it was climatically unfavourable for farming. Exceptions were made for the displaced peoples from Petsamo, Salla and Kuusamo. Thirdly, Swedish-speaking parishes were generally excluded from the resettlement scheme; though a small number of displaced Swedish-speaking peoples from the coastal tracts of Porkkala were absorbed by them. Four-fifths of the displaced people were countryfolk. Displaced townsfolk were absorbed principally in urban areas: about 25,000 evacuees from rural areas also chose to be resettled in towns. In some cases entire new districts were created in existing towns. For example, a new suburb was created in Lahti to accommodate a substantial number of evacuees from Viipuri. Elsewhere, virtually new towns were built immediately across the border, e.g. Uusi Värtsila in Karelia. Displaced fisherfolk from the ceded coastlands and islands of the Gulf of Finland presented a small-scale, but different, problem. They were Finnish-speaking and most of Finland's south and west coasts were occupied by Swedish-speaking fishing communities. A small territorial bonus was available in the returned Hanko peninsula, but so much restoration was required to make it inhabitable that it was an immediate liability rather than an asset. As in 1940 substantial numbers of livestock also moved out of the ceded areas and gave rise to pressure on winter accommodation.

The experience of resettlement, which is only a generation away, remains a vivid memory for hundreds of thousands of Finns. Four considerations weighed heavily at the personal and national level simultaneously. They were time, money, priorities and equipment. Although in retrospect rehabilitation in Finland appears to have been undertaken speedily, at the time of the operation seeming delays caused much restlessness and frustration. In general urban evacuees and industrial workers were accommodated more quickly than farmers. Indeed the permanent resettlement of displaced farmers was to take eight years to complete. It implied major redistributions of land ownership and land use. These could be more easily undertaken in some areas than in others – and in any case all forms of outdoor activity were subject to the inexorable seasonal rhythm. To keep labour fully and purposefully occupied between the time of displacement and time of resettlement was difficult. In the process a considerable percentage of displaced farmers – especially younger ones – suffered a migratory existence in reception camps for several years. Not surprisingly many grew tired of waiting and took other employment.

The displaced people were dispossessed people. Compensation was paid for by a capital levy which was progressive in its incidence. Displaced farmers, unlike industrial employees and those engaged in services, found themselves robbed of income as well as capital. As a result day-to-day income had to be provided until their new farms yielded a living. This was largely met through a series of subsidies for land clearance, ploughing, ditch digging, erection of farm buildings and related activities. Timber felled from cleared land provided limited revenue. Income was also supplemented by winter work in the forests for the state and the timber companies.

Complementary to the compensation legislation were the Land Resettlement Acts which made provision for the acquisition of land to accommodate displaced farmers. The state is Finland's most extensive landowner, but most of its domain is in the northern third of the country and unsuitably located for farming. In the plans for land acquisition, public property was, in general, acquired before private property. Where state land was available in the reception areas it was subjected to the heaviest demands for resettlement: thereafter, the properties of parish and ecclesiastical authorities. Private landowners, especially the joint stock companies, were nevertheless compelled to give up extensive areas of both forest and arable land. Landowners in Swedish-speaking areas paid a special levy instead of admitting refugees and the proceeds from this were used to pay for the costs of land clearance in other parts of the country. Altogether more than 30,000 new farmsteads were required – a number equivalent to a tenth of all the farms in pre-war Finland. The new farms were created out of new holdings. New holdings were called 'cold farms' (*kylmät tilat*). Division of existing farmlands, which took place most commonly in the south-west, resulted in the immediate availability of cultivable land. The owner of a 'cold farm' had to start as a pioneer in a forest lot.

Priorities had to be decided at all levels, and decisions made for inevitable disagreements. In the salvage operation of the resettlement social need had to take precedence over economic considerations. This produced friction at the administrative and academic level because the general principles of rural resettlement ran counter to long-term economic interests. First, they broke up the larger, more economic and frequently more progressive farm units and substituted for them smaller and less efficient units. Secondly, they initiated a major assault on the woodlands at a time when the value of softwood timber was rising relatively more swiftly than the value of farm products. Thirdly, they tended to shift the geographical centre of investment in farming away from the south-west – and accordingly to areas where the return on capital was lower. While these decisions racked policy-making circles, the individual farmer was simultaneously confronted with distracting divisions at his lowlier level. Everything was needed at the same time. As a general principle the *sauna* was built first (or, at least, a timber cabin which was the family's first shelter and later became the *sauna*); next the stable; then the family home. Land clearance and improvement necessarily took second place to shelter for man and beast. It might be several years before a hectare of arable land was ready for its first crop of oats, barley or rye.

At every step resettlement operations were retarded by shortage of capital equipment. Tractors became increasingly available, but heavy land clearance and road-building machines were very limited. Road construction commonly had to precede the establishment of new holdings. A state-supported but privately operated land clearance company, *Pellonraivaus Oy.*, was established. It provided regional pools of large-scale equipment, the disposition of which virtually resembled military operations. Supply never equalled demand because the machinery most urgently needed was usually only produced in the U.S.A. Demand for it was also widespread throughout Europe and Finland's dollar stocks were in any case in very short supply. As a result, and almost invariably in the earlier stages of resettlement, land clearance was undertaken in the traditional manner.

In this atmosphere of frustration with the best will in the world it was difficult to avoid social friction. There was friction, open or concealed, between many established farming communities and the intrusive settlers. The causes were both superficial and fundamental. It was not easy to see strangers felling a carefully husbanded timber stand or indifferently tilling a formerly well-managed plot – especially when they spoke with a pronouncedly different dialect, practised different customs and (bearing in mind the experiences that most of them had suffered) looked a different breed of men. For a considerable number there was another distinction. They had been brought up with a different form of the Christian faith for most of Finland's 75,000 adherents to the Orthodox Church lived in Karelia. The diaspora called for the creation of a new network of parishes, the construction of new churches, the provision of special Orthodox sections in local cemeteries. Here and there it yielded even more colourful features – the Orthodox archbishopric, from its museum of ecclesiastical treasures to its sober record books of the census, established itself in Kuopio; the monks of Valamo transported bells as well as books and candles from their Ladogan island retreat to the cramped confines of a manor house in Heinävesi. But whether or not they were strictly Lutheran and indistinguishable from the natives of the reception areas, the displaced farmers were inevitably the outward and visible signs of the war lost to Russia. Even though the intruders were fellow-countrymen who, as a result of living on the frontiers of the homeland had frequently lost all, it made it no easier for the established farmers to relinquish a part of their possessions for them.

Members of the armed forces engaged in the front line during the war were also given the right to acquire a stake in the land. The widows of men killed in action had the same privilege. Both groups availed themselves of the opportunity and added to the pressure of demand for new holdings.

By the end of the resettlement operation more than 10,000 cold farms had been established. As a result of the land reclamation associated with them and of extensions to the arable area on divided holdings, much of the Finnish countryside took on the appearance of a pioneer landscape during the decade following the war. Indeed the resettlement gave rise to the most intensive episode of land clearance experienced in Finland's history: in the reception area all parishes were affected by it. The episode provided the historian with the chance to see re-enacted the equivalent to forested Canada's colonial settlement – perhaps even the externals of the great

Rodungszeit of mediaeval Europe. For, during its early stages, Finnish land reclamation was conducted in the same elementary manner – by men, animals and fire.

It is true that many of the displaced farmers (and their wives) had had personal experience of land clearing, so that the challenge of the unbroken forest and undrained swamp was not wholly strange. But the task was undertaken in unfamiliar circumstances. And the scale of the enterprise differed. To carve a new farm piecemeal from the woodland was an object of a different order from adding a hectare or two to an already established farm. The rough and unkempt clearings, burnt over by fire, their top soil churned up by bull-dozers and exposing nests of boulders, frequently looked like battlefields around the raw unpainted clapboard buildings. They were to take a generation to acquire maturity. It is a miracle that not more than one in twenty-five of the new holdings failed.

Yet the price paid for winning a few hectares from the wilderness stamped many with the signs of premature old age. 'The years that the forest has eaten up' (as Paul Waineman expressed it on an earlier occasion) were manifest again. 'When the rye blooms and the ears of corn ripen in our fields, let us call to mind these first martyrs of colonisation', wrote Juhani Aho in his short story *Pioneers*. Aho was fixing the legend of Finland's voluntary pioneers: the displaced farmers were involuntary pioneers. They, too, had a legend to fix. The generation born on the new holding was to feel little allegiance to or interest in the ceded farmstead that it never knew. But memories died hard in the older generations. Faded photographs remained to echo the roll call of the ceded parishes – from Impilahti to Suistamo, from Äyrypää to Säkkijärvi; to recall the knapsack life of the refugee and his prickly reception by the new community; to stir the inescapable yearning for the lost Eden of what the English encyclopaedist Millar had called 'Corelia the Fair'.

The Impact of the Reparations

The reparations demanded by the U.S.S.R. had to be paid in kind and according to rigorously defined schedules and categories. Deliveries were precisely identified on a monthly basis and any delay in delivery of a quota entailed a fine. By the 1944 agreement deliveries were to be completed in six years. In December 1945 the period over which they were spread was extended to eight years. At the half-way point in 1948 a substantial reduction in the total was made, together with modifications in delivery dates. The upshot of these arrangements was that by four years after the end of hostilities two-thirds of the reparations had been paid.

In the same way as the resettlement of the displaced farmers fundamentally disturbed Finland's agricultural economy, the reparations programme warped its industrial structure. More than two-thirds of the items included in the reparations schedules derived from the metallurgical and mechanical industries; less than a quarter were products of softwood origin. A major diversion of capital to the metallurgical industries was consequently forced upon the country. At the same time expansion in this sector had to be effected with the greatest possible despatch. The metallurgical category embraced an enormous range of items. Most were capital goods, the production of which assumed a diversity of skills and called for the assembly of an immense variety of component parts. These components had frequently to be imported from western Europe or North America. They were converted into engines and rolling stock, electrical components and power plants. A variety of complete softwood processing plants was also included. Prefabricated houses (and plants for their production) were complemented by wooden barges and ships for use on Russia's inland waterways. In part payment of the reparations bill Finland also made over much of its mercantile marine, including the modest flagship of its passenger fleet and its principal icebreakers. A new Soviet embassy was also paid for from the same source. Its classical, grey granite façade is a permanent memorial in the old residential suburb of Kaivopuisto to the reparation programme.

Finland's ability to conform to the reparations schedule was affected by a variety of broader considerations. For example, the productivity of many industrial plants suffered because of lack of wartime maintenance. Again, punctual delivery of reparations was both dependent upon the maintenance of satisfactory labour relations at home and the uninterrupted flow of essential materials from overseas. As with many other countries Finland also suffered a shortage of energy supplies.

Not surprisingly by the end of the reparations period the metallurgical industries had taken precedence over the softwood group as the principal employer of industrial labour. Most of the plants developed out of already existing concerns, so that the growth of metallurgy reinforced the disproportionate concentration in the south-west. Helsinki and Tampere in particular felt the expansive effects. Since Finland is not well endowed with mineral resources, the metallurgical developments depended to a large degree upon the import of either semi-processed materials or component parts. Even mineral exploitations which had been opened up before the war were limited in either the volume or the variety of the production. Outokumpu was the exception, with copper deposits as large as any in Europe and an output of an international order. Its ores played a critical role in supplying raw materials for the wire and cable industries.

Although it would have been incidental to needs in the context of the reparations, the loss of Petsamo robbed Finland of one of its most valuable mineral deposits. Concessions to develop Petsamo's nickel ores had already been acquired by Canadian Nickel Mond in the immediate pre-war years. Throughout the duration of hostilities they were both the object of international interest and negotiation. The territorial adjustment of 1944 transferred them to the U.S.S.R. which made an outright payment to the Canadian company of $10 million as compensation for them.

Eight years to the day after the end of hostilities the last deliveries arrived in the U.S.S.R. Economists were left to count the cost – a cost inseparable from the domestic spiral of inflation and from independent inflationary tendencies in critical countries of supply. In changing monetary terms conservative estimates place the ultimate bill at nearly double that originally stipulated. After 1952 the members of the Soviet Control Commission withdrew and the 400 civil servants who ran the Finnish War Reparations Industries Commission were gradually disbanded.

Throughout the reparations period, Finland had had an equally critical complementary task – to restore exports and to maintain a firmly positive balance of trade. All its traditional markets in western Europe were hungry for Finnish softwood products but all suffered shortage of foreign exchange. After 1947 the American programme of Marshall Aid helped individual European economies. For political reasons Finland declined to accept the invitation to participate although it benefited indirectly. Between 1946 and 1952 Finland received generous credits through the Export-Import Bank and the International Bank for Reconstruction and Development. Great Britain was speedily restored to its place as Finland's leading market in the west and the beginnings of a significant increase in exports to America were discernible.

The most striking change was the emergence of the U.S.S.R. as an export market. During the inter-war years Russo-Finnish trade had been negligible, but in a number of years between 1944 and 1950 and independently of the reparations Russia absorbed more Finnish exports than any other country. The restoration of Russia to the Finnish trading picture was an unexpected consequence of the peace. It carried with it the seeds of a new economic dependence on its eastern neighbour. The situation became the more critical when reparations deliveries were concluded, and Finland found itself with a substantial industrial plant tied to the Russian market and unable to compete successfully in other markets. The resuscitation of trade with Russia, despite restrictions on the convertibility of the rouble, has brought considerable advantages to Finland. It has added a cosmopolitan touch to the street scene, where the Russian car is popular; provided useful supplementary fodder grains for the farmer; and become a principal source of petroleum imports. But by comparison with the trading relations with other countries those with the U.S.S.R. marry more closely politics and economics.

The Political Pendulum

The social and economic upheaval had its direct influence upon domestic politics. First it stimulated a larger percentage of the electorate to go to the polls in national, local and presidential elections. Secondly it led to adjustments in representation. This was principally because it brought into the open the Communist Party (*Suomen Kommunisti Puolue*) and led to the rise of a powerful but somewhat amorphous party of fellow travellers, the Finnish People's Democratic Party (*Suomen Kansan Demokraattinen Liitto*). The S.K.D.L. established itself in the first post-war election of 1945 as one of the three leading parties in the *Eduskunta*. It gained 49 seats – against the Social Democrats' 50, the Agrarians' 49, National Union 28, Swedish Party 14, Progressives 9 and others one. Although attempts by the Communist Party to capture the Social Democratic Party in the immediate post-war years were unsuccessful, left-wing Social Democratic members shifted their allegiance to the S.K.D.L., thereby reducing the power of the party which had prevailed in the inter-war years. In the elections since 1945 the maximum variation in the number of seats obtained by the three principal parties has not exceeded twelve, but this is a sufficiently pronounced swing to shift the balance of governmental power.

In the immediate post-war years there were attempts to bring together the three leading parties in a 'popular front' which would make for maximum cooperation in the face of the national crisis. But Agrarians, Social Democrats and Communists made uneasy bedfellows. For a while, after 1950, there emerged a stronger coalition of Agrarians and Social Democrats under the premiership of U. K. Kekkonen. Divisions in the Social Democratic Party subsequently reduced its strength, so that the Agrarians have played the principal role in drawing together governments over the last decade. Minority or 'caretaker' governments have held office while the major parties have compromised over their differences. The majority of post-war cabinets have included non-party experts. Indeed during the brief von Fieandt government of 1957–58, the cabinet consisted exclusively of them; while the five-month government of its successor also drew a majority of its members from outside the *Eduskunta*. Such members have included civil servants, bankers, university professors and trade unionists. The frequency of post-war cabinets has continued much the same as in the pre-war years. Their comings and goings, analysed together with a range of other political information by J. Nousiainen in his comprehensive study of the Finnish political system, average about once a year. His analysis also indicates that while governments change, Ministers frequently remain.

Until he retired in 1956 the successive coalitions ruled under the presidency of J. Paasikivi, a National Union or Conservative Party leader who served two terms of office. He was succeeded by U. K. Kekkonen, an Agrarian, who entered his third term of office in 1968. During his first term of office Paasikivi clearly defined his policy of friendship and cooperation with the U.S.S.R. In his public speeches at the time of the 1945 election he urged the nation to refrain from all action that could offend the U.S.S.R. Although they failed to take over the Social Democratic Party and although they were unsuccessful in their attempts to capture the Confederation of Finnish Trade Unions, the Communists entered the first post-war government (1946–48) after Paasikivi became President. Six out of the eighteen cabinet seats were allotted to members of the S.K.D.L. The Prime Minister, Mauno Pekkala, and Minister of the Interior, Yrjö Leino, were both members of the party. In addition, Leino was married to Hertta Kuusinen, leader of the Communists in the *Eduskunta* and daughter of Otto Kuusinen, leader of the Terijoki puppet government and subsequently president of the Karelian S.S.R.

In the final instance members of the S.K.D.L. played their hands too hard. Leino had already made himself widely disliked in 1945 because of the part that he had taken in the extradition of a group of émigré Russians. On the demand of the Soviet Control Commission twenty Russians who were resident in Finland and some of whom were Finnish citizens, were returned to the U.S.S.R. This unconstitutional and undemocratic act was not allowed to rest and, although a parliamentary committee found the ministerial authorities guilty of a breach of conduct, the Prime Minister upheld Leino. Nor did the fulsome speeches given by S.K.D.L. cabinet members at the conclusion of the formal Peace Treaty in 1947 add to their popularity. A political *coup* was feared, Leino was dismissed from office and, in the ensuing elections of July 1948, the S.K.D.L. forfeited a substantial number of seats.

At the time, the generous allocation of cabinet offices to members of the S.K.D.L. seemed fitting. But the admission of S.K.D.L. members to the cabinet was not repeated for two decades – and then in reduced numbers. In 1948, against the background of similarly sympathetic attitudes to the Communist Party and with similar infiltration, the control of Czechoslovakia was taken over by a minority Communist group. The process could easily have been repeated in Finland. The inner story of its prevention has remained discreetly untold.

While elections in Finland are as widely based and free as those in any country in the world, post-war Finnish governments have been continuously aware of pressures from the U.S.S.R. Sometimes these have taken the form of open protest. During the predominantly Social Democratic government led by K. A. Fagerholm in 1958, the U.S.S.R. was outspoken in its criticism, obstructed Fenno-Russian commercial negotiations and pointedly left Helsinki without an ambassador. Sometimes the pressures have been indirect, as in 1962, when Finland's foreign policy was questioned by the U.S.S.R. and elections were postponed. During the incidence of these external pressures all organs of the press have continued without censorship, though the U.S.S.R. has inevitably achieved at least a part of the object of its particular exercise. Two general principles have emerged in domestic political manoeuvres – first the attempt on the part of the U.S.S.R. to deny power to the Social Democratic Party: secondly the attempt on the part of most Finnish parliamentarians to prevent the S.K.D.L. from holding cabinet positions.

Among the political parties the S.K.D.L. may be the most demonstrative and most obstructive, but it makes its distinctive contribution to the domestic scene. Its House of Culture, designed by Aalto in 1958, is one of the most attractive places of assembly in the capital and it accommodates a steady stream of distinguished Soviet artists. May Day finds the members of the S.K.D.L. filling the streets of Helsinki with their long, colourful procession. Red flag and brass band have their complement, for the white-capped students begin May morning (or conclude a Walpurgis night of revelry) with rival processions through streets where blue-and-white flags fly on all public buildings.

The Search for Neutrality

Another consequence of the peace was that Finland had to adjust its relations with its neighbours and, more importantly, to accommodate itself to existence between the new large power blocs. During the inter-war years, Finland had aspired to neutrality; in 1939 it had affirmed this publicly; after 1944, the effects of its location between eastern and western Europe swiftly asserted themselves. During 1947 and 1948 both eastern and western neighbours began to consolidate their situations. The Scandinavians discussed the possibility of a neutral group in northern Europe; the U.S.S.R. began to formalise its military and strategic relations with its border states. Despite sympathy for the Scandinavian plan Finland had no alternative but to enter into an 'Agreement of Friendship, Co-operation and Mutual Assistance' with the U.S.S.R., signed in Moscow in April 1948. The agreement was to last in the first instance for ten years and to be renewable at five-yearly intervals. It was of a similar character to pacts offered by the U.S.S.R. to Romania and Hungary.

The agreement, brief in content and terse in statement, was of an essentially defensive character. It contained four principal clauses. First the High Contracting Parties agreed that if Finland or the Soviet Union through Finland was attacked 'by Germany or any state allied with the latter', Finland would repel the aggressor 'if necessary, with the assistance of, or jointly with, the Soviet Union'. Secondly, neither party would conclude an alliance or join any coalition directed against the other. Thirdly, both parties agreed to support loyally the maintenance of peace and security in accordance with the aims of the United Nations Organisation. Fourthly, the parties pledged themselves 'to observe the principle of mutual respect of sovereignty and integrity and that of non-interference in the internal affairs of the other state'. The agreement contained no clauses which conflicted with the Finnish ideal of neutrality; but it was a clear expression of the Soviet sphere of influence in northern Europe and Finland's foreign relations could only be conducted in terms of it. In the interplay of Fenno-Scandinavian relations Moscow blew hot and cold, both predictably and unpredictably.

The failure of the Scandinavian states to draw Finland into their proposed neutral bloc made it impossible to bring Finland into the Joint Scandinavian Committee for Economic Cooperation. This committee, established in 1948, sought to lay the foundations for a virtual economic union of the participating countries. It was not until 1955 that Finland was able to establish an official relationship with the Scandinavian community by joining the Nordic Council which had been established in 1953. It joined on condition that its sixteen delegates should not be required to discuss military policy. Finland attended its first meeting in Copenhagen the next year and in 1957 invited the representatives of the other countries of Norden to Helsinki. The Council meets annually.

In the same year that Finland became a member of the Nordic Council, it reaffirmed the Treaty of Friendship with the U.S.S.R. and extended it for twenty years. As an associated gesture of goodwill the U.S.S.R. withdrew from the Porkkala base. Porkkala had been a thorn in the flesh, not least from the obstacle that it presented to communications. Shipping had to give its coastal waters wide clearance, aircraft had to avoid it; while only iron-shuttered coaches hauled by Russian-driven engines were allowed to use the track of the Helsinki–Turku railway line that passed through the peninsula. When Finnish troops took over in January 1956, a fundamental problem in rehabilitation as well as resettlement was presented. No public record exists of the bizarre spectacle that was encountered by returning Finns – the reversion of farmland to wilderness, the reversion of property to slum, signs of a very dense military population, the broad new cobbled highways. The main point was the restoration of the ceded territory; time and money could put the rest right.

By the 1960s new patterns of organisation were showing themselves in Europe and it was imperative that Finland should review its position in relation to them. This implied further tensions with the U.S.S.R., the first evidence of which came in October 1961. Helsinki received a Russian note directing the attention of Finland to the hazards caused by the North Atlantic Treaty Organisation. Accusing fingers were pointed at Norway and Denmark whose association with the Atlantic alliance was deemed to constitute a threat to the security of the U.S.S.R. In spite of Sweden's neutrality, attention was directed to its arms manufactures and to the contribution that they were making to the rearming of West Germany. The new phase of Russian agitation probably had several motives. First, it was directed against Finland's proposed adherence to a broad new agreement for cooperation between the five countries of Norden. In spite of the disapproving attitude of the Soviets a signature was appended in March 1962. The forty articles identified in it enabled Finland to share in one of the most liberal and lively international communities in the world. The agreement paved the way for a great range of measures to promote the closer unity of the countries of Norden. From the abandonment of passports to the establishment of a common labour market the restraints upon personal mobility between the countries of Norden have been reduced to a minimum. A second motive for Russian pressures in 1961–62 was the forthcoming presidential election. When the opposition candidate discreetly withdrew, the field was left clear for the re-election of U. K. Kekkonen. A third motive was probably to impress upon Finland the unwisdom of attempting to associate itself with the emerging European Free Trade Area.

Following the Treaty of Rome in 1957 the European Economic Community came into existence in 1958; E.F.T.A. came into being in 1960. An inner six were thus balanced by an outer seven, with Denmark, Norway and Sweden tied to the latter from the outset. In 1961 Finland was admitted as an associate member of E.F.T.A. Through this affiliation Finland acquired all of the advantages of the free trade area without suffering any of the disadvantages resulting from its existing arrangements with Russia.

Several broad generalisations may be attempted about Finland's role in international relations since 1944. First, it has been necessarily a follower and not a leader; though by the middle 1960s, against the background of its distinctive relationship to the U.S.S.R. and through the intermediacy of a strong President, it began to explore anew the ground for a neutral Nordic group. However, the arguments were insufficiently persuasive either to woo Norway and

Denmark from N.A.T.O. or to encourage them to exchange their N.A.T.O. membership for mutual assistance pacts in the west resembling that between Finland and the U.S.S.R. A second generalisation is that Finland has been more aware than previously of changes in the location of world tension. For example, Russian concern over its Far Eastern relationships has tended to reduce stress along its western borders. Thirdly, Finland has been increasingly conscious of the effects of American policy upon its situation; though they are indirect rather than direct because the American sphere of influence does not extend into the Baltic. All in all the degree of success achieved by Finland in its post-war European relations represents a victory for pragmatism. With minimal room for manoeuvre, Finland has achieved maximum results. Each successive development in post-war Europe seems to have offered a more difficult challenge to Finland, yet none has been insurmountable. In the face of this it is unlikely that Finland would fail to accommodate itself to any unification between the members of E.E.C. and E.F.T.A.

A century ago in his lectures to history students in the University of Helsinki, Zachris Topelius followed a Sprengtporten line and declared that Finland must be neutral in international affairs, but that this was impossible unless Finland were a sovereign state. In union with either of its two neighbours it was powerless to escape involvement. Free from both of them, he argued that it might be in a position to act as a bridge as well as an effective buffer between them. In 1917, Finland achieved its political freedom: in 1944, it succeeded in maintaining it. Yet ultimately its liberties depend upon the sanctions of both eastern and western Europe. It is integrated with both of them and committed to both of them. In theory, because of this integration and commitment, independent Finland finds that it has acquired a double function. A century after Topelius it is a real, if minor, bridge between eastern and western Europe; a real, but by no means negligible, buffer, to absorb the shocks arising out of their differences.

From Assignment to Achievement

Having escaped extinction in war Finland had subsequently to resist absorption in peace. The most immediate method of resistance was the payment in kind of the material goods demanded as war reparations. The first eight years of peace were a kind of treadmill during which the country's efforts were expended with relatively little domestic benefit. The ordeal of the peace was the more acute because it introduced crises of growth and development inseparable from the country's conversion to industry and urbanisation. By comparison with the industrial and urban transformation in many countries that of Finland was abrupt. It was abrupt partly because of the pressure of the reparations programme. The experience produced structural conflicts in Finland's society and economy. They were different from, but in their own ways no less exaggerated than, those in larger and more densely peopled lands. The experience was paid for in part by fierce inflation. Its measure may be assessed by the fact that on 1 January 1963 a new silver mark was introduced. It had the equivalent value to one hundred old marks. Devaluation had succeeded to inflation.

With the release from the servitude of reparations Finland sensed an escape from assignment. It would not be an exaggeration to say that, by any standard and in a variety of fields, it leapt forward to an age of achievement. The achievement has been manifested externally in an immense building programme which has changed the face of most cities and towns as well as giving rise to new settlements. The programme has reached its climax in Helsinki, which planners consider has attained an optimum size. In an attempt to restrict its growth beyond half a million inhabitants, they have established a major garden city to the west in Tapiola (Sw. Hagalund) and conceived a semicircle of seven satellite towns around the capital. In addition new port facilities are projected for Porkkala peninsula; while the civil service is disturbed by discussions to shift the principal administrative offices from Helsinki to the southern interior city of Jyväskylä.

These developments take place in a society which the stresses of war and the strains of peace have done much to integrate. Finnish society has been essentially egalitarian since the old estates ceased to exist and since the rise of a comprehensive, highly centralised system of state education. In addition, such extremes of wealth and poverty as remained before 1939 have been largely levelled through schemes of social benefit and through a steeply graduated income tax, the incidence of which was exaggerated at the end of the war by a capital levy. Generous housing subsidies, through the ARAVA scheme which was established in 1949, have done much to reduce the differential in housing conditions between different income brackets. Egalitarian though it may be, Finnish society has its own particular social distinctions; but they are expressed less in terms of residential patterns, appearances and accents than in many countries. The situation is explained partly by the recency of urban development and the persistently close links between town and country. By contrast with the reactions of the town dwellers in a country such as Britain, the seasonal silences of the wilderness are as continuingly attractive for most Finns as the siren songs of the city. In an urban society where the backwoods philosophisings of authors such as Veikko Huovinen claim a substantial following, the development of elaborate class distinctions makes little headway.

Nevertheless, as in the Scandinavian countries at large, Finland has a proliferation of titles. But the titles that follow the Finn from the telephone catalogue to the tombstone have a functional rather than a social purpose. For the most part they identify his trade or profession. His wife may be distinguished by the feminine form of his title (except that she may have a title in her own right). There is also a range of civic titles, most dignified of which is that of Counsellor (F. *Neuvos*: Sw. *Rådet*), adjectivally qualified according to the profession of the citizen – for example, mining counsellor (F. *Vuorineuvos*: Sw. *Bergsrådet*). Since 1943, civic titles have carried an annual tax.

Contemporary society has two other characteristics. First, it remains a society in which women are as emancipated as those anywhere in the world. They engage in almost all trades as well as professions. They sort logs, unload ships, lay bricks, and dominate banks and barbers' shops. A higher proportion – 45 per cent – of married women work than in most countries. Yet in spite of the widespread employment of their talents, with 40 per cent of the labour force constituted by women (30 per cent in Sweden, 32 per cent in the United States), Finland is ultimately pervaded by what Ganivet politely called seventy years ago *de precedencia masculina.*

The second characteristic is the secularisation of society. Ecclesiastically speaking, Finland is full of paradoxes. The country displays a situation in which church attendance is less than a tenth of the possible, yet where 95 per cent of the population are nominally Lutheran, where a church tax is retained, where a flourishing *rippikoulu* prepares for the religious and social event of the confirmation, where church feast days (Roman and Orthodox as well as Lutheran) still serve for public holidays, where blasphemy remains a punishable offence to give rise to the occasional *cause célèbre*, and where death, advertised in spacious obituaries, is followed by large funerals and the panoply of heavy mourning. The range of churchmanship in worship is considerable, from black-and-white pietism to the flash of vestment and intrusive puff of incense. The clergy, who occupy a strong position in society, range from the oecumenically progressive who have searched for inter-communion with Churches outside Finland to the narrowly reactionary. Church buildings vary from the superbly restored mediaeval, through the well-preserved neo-classical structures of Engel (as in Pielisjärvi and Leppävirta), to the vigorously functional of Erik Bryggman (seen in Honkanummi chapel), the imaginatively cubist of Alvar Aalto (reaching extreme expression in Vuoksenniska) and the unusual rhomboidal structure of Reima Pietilä in Tampere. The Church of Finland has not yielded historically to schism or to non-conformity. Finland may have relatively few practising Christians, but Lutheranism is a powerful subconscious element in its thinking and acting.

This, coupled with the sense of achievement in the material sphere, helps the Finn to tolerate rather than to resist, to absorb rather than to reject, the stream of external political influences from which there is no ultimate escape. The sense of achievement is the more important because it extends beyond the domestic field to the outside world. It is mentally as well as materially important for Finland that its products should find satisfied customers beyond its shores. The more that Finland can give of that which is distinctly Finnish, the deeper the sense of achievement and the stronger the resistance to absorption.

Chapter 8

The Retort of Time

Dream and Tradition

Modern Finland, larger in size than at the ebb of its fortunes but smaller than at their flood tide, has a character compounded from five principal experiences. They embrace a remote Fenno-Ugrian prehistory, the myths of which have been successfully fostered to play a powerful role in the rise of the contemporary state; a saga of spacious times, when Finland was an integral part of Sweden, was cast in a west European mould and shared in the expansive mood of a great European power; an age of apocalypse in which it bore the physical brunt of Sweden's waning fortunes; an episode as a Grand Duchy of Russia, with the advantages as well as the disadvantages of association with an imperial autocracy; and half a century of uneasy independence. From each of these experiences Finland has derived distinctive features, traditions and dreams.

The relict features from all but the last two of these episodes are not as widely evident in Finland as in most European countries. The traditions that distinguish Finland may also be less well defined than those of other lands. Some, happily, have disappeared. For example, Lahtinen (one of Väinö Linna's soldiers) could no longer level at society the bitter complaint that 'Hunger has been turned into a tradition in Finland'. The dreams continue and few generations of Finns have been privileged to see their fulfilment so completely as the last. None, at any rate, has had the prospect of living longer to enjoy the benefits of fulfilment. Life expectancy in Finland is seventy years today: in 1900 it was forty-five years.

The purpose of this chapter is to consider something of the character and consequences of this realisation. In character, it amounts to a technical revolution. The technical facilities that have become available over the last generation have had relatively more significance for Finland than for many countries. They have broadened and deepened its possibilities by making it more habitable and more amenable. Above all they have given new values to its limited resource base. In part they have fallen on prepared ground, because technical education in Finland was well established in the inter-war years. There have been a number of consequences – the application of new methods in many areas of production, widespread innovation leading to variations on the themes of the new techniques, a new appreciation of scale as a factor in almost all activities, new forms of international integration, and correspondingly greater international dependence. The revolution has also had social implications. Established institutions and values have been questioned. History has been rewritten. Young states, such as Finland, incline to greater extremes in these processes than more mature states; they are both more sensitive and more ruthless. They are more sensitive about the critical appraisal of their institutions by the outside world, but they are more rigorous in their self-examination. The essence of all nations is continuously distilled in the retort of time: that of Finland never with greater care than in the last generation.

Attachment to the Land

Among the most abiding Finnish traditions is attachment to the land. One of the fondest and most widespread desires is to have a stake in it. Land ownership has always been broadly based in Finland; the base continues to broaden. Attachment to the land is common to people with a wide range of political attitudes and human attributes. People may leave the countryside but one of their first acts when they acquire a little money is to buy a plot of their own. Their names are mostly names from the land – the names of family farms. In time of stress the land has been a sheet anchor. During the Winter War and the Continuation War many Finns defended their soil as if it were near sacred, while those who had none of their own were given the means to acquire it with the coming of peace. Finland is a country with few impressive national monuments and its contemporary countryside reflects only meagrely the successive stages of its evolution. The principal memorial to the energies of the past is the cultivated lands. They are emblematic of generations of pioneers and improvers. 'Woe unto that people, woe unto that country, which loses its love for the land. When that is lost, the yeoman class (*bondesståndet*) goes under, and when in turn it is lost, a nation stands on the edge of the pit.' Hannes Gebhard's words still claim respect among the yeoman farmers, but there is a much broader attachment to the land than in his day.

The attachment is inseparable from the fact that land can still be legally acquired from the wilderness and won from it. Nineteenth-century romanticists made play with the symbolism of *grinden, vägen, skogen* – the gateway, road and woodland. It was (and is) a relatively short journey through the gate (even the city doorway) and down the road to virgin forest. It is technically possible for Finns to follow it if they so wish. For this reason mid-twentieth-century Finland is exceptional in Europe in that it savours continuingly the bittersweet experience of pioneering. The urge in at least some members of the rising generation to pitch their camps beyond the next hill recalls the mood expressed by P. A. Sjögren in a manuscript poem from his early days:

Die Phantasie auf ihren golden Flügeln
getragen, spielt hinter jenen Hügeln.

(Fancy on its golden wings, plays behind every hill.)

Yet, if the romantic drama of pioneering remains much the same, the properties in which it is dressed are different. The pioneer can no longer be a nonconformist, for he must in part conform to the rules of the state that underwrites his enterprise. But if the simple life is no longer simple, at least it has the ultimate assurance of security.

The farmlands, and the associated forests to which the Finn is so deeply attached, differ regionally in form and extent. In south-western Finland it is the extensiveness of arable land that impresses. Limited barbed wire or post-and-wire fences do little to intercept the openness of the countryside, while the thickets of split-rail fences that obscured the landscape of Ostrobothnia are disappearing as holdings are being gradually reorganised. Coastal Finland has the greatest share of the good earth of Finland. In the south-west in particular, it has been made better by long cultivation. It is being improved with greater intensity than the farmland in most parts of the country. The seams of the open ditches, that quilt the farmland as it is seen from the air, are slowly being replaced by tile drainage. Open ditches remain the distinguishing feature of another type of open landscape – the extensive peatlands of northern Ostrobothnia. Local rhymesters may claim that they have not their like in all Finland; but it is kindlier and mature 'peninsular Finland' that is the dream land of the arable farmer.

Interior Finland has its open vistas, too – but they are lakescapes rather than landscapes. Arable land contracts and is hemmed in by water and wood. Cultivated land is richest and most extensive on the lake terraces. It blossoms in clearings about which the sawtooth-edge of the spruce woods is nearer or more distantly a natural picket fence. Eastwards and northwards the impact of man upon the land is measured by islands of cultivation in the sea of forests or of swamps. All parts of Finland – not excluding the fells of Lapland – reflect some attempt on the part of man to reclaim wasteland.

The centuries of effort put into the tilled land are concealed, though the trained eye can detect the occasional detail of past cultivation systems. Prehistoric, dark-age, mediaeval and Renaissance features which are inscribed freely upon the landscapes of much of Europe are rarely visible in Finland. They have been both obliterated by the intensive processes of contemporary cultivation and obscured by the return of woodland and swamp. One important fact is that, in contrast to the British Isles where centuries-old permanent grass has preserved the outlines of these features, Finland has no 'permanent grass' save in its water meadows. As a result, the clustered mounds of Åland's prehistoric cemeteries are overgrown with spruce, birch and rowan; while pines have littered their needles for a millennium upon the outline of its boat-burial sites. The boulders piled into fortifications by dark-age settlers, the rough-hewn granite strong points of Russian forces in south-east Finland from the eighteenth century, the local pillboxes of Red and White troops from the Civil War, the residual outposts from the Winter War and the Continuation War are all lost in the forest. They are sought out by archaeologist, historian or sentimental pilgrim, but they rarely announce themselves to prompt the curiosity of all as in countries where the timber cover is scanty. While many Finns are haunted by a sense of the past, the externals of daily life are curiously free from its sights and signs. This irony is coupled with another. For there is a school of thought which rejects at least a part of the past and considers that it is not fitting for a state that describes itself as modern to make a fetish of antiquity.

The mid-twentieth century has seen the climax of agricultural endeavour in Finland. It is unlikely that the contemporary figure of 2.7 million hectares of cultivated land will be exceeded for two reasons. First, although local reclamation will continue, it is likely to be more than offset by schemes for reafforestation. Indeed, following the example of Sweden there are long-term plans for the extensive conversion of arable to woodland. Secondly, the loss of farmland to building sites and highways in south-west Finland approaches figures comparable to those in other west European countries.

The climax has been the result of a mechanical and scientific revolution. Since the late 1940s Finnish agriculture has undergone a mechanical transformation. For example, the tractor, with its variety of appliances, has become a feature of most farms; the combine-harvester has been brought within the reach of many others; milking machines are ubiquitous. Machines are numbered by the hundred thousand in contrast to the ten thousand of the mid-forties. The time lag in mechanisation by comparison with the other countries of Norden has been made good. Sometimes, mechanisation has been brought on by the 'flight from the land': sometimes, it has prompted the flight. In addition, partly because a certain prestige adheres to mechanical equipment, some farm units are over-mechanised.

The scientific revolution has been of no less consequence. As a mixed-farming country concentrating upon dairying, Finland has taken full advantage of international improvements in the hybridisation of stock and crop, in new rotation practices, in new forms of fertilisation and in land drainage methods. At the same time it has made its own contributions to research in these fields. An example is provided by the system of chemical conservation of fodderstuffs, named A.I.V. after its discoverer, the Nobel prize-winner Artturi Virtanen. More swiftly ripening grains have provided fuller opportunities for cereal cultivation. Much more important are the new strains of grasses and legumes that have greatly increased the yields of the leys and the carrying capacity of land. The range and efficiency of kale, rape and beet have been extended. Among animals high-quality bulls have had especial importance for the standard of dairy herds. In the interests of economy they are not infrequently cooperatively owned; in the interests of efficiency artificial insemination is widely practised. Milk yields have risen to the same level as those in the other countries of Norden. Pig production is complementary to dairy production, as in Denmark. Sheep rearing, an old-established Finnish industry, is less efficient and popular than dairying: its possibilities in the present farming structure await fuller exploration. And round the margins of the traditional farm scene are the coastal smallholders thriving upon the returns from their millions of variously-coloured mink and the horticulturalists who, especially in Ostrobothnia, have put acres under glass.

Not surprisingly, over-production has become a problem in some sectors of agriculture. This is especially true in dairying, the activity which suits Finland best both because of its climate and because of the structure of its farms. Finland has more than enough milk, butter and cheese to meet domestic needs – at least at the current rate of consumption. Butter can only be exported if there are export subsidies: cheese competes successfully in the international market. Emmenthal type, for example, is a serious competitor with the original Swiss product as well as with that from France.

All of these developments are taking place within a farming framework which suffers from problems of scale. Finland is a country of smallholders and too many of its holdings fall short of the optimum economic size. As a result of the resettlement programme further reductions in size took place. It is true that most Finnish farms have a stand of timber, so that the absolute extent of the arable area is not the only criterion for assessment. But, in spite of this, farm economists would argue, for example, that it is uneconomic to have a tractor for an arable area of less than 15 hectares. One consequence of farm size is the lower standard of living in many country areas. Finland is without urban slums but their counterpart can be found in rural areas. So far Finland has not initiated the radical legislation which has been adopted in Sweden to prevent further division of existing holdings, to control the sale of farmland entering the market and to encourage amalgamation. In some parts, Ostrobothnia for example, fragmentation of farm holdings may approach the *Parzellwirtschaft* of Germany; but this is not common.

Changes in the character and practice of Finnish agriculture have had their effect upon the input of labour. Formerly, there was a pronounced seasonal rhythm in the demand for labour. Winter unemployment was a distinctive rural feature – and there was, in addition, much concealed unemployment. Improved animal husbandry with year-round calving and sustained milk yields, indoor piggeries and winter-heated poultry runs, have smoothed out seasonal variations in the demand for labour. The work load in rural areas still reaches haymaking and harvesting peaks, though it is reduced through labour-saving machinery. Machinery also increases the certainty of the harvest in an environment where the frost hazard is especially great.

Farming in Finland is subsidised. Assistance is both general and regional; but the budgetary allocations are flexible in their distribution, varying according to temporal as well as local circumstance. Among general supports are those given for improvement schemes such as land reclamation and drainage. Production premiums are given on domestic wool and rye (according to its quality in relation to area of cultivation). For milk production, seven zones are identified (in 1967, support given within them ranged from 6.65 to 1.9 pennies per litre): milk transport costs were also subsidised at two different rates in two different zones. The north-eastern third of the country, which has only been brought effectively into the *oecumene* in post-war years, is especially dependent upon supports. Among them subsidised freight rates for grains, fodder, fertilisers, acids and food-stuffs are critical. Reimbursement of the cost of drainage, up to 45 per cent in the south, is up to 75 per cent in the north and north-east. Subsidised transport is also vital for the skerries, where farming continues to retreat from the less accessible islands. Indirect help is given to farmers through a denser, faster and better maintained road network, through new bridges and ferries to the islands and new railways to the northlands. In this way isolation is reduced. At the same time greater accessibility speeds milk collection, favours the nationalisation of dairies through the extension of their service areas and eases the operation of mobile shops and other delivery services.

There is a growing attachment of farmers to their forests. The proportion of woodland to cultivated land increases from coast to interior and from south-west to north-east. By area about half of Finland's woodlands are owned by farmers. The state owns about a third; private corporations (including the Church and local authorities) the remainder. Most of the privately owned woodlands are in the south-western two-thirds of Finland. These are inherently the most productive areas of woodland; but they are also the areas most altered by man. Removal of the timber cover reaches its maximum in the south-western third. Destruction of timber cover has taken place with different degrees of regional intensity. For example, generations of tar burning in Ostrobothnia have diminished supplies of merchantable timber over wide areas; while the firing of woodland for cultivation in Karelia has left extensive areas bereft of mature conifers. First growth deciduous woodland, of little or no commercial value, distinguishes broad tracts of country. To the botanist and forester they speak of the recency of primitive farming practices.

The privately owned timber stands of the south-west are also the most fragmented in ownership. Their quality varies greatly and includes some of the best and some of the worst woodland in Finland. Poor management is explained by a number of facts. For example, woodland grazing, with all of its deleterious consequences for regeneration, has only been effectively combated in the post-war years. Again, the wood lot is all too often regarded as a source of ready capital which can be used to pay for new buildings, equipment, cars and more expensive consumer goods. Silviculturalists who challenge this attitude have naturally been among the vocal minority who protested that clearance for resettlement was against the long-term national interests.

The post-war years have witnessed an intensification of silvicultural research, education and propaganda. Finland is one of the leading countries in the world in research into coniferous woodlands and the economics of forest management. Its experts have an international reputation. It is among the few countries that have detailed forest inventories from the past as well as running inventories from which actual and potential yields can be assessed. Forestry education for the farmer as distinct from the university man has lagged behind agricultural education, though the forest advisory service is old-established and forestry journals have large circulations. Forestry schools for smallholders now supplement those devoted to agriculture. Gradually, a silvicultural *légende* is being developed. The annual conference of *Metsäliitto*, the private foresters' society, is attended by thousands of active members. Most are practical men of the trees. As a result of their collective endeavours discriminatory felling, trimming, draining, planting and remedial burning urge forward forest improvements. The returns are quicker in the south, where pulp wood achieves maturity in thirty years: it may take twice as long in the north.

Meanwhile, in the state-owned and company-owned woodlands extensive operations contrast with the limited activities of the smallholders. Current expansion has been made possible largely through improved communications. The annual construction of scores of miles of roads, especially in the north-east, has brought virtually the whole of wooded Finland into the territory of economic exploitation. As recently as the mid-1950s, a so-called *nol* area was identified within which timber had no industrial value.

With the rising demand for timber a comprehensive scheme for forest improvement has been initiated. The so-called MERA programme looks to the replacement of poor, slow-growing stands with more swiftly growing timber. It is investing heavily in extensive drainage, in widespread re-seeding; in the maintenance of experimental plots, nurseries and research stations; and in collaboration with the conservationists. The programme calls for the recruitment of an increasing amount of full-time labour in addition to the continuing winter supplement of tens of thousands of lumberjacks. The recruits are principally smallholders, who work in the state- and company-owned forests for varying periods annually. Although fewer of them take horses than previously because of the widespread mechanisation of operations, tractors are not absolutely substitutable for horses. Permanent logging camps, subject to strict rules and inspection, are supplemented by mobile caravan encampments, which reduce travelling time to and from the place of work. The motor saw has largely replaced the traditional axe and cross-saw. Motor lorries – many privately owned by farmers – transport logs, poles and pulp wood from forest sites to processing centres throughout the year. Summer floatage operations continue along a network of timber flumes and of improved water courses, across the broad lakes and into elaborate sorting basins. The handling of logs in large bundles on lorry and rail, in river and on lake, increasingly replaces traditional methods of movement. As a result of all these changes both felling and transport operations have shown an enormous increase in productivity per operator since the war.

In contemporary Finland, farmland and forest land compete increasingly for the attention of economist and politician. The forest lies behind the nation's largest industries and is the ultimate source of its material wealth. The annual demand for its raw materials has grown so swiftly since the war that it has overtaken the annual yield of timber. And, in contrast to the demand for farm products, the market for timber products continues to expand. Both nationally and internationally it is in Finland's interest to concentrate its attention chiefly on the timber crop. The situation produces continuing dilemmas for members of select committees who recommend policies and for the politicians who are forced to compromise over their recommendations. Many Finnish farmers can quote Kaarlo Kvamso's jingle about their fictional prototype Jaakkima Berends:

Se on talonpojan työksi	It is through the farmer's work that
Aina tullut suomenmaas;	everything is produced for Finland:
Minkä herra maahan syöksi	whatever the rest of the people eat
Rakens talonpoika taas.	comes ultimately from him.

Although the farmer is subsidised for his labour, the jingle retains more than a half-truth. Manufacturing industry cannot escape its dependence on forest, field and mine. Finland's primary pursuits accordingly grow in significance as manufacturing grows.

The Contribution of Contemporary Industry

Within a generation Finland has become an industrial country. The balance of employment has shifted from the field and forest to the factory. For its raw materials, Finnish manufacturing industry looks first to the forest. Timber processing, to one degree of refinement or another, accounts for the greatest output by value, though metallurgical and engineering industries claim a larger number of employees. The locations of the softwood industries are chiefly a reflection of either proximity to or accessibility to the gathering grounds of their raw materials. Easy large-scale water transport is still important. Softwood processing has its lowest rate of concentration in the south-west. Elsewhere, save in the province of Lappi, wood processing industries are widely scattered. The largest plants are located on the south shore of Lake Saimaa – with its Vuoksi river outlet (where the Lappeenranta–Vuoksenniska–Imatra area is one of Finland's centres of industrial growth); in the lower reaches of Kymi valley at the approaches to Kotka; and at the head of the Gulf of Bothnia around Oulu and Kemi.

In many areas, the softwood factory has developed into a complex of plants. In the interests of economy a diversity of processes is now frequently concentrated on one site. They may include saw-milling, pulp manufacture (usually either mechanical or chemical, rather than both), the production of several kinds of paper and the reduction of chemical by-products (especially alcohol). At the same time the company town or mill town has become a distinguishing feature of the countryside: in this, Finland resembles Canada, Norway and Sweden.

The wood processing industries blend old and new. Where old activities remain, new have been commonly grafted on to them. Several examples must suffice. First, the plywood and veneer plants, with their improved and diversified laminates, contribute new materials for the building and furniture industries. At the same time as Finland continues as the Old World's principal supplier of plywood, designers such as Tapio Wirkkala can employ its laminates for domestic and ornamental use to achieve laurels at international exhibitions. Secondly, large-scale pulp, paper and sawngood mills remain absolutely dominant, because they produce the principal commodities demanded by the export market. In general their products are only semi-finished, since importing countries (of which Britain is the largest) usually levy tariffs of varying severity upon more refined goods. In seeking ways of escape Finland has found in the wall-board industry a satisfying and remunerative activity to diversify its markets. Thirdly, familiar deal boards still move out of most of Finland's harbours, but sawn timber is also refined into a great range of products before export. For instance the reparations programme gave considerable impetus to the production of prefabricated houses. Houses for assembly are delivered from the factory and erected on their sites without the intermediacy of contractors – to Sweden as well as the home market. Pre-fabricated *saunas* have developed a world market since 1948. It is in keeping with modern Finland's concern with efficiency that both architect and manufacturer should look constantly at function and design. New ways of using old materials are constantly sought. The results may be seen in such contrasting structures as the monumental games hall at Otaniemi Technical Town outside Helsinki, its roof a forest of aesthetically dove-tailed timbers, and the range of cunningly devised utilitarian furniture. Nor can the use of laminates in ski manufacturing and pleasure-boat building be overlooked. Both yield exports in their own right. Such achievements are the logical extension of the 'wooden' culture preserved in Finnish folk museums.

The scale and variety of contemporary activities have had many implications. For example, shortage of softwood timber anticipates both the possibility of import and the substitution of hardwoods. Birchwood is already employed by the pulp industry. Again, large-scale manufacturing industry presumes an abundant supply of energy together with metallurgical and engineering industries capable of sustaining its needs. In addition, and because of Finland's geographical setting, it demands a greater frequency and regularity of shipping services.

The metallurgical industries, transformed in response to reparations and subsequently looking in part to contract orders from the U.S.S.R., also blend the traditional and the new. They are developed upon the bases of ore production of modest pretensions. The copper of Outokumpu, refined principally at Harjavalta, is the largest source. A roll call of Finnish mining sites – such as Orijärvi (lead), Nivala and Kotalahti (nickel), Mätäsvaara (molybdenum), Ylöjärvi (wolfram), Otanmäki (vanadium) – makes little impact on the outer world. Geological prospecting suggests that Finland has a diversity of minor ore bodies rather than major deposits. The mining of iron ore has proved uneconomic at Nynäs in Åland and Jussarö, off the south-west coast. Lapland's iron is currently worked on a small scale in the Torni and Kemi valleys. Together with ores from north Savo those of Lapland are oriented to Rautarukki, the site of the government-sponsored iron and steel plant outside Raahe. Rautarukki plant, comparable in size and function to those at Norway's Mo i Rana and Sweden's Luleå, employs 2,000 and has a capacity of 500,000 tons p.a. It is intended to meet the needs of a domestic market which is inadequately supplied by the existing group of small steel plants that rely upon imported ingots and scrap.

The blending of old and new is seen again in the transport industries. Increased supplies of steel are fundamental to the modernisation and extension of the railroad network. The old-established engineering workshops at Tampere have become the construction centre for diesel locomotives, railcars and increasingly varied rolling stock. The juxtaposition of old and new is even more striking in the shipbuilding wharves on the Aura at Turku and Hietalahti at Helsinki. Repair and conversion are complemented by a newly acquired specialisation in ship construction. Four particular examples may be mentioned. First, there are the trans-Baltic ferries that shuttle between Finland, Sweden, West Germany and Denmark. They are the pride of the Baltic fleet, carry a large summer tourist trade and bear an aura of prestige. Secondly, there is a fleet of cargo vessels which has been especially constructed to meet the needs of paper and pulp exporters. They ply throughout the year on services between Kotka and Hamina and the ports of western Europe. Thirdly, there are the icebreakers, constructed in the wharves of Helsinki and Turku, and already enjoying an international reputation. Since 1955 orders for vessels ranging from 10,000 to 35,000 h.p. have come from the U.S.S.R., West Germany, Sweden, and the U.S.A. Finnish icebreakers delivered to the U.S.S.R. operate in the Arctic as well as the Gulf of Finland. No country in the world has acquired more expertise in this work than Finland. Finally, Finland has been constructing large floating 'lodging houses', each capable of accommodating some hundreds of residents, for use on Russia's internal waterways. These very substantial Russian orders have frequently accounted for a high percentage of orders on the books of individual companies.

Against the background of domestic needs post-war Finland has evolved its own plants for the manufacture of agricultural machinery. Its experiences match those of Denmark and Sweden, and the size and cost of equipment has been scaled down to the needs of the smaller fields and more slender purses of the *talonpojat*. Long-established steel factories, such as those of Fiskars and Hackman, have added tableware and culinary ware to the barbed wire and day-to-day tools used in farm and garden.

The electro-technical industries, concentrated chiefly in the capital, where *Oy. Strömberg Ab.* (founded in 1889) is one of the largest single employers of labour, provide increasingly the equipment needed to produce electrical energy and the means for its nation-wide transmission. Since the middle 1950s considerable expertise has been acquired in the production and assembly of generators and transformers. A contributory factor to Finland's success in this field has been a long-standing interest in the processing of copper, especially for the manufacture of wires and cables. Copper is very much a national metal. It is imaginatively employed by architects – not merely for roofing, where the aesthetically 'weathered' green can be chemically induced, but as a facing for buildings. Designers fashion it anew into utensils, household equipment and ornaments – probably deriving some of their inspiration from the copper kettle, which is sacred to the brewing of Finland's national beverage.

Since 1944 development has been more fundamental and more diversified in the metallurgical sector of manufacturing than in any other. Because it provides the machinery for other industries, it has been basic to the conversion of Finland into an industrial state.

The transformation of other industries in which traditional machinery, tools and appliances are still employed springs from a reassessment of design and a reorientation of markets. While design is fundamental to all industries, it is especially critical for textiles, ceramics and glassware. It is the more critical if the producing plants are to acquire and maintain a fair size. In Tampere, Finland has Norden's largest textile city; in Riihimäki, it has a glassworks of a stature comparable to most of the leading Scandinavian plants; in Arabia, Helsinki claims Europe's largest porcelain factory. Imported cotton has been and remains the principal raw material for textiles, with domestic wool, flax and synthetic fibres ancillary to it. The fortunes of most branches of Finland's textile industry have fluctuated in the years since independence. Revival is owed principally to specialisation and to appealing design. For example, contemporary cotton fabrics compete successfully with those of the rest of Scandinavia and are not easy to distinguish from them. Again, the decline in demand for woollen clothing has been more than offset by the rise of an export market for the colourful new Finnish blankets; while a profitable ski-clothing industry has grown out of the necessity to make winter clothing.

Finland is learning much from its Scandinavian neighbours about the art of selling itself and its products. It is a far cry from the first industrial exhibition of 1876 to the full-time team of artists and organisers who deal professionally with displays for contemporary trade fairs.

With the growth in size of Finnish manufacturing complexes and the accumulation of organisational experience, Finland has also followed Sweden and Denmark into the international marketing of large-scale capital units. Entire power plants and smelting units, paper and pulp factories, sawmills and plywood units are exported and assembled in the country of purchase. Even trainee schemes for their operatives may be initiated. Finland has made its mark by the sale of copper smelters to Japan, India and Romania; pulp and paper plants to countries in Europe, Africa, south-east Asia and Latin America. In its own limited way, it has become very much a workshop of the world.

Industrial expansion and agricultural mechanisation have only been possible with the introduction of new forms of energy. Since the days when running water and wind were superseded by steam, Finland has suffered shortages of energy. Deficiencies in wood fuel were first made good by imported coal, principally from Germany and Great Britain. With the development of hydro-electricity Finland's power budget was more satisfactorily balanced, though only by the establishment of a multiplicity of relatively small-scale plants, since Finland lacks large-scale sites. The immediate post-war years found

Finland with a greatly increased demand for energy and manifold supply problems. They sprang from the loss of plant and of power sites to the U.S.S.R. in the Vuoksi valley, from obsolescent equipment, and in any case from a fundamental deficiency of power stations. Within twenty years the character of Finnish energy production was completely transformed.

Transformation was rooted first in a number of major integrated hydro-electric power schemes. A veritable *koskensota*, or battle for water-power sites, broke out between rival power companies. The complete development of Oulu river power enabled north Finland to redress energy losses in Karelia. The Kemi river system, which is the richest source of hydro-electric energy in Finland, is the subject of integrated development embracing more than a score of sites. The border rivers with Sweden, Tornijoki and Konkamajoki, are the only significant Finnish watercourses lacking development. As with Sweden, Finland's principal surplus hydro-electric supplies are in the northern half of the country: its principal seats of demand in the southern third. Increasingly efficient long-distance transmission and a national grid help to remedy the defect.

Yet Finland cannot aspire to independence in energy production. Only a half of its needs derive from water turbines. Indeed, the more the modern industrial state with its associated high living standards is manifest, the more the deficiency is apparent. In the second place its situation has been transformed through the large-scale production of thermal energy. Coal is widely employed with Poland as a leading source of supply; but an increasing part of modern Finland's energy derives from oil-fired electricity plants. The larger of these are concentrated in the south-west. During the twenty years following 1945 electricity consumption increased by more than fivefold, representing a growth rate of more than 8 per cent annually.

The nature of the market gives rise to two particular difficulties. First there is a widely varying seasonal rate of demand, with a midwinter peak and a midsummer trough, when holidays as well as daylight and temperature reduce demand. This means that an approximate 30 per cent excess power capacity above the minimum must be maintained. Secondly, although electrification of the countryside as with the rest of Norden is virtually complete, the dispersal of settlement and of activity in the north-eastern two-thirds of the country makes for correspondingly high distribution costs.

In the same way as the rising domestic demand for steel has made it feasible to establish a large steel plant, so the expanding demand for oil and oil products has made it economic to build refineries. Finland's two principal refineries are located at Naantali near Turku and Stensund near Porvoo. The increasing use of oil introduces new physical, as well as economic and political, problems. Among them is the need for storage, because supplies can be interrupted by the winter closure of shipping routes. The logbooks of tankers bringing supplies to the ice-beleaguered coast of Finland in the late winter of 1965–66 recorded Arctic or Antarctic experiences rather than European. Economically oil imports play a powerful role in the balance of payments. Fuels, principally oil and oil products, account for a tenth of Finland's imports by value. Politically, the sources of supply are sensitive. Much of Finland's oil comes from the U.S.S.R., which now has a Black Sea–Baltic pipeline with a terminal at Liepaja in the Lithuanian S.S.R.

Bearing in mind the new dependence that Finland has upon imported oil and not forgetting the pressures of forest economists to reduce the continuingly heavy consumption of wood fuel, it is not surprising that Finland should toy with atomic power as a source of energy. A power station, to be located at Loviisa, is scheduled to begin operations in 1972, and a second plant may possibly be located at Kotka. It has also been suggested that a pipeline for natural gas imports from the U.S.S.R. might be built.

The changing structure of industry and its new international relationships have entailed changes in organisation. Thus, there has been widespread linkage and integration between industrial concerns, with strategic consortiums which enable the pooling of capital for major enterprises. *Oy. Värtsilä Ab.* and *Oy. Rauma-Repola Ab.* provide illustrations of these ramifications. *Värtsilä* takes its name from the small Karelian town where it had its origins in a mechanical workshop. Its tentacles now stretch far beyond the metallurgical pursuits that were its original interest and which are continued in its small Kotka factory (*c.* 200 employees) into the realms of shipbuilding and ceramics. They embrace Finland's two largest shipbuilding wharves – in Helsinki (*c.* 1,400 employees) and Turku (*c.* 4,000), workshops in Kokkola (*c.* 800), Vaasa (*c.* 500) and Dalsbruk (*c.* 800); the Arabia ceramic plant (*c.* 1,400), Turku porcelain factory (*c.* 200) and Nuutajärvi glassworks (*c.* 200). *Värtsilä* is also a member of one of Finland's private atomic energy consortiums. *Rauma-Repola* shows the same integrating tendencies. It is Europe's largest producer and exporter of sawn goods, has industrial enterprises in fifteen different places and employs a labour force of about 8,000. To its original softwood factories have been added metallurgical establishments. These have developed on a sufficient scale for *Rauma-Repola* to compete in the world market for the sale of entire softwood processing plants. At the same time, the company has expanded its shipbuilding yards to meet a substantial Russian market for small tankers and barges.

In the promotion, distribution and maintenance of Finnish industry the state continues to play a critical role. As the principal source of capital accumulation for investment, its influence is felt both directly and indirectly. For example, it is directly concerned with the location of new industrial plants. The decisions in the 1960s to establish an iron and steel plant near Raahe and subsequently a softwood mill in Kemijärvi are typical. An example of indirect control may be found in the decisions about the State Railways, the changing network of which automatically affects the fortunes and siting of industrial enterprises. The state-owned energy company, *Imatra Voima Oy.*, has been behind the development of the Kemi river system. It has also entered into vigorous competition with private power consortiums over the provision and location of atomic energy plants. As in the rest of Norden, the Finnish state has invested widely in the shares of private industrial companies so that it may have strong voting powers in their boardrooms. Its indirect control is also exerted through the National Bank of Finland, which in turn plays a decisive part in the negotiation of the international loans that are increasingly the life blood of Finnish development. Given this situation, decisions upon industrial developments may be the result of political rather than of economic argument. For example, the government considers direct foreign investment inadvisable in the forest and mining industries – this because of the limited nature of Finland's raw material basis.

The growth in size of the more successful industrial and commercial units prompts anxious enquiry about the size and scale of operations in other areas of activity. In addition to agriculture, local government is an area where structural reorganisation appears to be urgent. There are large numbers of rural communes the efficiency of which is hampered by population deficiency (and correspondingly limited financial resources), by geographical size and by physical shape. The average size of communes has tended to diminish over the last half-century. So has the total population inhabiting communes in the range of 2,000–4,000 inhabitants. In Sweden there has been widespread reform of local government areas, especially with a view to the more effective grouping of population within them. The Swedish example of inter-communal grouping for particular purposes has done much to direct Finnish attention to a developing defect in its local government structure. At the same time, inter-communal grouping is intended to employ more efficiently the 55,000 local government officers employed in their administration.

Inequalities of Opportunity

Both the physical circumstances of Finland and the course of its historical evolution make for inherent regional differences of opportunity. The differences have been exaggerated rather than relieved by the rise of industry and associated urbanisation. As a result three economic regions have emerged – a developed south-western corner, an under-developed northern and eastern third, and an intermediary transitional zone. The principal criterion for identifying them is population distribution. For Finland at large it is 14 per square kilometre; for the south-western quarter it rises to fifty; for the north-eastern third it falls below five. Ilmari Hustich has shown how population concentrates increasingly in the south-western corner. In the late nineteenth century, half of the country's population was settled in the south-western third; today, half is concentrated in the south-western quarter. It occupies that part of peninsular Finland defined by a line linking Pori, Tampere, Lahti and Kotka. The concentration is pronouncedly coastal. Finland's population drift to the south-west is the counterpart of Norway's drift to the south and Britain's drift to the south-east. It is a drift to the most pivotal part of the country so far as external relations are concerned.

Income levels repeat the regional variations in opportunity. Detailed studies on a commune basis by Lars Wahlbeck and Kai Palmgren indicate a further close correlation between income levels, percentage of inhabitants with a secondary school background and percentage of employees engaged in service industries. All add up to fundamental differences in the standard of living. And the effects are cumulative, with the pace of development of rather more than 200 communes located in the north and east, falling behind that of the leaders in the south-west.

By almost any set of criteria, Finland has an extensive underdeveloped area in the north and east. Appreciation of the declining gradient of opportunity from south-west to north-east has been sharpened as a result of the greater mobility of population. Attitudes to the situation range widely. The spectrum of opinion among the northerners extends from those who wish to preserve their isolation to those who actively encourage southern developers. Most are jealous of the manner in which developers appear to intrude upon their countryside and to extract its raw materials for their benefit. At the same time all are aware of the subsidies that aid their daily lives and there is steady political pressure to increase them. Among those who live outside the under-developed areas, most would admit that the economy of the north country must be underwritten. It is the amount allocated and the manner in which it is used that occasion argument. It is theoretically arguable that there is disproportionate investment in the provinces of Lappi and Oulu, since returns from much of it are likely to be lower than if corresponding sums were invested in other parts of Finland. Certainly much of the capital channelled into north Finnish investment looks to long-term rather than to short-term returns.

All of these arguments are supplemented by those of social desirability and political expediency. It is socially desirable that there should not be two nations in Finland – a richer south and a poorer north. It is politically expedient that the northerners should not suffer resentment towards the south. A scattered population living on the margins of authority inclines to display centrifugal tendencies. In addition many northerners are of radical persuasion. Voting patterns for the country display strong S.K.D.L. support in the rural areas of Lappi and Oulu.

There are additional problems. Among them is the administrative identification of the areas needing support. For better or for worse, commune boundaries tend to become the ultimate lines of division. Because of their arbitrary character they cannot fail to cause local – even regional – dissatisfaction. Sometimes there are indirect attempts at appeasement. Thus, north Savo and Kainu, adjacent to the inner reaches of the province of Oulu, have been given government assistance to establish softwood factories in order to diversify their predominantly farming economy. Within the north country, agricultural and transport subsidies are supplemented by adjustments to the salaries of civil servants and teachers. Additional emoluments to encourage and sustain recruitment take two forms – first, a general payment to compensate for the extra costs of combating the northern winter; secondly, specific payments in which criteria of isolation are employed.

The province of Lappi is isolated from the centres of control in Finland in the same way as the *fylker* of Finnmark and Troms and the *län* of Norrbotten are isolated from the heartlands of Norway and Sweden respectively. Collectively these four provinces form the core of a region known as *Nord Kalotten*. While Lapland is a concept that makes an impact upon the outer world out of all proportion to its real meaning, *Nord Kalotten* is still largely unknown. Yet the common interests and problems of its constituent parts give to them a community of feeling that has practical expression in the meetings of administrators and other groups directly concerned with high-latitude living.

Although there is a general drift of population from north to south, there is a lively short-term movement of Finns into the north country. But most Finns who visit the sub-Arctic third of their land are bent on pleasure rather than work. The northern fells have become a virtual year-round playground for many of the coastal fringe of city dwellers, and they have a more powerful appeal for the inhabitants of metropolitan Finland than the Scottish highlands for those of metropolitan England. The north country also has appeal as a great nature reserve. It contains extended protected areas – from the Pallastunturi national park on the Swedish borders to those on the Russian border which embrace the impressive gorges of Pitkäjoki and Oulankajoki. Summer tourist hotels are converted seasonally into winter resorts. Even the twilight weeks of midwinter have been converted into a tourist attraction. The northern third is the only part of Finland where there are significant elevations for ski-ing, and it is only in the fells of Lappi that obstructing tree vegetation yields to the low flora of the tundra. Centres such as Rukkatunturi and Kilpisjärvi are expressive of new demands for recreation but they also illustrate the new opportunities of the northland. Around them the antique and the modern join hands: the ski, which is the oldest aid to locomotion, meets the snowmobile and snowscooter.

The transient tourist is also juxtaposed with the persistent Lapp in the north country. Nine-tenths of the Lapp population live in Norway and Sweden, where the intrusion of the commercial upon their subsistence economy has had a more profound impact. As with Norway and Sweden, Finland has identified a *Same alue*, or Lapp territory, which is precisely mapped and ostensibly preserved for domesticated reindeer. There are about 150,000 reindeer in Finland and grazing grounds are probably over-stocked. In spite of these large herds, less than a tenth of the Lapps engage in the traditional husbandry. Most have settled down to a sedentary existence on holdings which, although marginal, enable them to escape the growing conflict between reindeer husbandry and the interests of water power, forestry and mining organisations. Yet at the same time as opportunities are restricted in one direction, they are broadened in others. For example, helicopters may be brought in from the army to help in the hunt against marauding wolves, while sausage machines in cooperatively owned slaughteries may diversify the marketable products of the reindeer. The commercialisation of his economy drains something of the colour from the life of the Lapp – not least in his substitution of factory-made, scientifically devised clothing for traditional garments.

The differential in development is not restricted to contrasts between the south-west and the north-east. The rise of opportunity has not been uniform throughout the south-west. The attractions of peninsular Finland have been no less powerful for the inhabitants of its adjacent archipelagos. In former times Finland's offshore islands were regarded as some of its most favoured settlement areas. The archipelagos of Åland and Turunmaa (Åboland) enjoy the mildest climate of any part of Finland and have fishing to supplement farming. Settlement was still expanding in them within living memory. Testimony is found in the substantial late-nineteenth-century farmhouses, with their associated land taxation documents, on the outer skerries of Saltvik and Eckerö. Both the pull of urban life and the lack of amenities in the islands have prompted depopulation and farm abandonment. In order to check migration both direct and indirect measures have been taken. Clearly the costs of educational, medical, electricity, telephone and steamer services cannot be borne by the local communities. The extent to which they should be underwritten is a constant matter for debate, especially when there are potential new users of deserted homesteads who demand no subsidies. For the retreat of permanent residents from the islands is counterbalanced by the advance of summer visitors to them. Opportunities for farming may have declined but those for holiday-making have been enhanced. Since the war the motor boat has been brought within the reach of a large proportion of the Finnish population. It has transformed summer access to the islands and also brought a seasonal migration from Sweden.

Industrialisation and urbanisation have introduced new problems of resource distribution. Ironically enough fresh water figures among them. In the context of the modern economy the Finnish lakes are not where they are wanted. Thus some of the country's major population centres lack satisfactory water resources. Helsinki is among them. With the waters of the Gulf of Finland everywhere in sight around its fretted seaboard, inhabitants of the capital might well repeat the Ancient Mariner's lament – especially in dry summers, when the Vanda river runs low and the chlorine content of drinking water is increased. Turku, too, has intermittent reason for remembering the comment of a Finnish humorist that Finland has many lakes but little water. The situation around the coastal plains is aggravated by regional and local problems of water balance which result from the lowering of water tables through drainage schemes. Water pollution seriously reduces the number of lakes that might otherwise be considered for reservoirs. Paradoxically, Finns are creating new lakes. Fresh-water bodies are being established behind coastal barrages at Larsmo and Uusikaupunki. The largest artificial lakes are being constructed in the swampy Lapland fells at Porttipahta and Lokka to regulate the flow of the Kemi river and its tributaries.

The fact that so many problems arise from maldistribution of opportunity is in itself an indication of the advanced stage of development of the Finnish economy. Solutions call for increasingly detailed surveys (from the speedier mapping of critical land surfaces by photogrammetric methods to the computerisation of statistics), for the presentation of results in a significant and readily assimilable form, and for the formulation of plans of action. With such plans in mind Finland's diverse scientific institutes were integrated in 1961 into six research councils, each with a chairman directly appointed by the President. The object of the councils that grapple with these inherent problems is to increase the efficiency of the country. At the same time they help to create a new climate of security.

A Climate of Security

In the 1880s the Finnish philosopher Hjalmar Neiglick wrote to K. A. Tavastjerna that the Finns are 'a people whose geographical setting is abominable and whose situation on the cultural map is even more so'. A direct consequence has been the climate of insecurity in which the nation has been reared. This cannot be eliminated but its effects can be eased. The means for creating greater physical security were never more abundant than today. First, technical invention has enabled a buffer to be set between the Finn and his physical environment. Secondly, the revolution in communications has transformed the speed of diffusion of cultural ideas and processes. Thirdly, Finland's political integration with the neighbouring countries of Norden and with Russia has never been fuller.

Technical invention cannot alter Finland's setting in space or change its climate, but it makes for infinitely greater tolerance of it and manoeuvrability within it. The challenge of high-latitude living has been met. It has been achieved principally through new forms of creating, distributing and conserving energy. There is, theoretically, a ubiquity of energy for heating and lighting in modern Finland. It is a measure of material progress that demand for it increases at about 8–9 per cent annually. A proportion of the increase is met by greater efficiency in production, distribution and conservation. New building methods, such as the widespread employment of double – even treble – glass, reduce heat loss. Side by side with mechanically produced energy, improved calorie intake has transformed personal energy. Under-nourishment has been completely overcome. In the face of shop windows, crowded with the products of the world, it is difficult to realise that, within the span of a human life, Finland has suffered major famines.

One consequence of the new forces of energy that have been released is to reduce the impact of seasonal change upon economy and society. Generally speaking, the closer the Finn lives to and works with nature, the more pronounced the rhythm of seasonal adjustment. The transfer of labour from primary production to manufacturing industry and to service activities has eased seasonal unemployment and under-employment. Old-established rhythms remain in forestry and farming, but in other industries sensitive formerly to climatic conditions they have been substantially reduced. Building and constructional work are now lively throughout the winter thanks to new technical devices and to regional and seasonal subsidies aimed at arresting unemployment. Technical devices include the employment of quick-drying cements and the creation of artificial climates around constructional sites. In the struggle against low temperatures, hot-air machines operate in buildings which may be swathed in their entirety in plastic or paper sheeting.

Additional building costs attributable to winter conditions may amount to a quarter above the normal. In higher latitudes the provision of lighting is important. To stimulate demand for labour in winter, public works programmes have become an accepted part of national policy. Building schemes qualify for special subsidies according to the months in which they are initiated – as early as August in the northern third of Finland: October, in the southern third.

Simultaneously the impact of winter has been reduced in the field of transport. Although it imposes its own special tax through the national budget, winter maintenance of highways with the aid of snow ploughs, scrapers and sanding machines is an easy matter. Finland's main highways are now negotiable throughout all winters. The same applies to rail traffic, so that overland transport schedules differ little in winter and summer. Locally, communications are subject to disturbance at the time of the thaw, but its impact has been dramatically reduced in the course of the last decade. With the introduction of new methods of road-making and surfacing, the effects of frost upheaval are limited to second- and third-class roads. At sea shipping schedules from the inner reaches of the Bothnian Gulf are seasonally interrupted, but the period during which harbours are accessible has been extended by weeks with the aid of icebreakers, ice-strengthened ships and ice forecasting. Most of the ports in metropolitan Finland – from Pori on the Gulf of Bothnia to Kotka on the Gulf of Finland – are kept open throughout the winter. As regular sailings of freight vessels have been guaranteed, problems of stock-piling and storage have diminished. For example, the statistics of paper and pulp exports show an even pattern throughout the year, in contrast to the pronounced seasonal variations that prevailed as recently as the middle 1950s. Passenger ferries are also guaranteed daily winter services to Sweden. Indeed the uncertainty of continuous winter shipping connections has been lifted out of a physical into a human context. By withdrawing labour from the icebreaker service, the seamen's union can close shipping lanes.

The mobilisation of energy has been especially critical for the rapid rise of urban areas. These are expressive of an almost American mobility of population as well as a rapid growth of population. Almost a million people, about a quarter of Finland's total, shifted their place of residence in the twenty years following the war. This new nomadism, as Ilmari Hustich calls it, is the more striking because of the centuries old immobility of the Finnish population. Movement to the town anticipates social instabilities. On the other hand and in contrast to many countries, the town appears to offer a secure retreat in a naturally hazardous environment. This seeming security is reinforced by the increasingly cosmopolitan air of most Finnish urban settlements. From the metropolitan south to the sub-Arctic north, they offer identical services and amenities to those provided in the towns of the rest of western Europe.

At the same time as migration to town and urban district continues, a greater degree of security is being diffused throughout the farming settlements. It is not only the greater certainty of returns born of easier communications, mechanical equipment, guaranteed prices, from improved crops (speedier ripening grains, for example) and stock (sturdier and more disease resistant animals). It is the new sense of security deriving from insurance schemes – among them, the introduction of compensation for frost damage. Frost damage is not restricted to spring and autumn hazards for summer frosts can be a widespread scourge, as in 1952 and 1956.

Meanwhile, schemes of social insurance have been broadened and deepened. The Acts covering national pensions in 1939, children's allowances, compulsory pension insurance and health insurance in 1964, are basic to the structure. The development of social insurance has been urged forward with especial vigour since the middle 1950s. It is inseparable from the tightening web of relations with the other countries of Norden; for the Scandinavians in general – and Sweden, in particular – have been pacemakers in many aspects of social security.

The most powerful impulse came with the establishment of the common labour market in 1954. Adherence to this led to generous transfers of Finnish labour to Sweden through the labour exchanges. There are probably about 100,000 Finns in Sweden – half of whom have entered formally as immigrants (many of whom, in turn, have been naturalised) and half of whom have moved on shorter-term contracts. The temporary migrants include a high proportion of Ålanders and Ostrobothnians. There are also old-established communities of Finnish-speaking people in Swedish Norrbotten, adjacent to Finland's north-west frontier. Complementary to the common labour market is a social security convention. Among its basic provisions are the payment of contributions and the receipt of unemployment benefits in accordance with the conditions prevailing in the insured person's place of work and residence. Because there is not complete identity in the social insurance payments and benefits throughout the countries of Norden, the convention makes provision for the benefits of the social security schemes available in the country of residence. Thus for Finnish nationals working in other countries of Norden, the host country meets the bill; for Scandinavians working in Finland, the Finnish state bears the ultimate financial responsibility.

The principle of reciprocity has further extensions. For example, compensation for permanent injury or to the next of kin in the event of fatal accident are payable by the host country. Medical expenses, including hospital charges required by members of the community of Norden visiting each other's countries, are similarly accommodated. In the north especially, hospital patients are taken to the nearest place of treatment regardless of frontiers. Under the health service consultations may take place and second opinions may be obtained across national borders. The near identity of Finnish medical training, the acceptance of Finnish medical qualifications in the other countries of Norden, the existence of a common pharmacopoeia, the standardisation of medical appliances, the existence since 1963 of a joint public health college at Göteborg in Sweden are further illustrations of the high degree of health security in which Finland shares. Finland is also a part of the single Scandinavian quarantine unit.

All these measures imply the existence and extension of a large body of similar laws. Finland's common legal tradition with Sweden and its long association with the conference of Scandinavian lawyers have facilitated the coordination of legislation made necessary by the social security programme. It shares increasingly in the jointly developed civil and criminal codes. In the civil field, for example, it has adopted the law of copyright and patents agreed by the other four countries. In the arrest and punishment of criminals, there is a large area of common practice. For example, a Finnish national may be extradited for a crime committed in one of the other countries of Norden – and vice versa. Again, a Finnish national who has committed a crime in one of the other countries of Norden may choose to serve his sentence in his home country. While the area of common legal practice broadens, there remain narrower fields which still lack uniformity. Thus, although intoxicated drivers are strictly punished – and the extension of Finland's airfields and highways owes much to their corrective labours – they are neither so severely tested nor so rigorously treated as, for example, in Sweden.

Finland shares unrestrainedly in all forms of Scandinavian cultural cooperation. The proliferation of inter-Nordic conferences held by professional and artistic bodies broadens the perspectives of Finnish life. At the same time it reduces misunderstanding and fosters similar standards. At the elementary school level, for example, Finland shared in the revision of textbooks and accepted the common Nordic interpretation of controversial matters. In the field of higher education it shares a common university entrance qualification and has coordinated its faculty requirements with those of other universities in Norden. Doctoral disputations call for interchange of examiners: appointments to university chairs, for the opinions of experts drawn from a pool of Nordic professors. Collaboration over the maintenance of standards becomes the more important as universities multiply. New Finnish universities include Jyväskyla (which was elevated to university status from a pedagogical institute), Oulu and institutes of university standing such as the School of Social Sciences in Tampere. Finland also shares in the new inter-Nordic research institutes and a joint Institute of Medical Science is attached to the University of Oulu. Yet, despite so much progress, student problems persist. Formerly, the school leaving examination guaranteed immediate entry to university: today most departments declare a *numerus clausus*. There are 40,000 university students, but pressure for additional places is strong enough to urge the establishment of new faculties in eastern Finland where the rival claims of Joensuu, Mikkeli, Kuopio, Savonlinna and Lappeenranta are hotly debated.

Closer association with the Nordic community is one among a number of factors which have reduced tensions in the language issue. Earlier emotional attitudes are succeeded by an increasingly rational approach. This is expressed in the codification of language practices. The Languages Act of 1962 identified unilingual and bilingual municipalities. A commune is defined as bilingual when at least ten per cent of the population employs the second language. The issue still remains sensitive in certain fields of activity, for example in appointment of local government officers whose language qualifications are the subject of special civil service regulations. Because of the high mobility of the Finnish population, language conditions are increasingly unstable. Accordingly, the Languages Act makes provision for a ten-yearly review of municipalities based upon census returns. In order to protect minorities fundamental changes in local language requirements do not take place immediately the threshold figure of ten per cent is reached. Thus a bilingual commune is not classified as unilingual unless the second language falls to at least 8 per cent, while a unilingual commune is not reclassified as bilingual unless the figure rises to at least 12 per cent. Certain cities are treated as exceptions. According to the criteria of the Languages Act, Helsinki, Turku and Vaasa are Finnish-speaking; but, because each has a large Swedish-speaking population and because each is in more direct contact with the rest of Scandinavia than most Finnish cities, it is agreed that they should remain bilingual. In addition it is argued that all three cities are the provincial capitals of administrative provinces which contain large Swedish-speaking minorities. The language status of the municipalities will be subject to review in 1972. At present 456 communes are listed as Finnish-speaking; forty-four as Swedish-speaking; forty-four as bilingual with a Swedish-speaking majority; and thirteen as bilingual with a Finnish-speaking majority.

The fact that Finland shares so fully in the Nordic network of professional and personal relations suggests at the same time a growing Russian tolerance. Without the slow movement forward from the compulsion of the reparations, through the ensuing sensitive (and for the Finnish economy often critical) trade agreements, through the pressures of the 'cold war' to a phase of relaxation, it would be difficult to write of a climate of security. The absolute volume of Finnish business conducted with Russia has never been greater in the history of the two countries. The share of the U.S.S.R. in the total exchange has averaged more than a sixth since 1944. All forms of exchange aid understanding; direct cooperation has an even greater potential.

For this reason enterprises such as the joint construction of the Ylä-Tuloma power station by the Imatra Power Company and the Soviet Teknopromeksport, and the joint Fenno-Soviet reconstruction of Saimaa canal have more than commercial significance. The Tuloma plant lies some 45 miles from Murmansk and a community of hundreds of Finnish engineers and workmen was established on the site after 1961. The work was completed in 1966. In November 1966 a special Finnish-Soviet Commission for Economic Cooperation was established.

The Saimaa canal, bisected by the new Karelian frontier, has been derelict and unused since the war. The Russian sector has now been leased to the Finnish state, which is responsible for its total restoration. The canal is 57 km. long and mostly in Russian territory. It has been deepened and improved by a labour force of 2,500 Finns and 1,200 Russians to accommodate seagoing craft loading up to 1,600 d.w.t. Harbour facilities are also available at Malyi Vysorskij (formerly Uuras) on Viipuri bay. In pre-war years about a million tons of shipping used the canal during the six months of open water. Following Finland's territorial losses in the south-east, highways were constructed to provide alternative outlets for softwood products from Saimaa shore to the harbours of Kotka and Hamina. Hamina, alone, deals with a tonnage equal to that carried on the pre-war Saimaa canal. The reopening of the canal will naturally affect the hinterlands of eastern Finland's two principal export harbours. Moreover, Kotka is now a virtual all-year harbour and icebreakers could do little to keep open a winter harbour on Viipuri bay. The restoration of the canal has been an expensive project, but the returns have to be assessed in terms of good neighbourliness as well as hard cash. It is a broad highway joining east and west – among those cooperative ventures that help Finland to absorb the intermittent bewilderment that springs from the unpredictability of Russian moves and motives.

Among the consequences of the greater atmosphere of security two may be mentioned – the development of a more expansive approach to living and the emergence of a greater sense of national assurance.

An aspect of the former is displayed in the increased international mobility of Finnish people. In the immediate post-war years movement abroad was not without an echo from earlier times of stress and there was an element of escape in it that was common to Europe. The stream of emigration continues for all sorts of reasons of attraction and propulsion. New worlds still beckon and North America attracts Finland's scientists and technicians no less than those of other European countries. But the volume of emigration has dwindled. At the same time, the stream of Finnish visitors abroad has become a torrent. Finns are clearly making up for lost time: for them, the going was never so good. Sufficient wealth has been accumulated for most ordinary people to give high priority in their spending to foreign travel. Nor are the operators of Finland's effective and dense domestic air network slow to encourage the movement. To follow the migratory birds to the legendary Finnish *lintukoti* on the shores of the Mediterranean or to escape the refrigerated north for the flaming poinsettias and waving banana palms of the Atlantic's fortunate isles is no longer the prerogative of the rich: nor is the shopping trip to Stockholm. Leningrad is only a bus ride away and Tallinn a four-hour steamer trip across the summer Baltic.

To balance the thousands bent on pleasure, a minority move abroad for study. Languages are vital to the Finn. Russian has little appeal, even among members of the S.K.D.L. English, which is also American, and German are most sought after. Thousands of Finnish girls seek *au pair* or similar posts in Britain and Germany with the doubtful motive of improving their languages. Expectations are not always fulfilled, partly because the 'dear octopus' of the Finnish family rarely releases its grip and wanderers are notoriously prone to homesickness. Each year some scores of students have reason to remember the generosity of the United States Advisory Commission on Educational Exchange which recommended in 1949 that Finnish payments on the debt incurred during the First World War be used to provide stipendia for study in the U.S.A. Finnish students also benefit from the Fulbright programme which was extended to Finland in 1952. While exchange restrictions are a minor tribulation for most Europeans, the Finnish government – although it may live upon the razor's edge of financial crises – maintains a generous attitude to foreign travel. In the national budget the balance of the tourist trade strikes a negative note – expenditure is usually twice as much as income.

The emergence of a greater feeling of national security is also closely related to the growing international role that Finland plays. It need no longer suffer from a small power complex or that of a state newly admitted to the comity of nations. So many scores of states have been born during Finland's fifty years of independence that by comparison it must be classified among the middle-aged. Furthermore, with a *per capita* gross national product which places it fifteenth in order of world status, the country becomes a model for others to follow. Its sense of achievement was further strengthened through entry to the United Nations in 1955. Finland had already benefited from and contributed to the United Nations Commission for technical assistance since 1949. Its contribution to the peace-keeping forces of Suez (1956), Lebanon (1961), Kashmir (1961) and Cyprus (1964) have added substantially to what Zachris Topelius called its balance in 'the credit book of the centuries'.

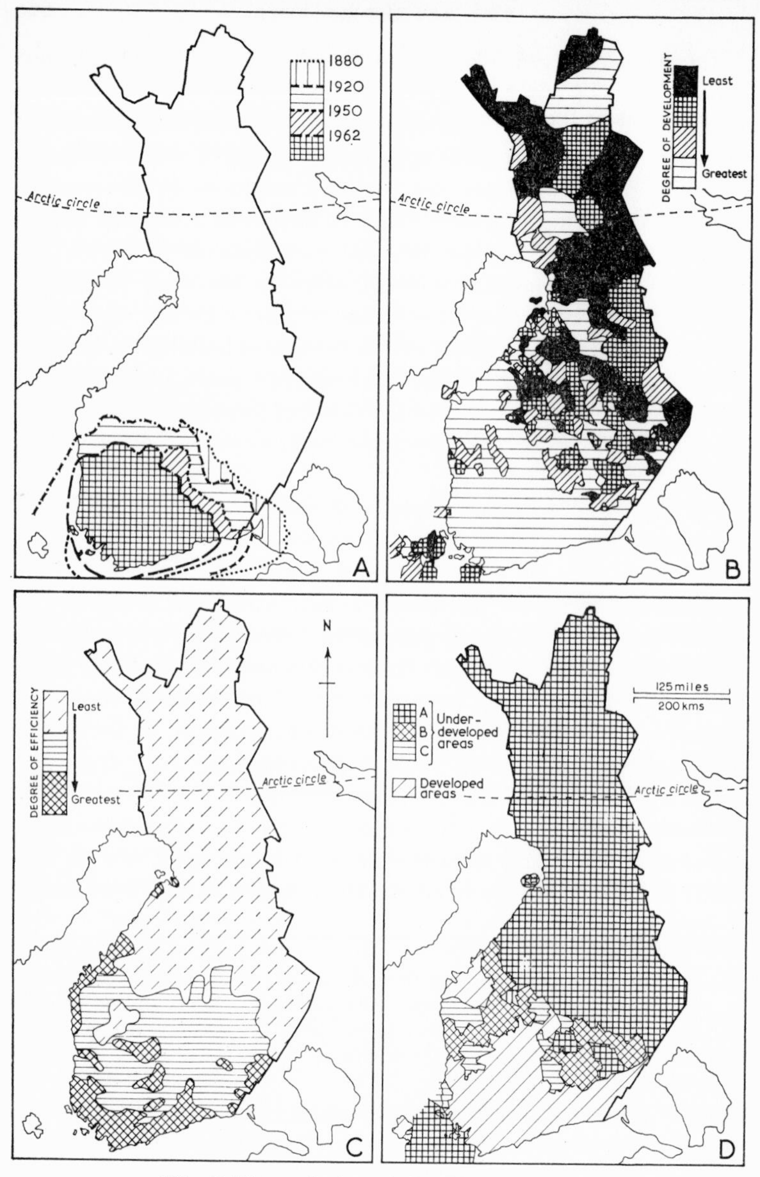

4. The Differentiation of the Finnish Economy

The four distribution maps show:

A The increasing concentration of Finland's population in the south-western third of the country. The shaded area indicates the area occupied by half of the total population (based on I. Hustich, *Finland förvandlas*, Helsinki, 1967).

Involvement in peace-keeping at the international level has turned the attention of some investigators to the nature and consequences of social friction inside Finland. It is clear that the maximisation of economic efficiency depends upon the reduction of social friction to a minimum. In analysing the regional variations in efficiency in contemporary Finnish society Olavi Riihinen has attempted to produce a formula which can be used as a national yardstick. His weighted criteria include such variables as the total population between 15–64 years of age, migration, *per capita* income, unemployment, expansiveness (as illustrated by the rate of building production) and availability of services. His conclusions are given a broad expression in Map 4; but, set against the detail of local government units, they help to focus attention upon the inefficient areas in the modern state.

All of these practical examples of Finland's search for efficiency, ingenious attempts at accommodation with its physical circumstance, cooperation with its neighbours and helpful contributions to the international scene, are interpreted as significant signs of stability by outside governments and organisations. These signs are of fundamental importance in another context. Finland is increasingly sensitive to the international long-term capital market and borrowing abroad is of growing importance for its development. At the end of 1966, among loans from foreign governments, those from the U.S.S.R., Sweden and the U.S.A. predominated. Two distinct types of loans additional to government credits are identified – state-guaranteed bonds and privately arranged investments. Among Finland's half dozen leading bonds are those floated in New York by the

---

B The differences in the degree of Finland's economic development as recognised by K. Palmgren. The information is drawn on the framework of communes, refers to the period 1955–60, and employs eighteen criteria (based on *Publications of the National Planning Bureau*, A. 15, Helsinki, 1964).

C The differences in efficiency in Finland calculated according to a group of economic and social criteria selected by O. Riihinen (simplified from *Teollistuvan yhteiskunnan allueellinen erilaistuneisuus*, Kuopio, 1965).

D The underdeveloped areas of Finland as identified by the Finnish government in 1966. A=underdeveloped areas as identified by the Miettunen committee in 1964. B=underdeveloped areas added by a government recommendation in 1965.

city of Helsinki in 1966 and the guaranteed bonds issued by the republic for European subscription in 1967. In 1966 large-scale private loans were made by American investors to *Kesko Oy.*, Pargas (Parainen) Cement Company, and the engineering company Rauma-Repola; by British and German investors jointly to the *Enso-Gutzeit* Company (Finland's largest), and by Swiss investors to *Huhtamäki-Yhtymä* of Turku. British credits were extended to Tampella of Tampere and to the United Paper Mills in 1967. Investment by outside nations is more than an expression of confidence in Finland. It is an expression of confidence in Finland's positive association with the U.S.S.R. The expansion of the Russian market, the size of Finland's trade with it and the proximity of Finnish industries to it are all inherent in the decisions of investors.

Processes of Re-appraisal

Changes in the economy and status of Finland have a growing impact upon attitudes to established institutions, to historical events and to national figures. All are subject to vigorous debate and re-assessment. Such processes are inherent in the conflict between the generations; but in the case of Finland they are inseparable from the degree of relative security in which many who debate them have been raised. There may have been tensions to disturb the adult world since 1944, but for the first time in the twentieth century, there has emerged a generation of young people who have not suffered the direct experience of a time of tribulation. Discussion takes place at a popular as well as an academic level; in detail and at large.

It is expressed first in changing attitudes towards the work and status of the 'founding fathers'. These attitudes are rooted in the discovery of new evidence as well as in shifting fashions. They are also based upon a broadening range of international experience and knowledge. Examples are manifold. Some discredit Elias Lönnrot's *Kalevala* for its synthetic character and misuse of the rich raw materials collected by its compiler. Others are opposed to the status accorded to the endeavours of the mid-nineteenth-century publicist I. W. Arwidsson. Some would put the neglected philologist P. A. Sjögren on a pedestal at least as high as that occupied by the enthnographer M. A. Castrén. Others would shift Johan Ludvig Runeberg from his plinth in the sunny centre of the Esplanade gardens in Helsinki. They would replace him with Finland's greatest bohemian, Eino Leino, who stands in nearby shade courted by the representatives of the beat generation. Some have their doubts about the hierarchy of bronze presidents who stand ranged before the classical façade of the Parliament House. Others would reduce the status of Marshal Mannerheim – 'half royal, half godhead', as Lady Diana Cooper described him. He is certainly one of Finland's enigmas. But the heroes of all countries come under intermittent scrutiny: it is a part of the risk that springs from living in high places. Usually they are secure in their seats for they are veteran campaigners and have emerged victorious from more formidable adversaries. There is even a renewing quality about some of them. The inspiration of Sibelius, for example, has produced in Eila Hiltunen's monumental 'cascade of sound' a memorial of unique merit.

In the second place the ferment of opinion froths around events. Nothing occasions livelier interest than the Civil War, defined with diminishing frequency as the War of Independence. The conflict can no longer be looked upon as the swirl of a wave on the margins of the maelström that engulfed St Petersburg. The search for disengagement from the emotions of the Civil War takes many forms. Its events are retold and revalued in both autobiography and fiction. The memoirs of men central to its actions, such as Arvo Tuominen, Oskari Tokio and Niilo Wälläri, reveal generous funds of humanity. They also disclose a rugged Finnish individuality which explains the ultimate inability of these leaders of the left to conform to Russian communism. In the field of fiction Väinö Linna has contributed much to the sympathetic reassessment of the background to many who followed the red banner during the Civil War. The episode in history has also assumed respectability for scholarly enquiry. Nothing could be more detached than Jaakko Paavolainen's clinical analysis of the nature of murder during the Red terror.

In the third place there is a reconsideration of the general picture of Finland – as projected both within and without. Finns were nurtured for decades on Zachris Topelius's *Book about our Country*. Its title has been adopted for a mid-twentieth-century impression of Finland by Jörn Donner. Part of his purpose is to reject old established formulae for the presentation of Finland. He is not alone in his attitude. In more than one quarter there is a revolt against the presentation of Finland in folkloristic, picturesque terms. Such a homespun image is dismissed derogatively as *tuohityö* (birch-bark work). Yet these touchstones from the past are fundamental to nationality. The alternative calls for a miracle of selection from among the many cosmopolitan and eclectic features that have invaded the modern state.

And, in any case, the picturesque survivals clearly make their contribution to the Finnish exchequer. The elements of the old formulae are powerful in their tourist appeal. They have colour. The heart of Helsinki throbs in few places more powerfully than in its daily market. Yet this survival of a 'peasant culture', anachronistically placed between the President's palace and the point of arrival of the principal shipping services, is viewed with disfavour by those who are sensitive about the image of a modern state. Disapproving eyes have cast upon Finland's four thousand gipsies who, congregating with a swish of black velvet skirts and bright bodices, are regarded as a rough edge to a tidy society. Their horse-trading activities have not been suppressed, but their practitioners are being slowly pressed into fixed abodes. The Lapps present a dilemma. They exert a widespread appeal but the handful who pursue the traditional life are rarely seen. Visitors' impressions usually derive from encounters with the less desirable fringe who inhabit roadside booths along the broad highways that cleave the superb Torni valley or thrust their way to the Norwegian border beyond Lake Inari.

Domestic differences of opinion help Finland to absorb the varying assessments of the outside world. These include a fair share of misrepresentation. The concept of Finland as a backward land remains widespread. There are still echoes of the anonymous 'native of Stockholm' who, writing in *Åbo Tidning* in 1800, described Finland as 'Sweden's ugly sister . . . a land of trolls and witches . . . the whole country a wild forest inhabited by bears and wolves'. However, given the present level of material achievement, such attitudes can be disregarded. Finland as a borderland, quickened and thrown into relief by the proximity of Russia, yields its regular harvest of colourful fiction. Not surprisingly it has been a playground for the spies and counter-spies of Len Deighton and Gavin Lyall. Yet although Finland's tranquil domesticity is the antithesis of their vigorous plots, the image that they create is on balance more acceptable than that of Anthony Glyn's in *I can take it all*. So much of Glyn's perceptive novel approaches the truth that it hurts the more in its cavalier treatment of a number of near-sacred Finnish subjects.

Finland as a setting for foreign fiction is matched by Finland as a subject of investigation by foreign scholars. The role of the republic during the Second World War has been looked at with fresh eyes by

C. Leonard Lundin of Indiana University; while Anthony Upton, a modern historian from the University of St Andrews, has concerned himself more narrowly with the crisis years of 1940–41. To these years also belongs the diplomacy of the Petsamo nickel deposits which has been a subject of enquiry by the Norwegian-born Canadian H. P. Krosby. In the artistic world, no one has claimed more attention than Jean Sibelius. The revaluation of his work by the American musicologist Harold Johnson, although less withering than that of Peter Heyworth, has provoked sharp resentment. It may be acknowledged by such critics as Eero Tervonen in *Finsk Tidskrift* (1967) that the examination of the Finnish situation by foreigners can frequently help Finns to appreciate more objectively the events and circumstances of their modern history. It may be that the translation of these books into Finnish and Swedish is an indication in its own right of the attention paid to them. It may be that they are the work of apologists who, if challenged themselves by anti-Finns, would spring to the defence of the country that they have seemingly attacked. But all of these studies challenge accepted Finnish points of view, and processes of re-appraisal at the international level are a relatively new experience for Finland. New experiences have yielded new reactions. Anthony Upton must be among the few foreigners to claim the distinction of being taken to task in a Finnish poem.

While the outer world has been reconsidering its judgement on events and personalities that are passing into Finnish history, it has been captivated by the imagination of a much contrasted trio of Finnish authors. Mika Waltari, Tove Jansson and Yrjö Kokko have all added a new dimension to Finnish literary experiences. Mika Waltari took to seven-league boots and escaped from the realities of rural Finland at an early stage in his career. In space the action of his novels spans the breadth of Europe and the Mediterranean; in time Waltari takes the centuries in his easy stride. Sinuhe roams the Egypt of the fourteenth century B.C.; Michael the Finn is engaged in adventures between Turku and the Porte in the sixteenth century; Turms the Eternal has an Etruscan background from the fifth century and Johannes Angelos experiences the siege of Constantinople in 1453. Waltari's exceptional gifts as a story-teller and his quality of verisimilitude have earned him an international reputation. Nor has popular success prevented his election to one of the twelve places in Finland's Academy. Yrjö Kokko's stories, capturing and adding to the magic of Lapland, are much slighter. But they have stimulated

Rudolf Koivu (an artist with a style akin to that of Arthur Rackham) to produce a memorable series of illustrations and Ahti Sonninen to compose a splendid score to the ballet springing from Kokko's story of Pessi and Illoisia. As for Tove Jansson, it is the whimsy of her Moomin family that has caught millions in its spell. While Finnish children thrill to the television heroes of the Western range, the Moomintrolls have exerted a complementary appeal throughout North America.

But the prodigality of Waltari and the popularity of Jansson are expressions of the Establishment. Even Linna, Rintala and Salama no longer represent the advance guard of authors. Fashions change, words are revalued. A new literary generation is cutting and thrusting its way forward. It is polemical and populist: it acknowledges the influence of eastern as well as western Europe: it looks to poetry and the theatre rather than to other literary forms. But because it speaks in Finnish, its impact is limited. For all the modern media of communication, men of letters must wait to be translated.

A Nation in the Making

Finland is one among 125 nations. In area, it is fifty-fifth in the world list: in population, it ranks seventy-fifth. It is highly unlikely that its area will increase – save by the natural process of uplift along the Ostrobothnian seaboard. But the more effective use of its living space is favoured by every technical device which accompanies the so-called poleward march of civilisation. Demographic optimists such as Zachris Topelius a hundred years ago and J. E. Rosberg in the earlier years of the twentieth century estimated that Finland was capable of supporting 15 million or more; but realistic contemporary forecasts anticipate no more than 5.5 million inhabitants in 1980. In crude arithmetic Finland is of very modest stature, with a gross income no greater than those of some of the world's larger commercial organisations.

Yet it is driven by a more powerful engine than that propelling any merchant house. C. B. Elliot, in his *Letters from Northern Europe* (London, 1832), put his finger on the first source of energy – attachment to the country. 'It is a happy circumstance that man is so constituted that the only charm required to attach him to any country is that it should be his own.' By European standards, the land to which the Finn was attached was of poor quality. 'His poor, hidden, holy native land', Runeberg called it in his poem *Julkvällen*

(Christmas Eve). 'Holy' was very much the operative word during the critically formative nineteenth century.

There was a second source of energy. Johannes Linnankoski identified Finland for his audience at the Snellman memorial gathering in 1906:

Tämä on kirren maa,	This is a land with frost in the ground,
Tämä on unelmien kansa.	These are people with dreams.

Dreams have been vital for the Finn. The private dream was usually to claim, own and cultivate a property of one's own: the public dream was to establish an independent state. If political geography means anything, it means the difference in the degree of development and organisation between Finland and Russian Karelia – even between Finland and Sweden's province of Norrland which lies in the same latitudes.

During many centuries the way forward for most Finns was to leave Finland. The culmination of a successful career lay in Stockholm until 1809; subsequently in St Petersburg. At a different social level towards the end of the nineteenth century many thousands emigrated to the New World in search of material success. Given national sovereignty the culmination of a successful career was to be found within the national borders. Finland has its 'brain drain', but it is of limited dimensions and insufficient to jeopardise national development. What Angel Ganivet chose to call its 'vibrant patriotism' has undergone metamorphosis in the last generation. It has been increasingly possible to divert the energies formerly squandered in anti-Russian feeling (even in antipathy towards Sweden) into more positive channels. Finland is flanked by neighbours that it is impossible to rival; but within limited areas of activity it is possible to gain satisfaction by beating the Swedes at their own game or indicating to the Russians the higher returns yielded by a different system of economic organisation. In so far as the compulsive elements in nationality can be sublimated in this manner, they pay tangible dividends.

Modern Finland is very much a nation in the making. It is under no illusions that, ultimately, compliance is the order of the day. Yet while complying physically, economically and politically, it does so with greater room for manoeuvre than at any time in its history. Finland is mature enough to accept its status and flexible enough in its thinking to adjust speedily to the swift changes of the modern world. Those who mould its fortunes might take comfort from the motto with which Michael Agricola ended the preface to his New Testament – nothing can be begun and perfected at the same time. So much has been begun and, despite vicissitudes, surprisingly much has approached perfection in a remarkably short time.

Bibliographical Appendix

This bibliography is only selective. For the most part it excludes books in Finnish and Swedish; though, where they are key volumes or where they have summaries in English, French or German, they have been included. The text incorporates many references to and quotations from manuscripts. It is not possible to refer to all of their sources individually. They are to be found in many collections in many places. Among collections used are those in the State Archives, University Library, Finnish Literary Society, National Museum and Land Survey Office – all in Helsinki; those in Turku at *Åbo Akademi* Library and *Finska Hushållnigssällskapet* (*Suomen Talousseura*) and those in the provincial cities of Mikkeli (which also include Viipuri city archive, evacuated there after the war), Kuopio, Vaasa, Oulu and Turku. Among parish archives employed are those of Kuusamo, Nurmes, Saltvik and Joroinen; among commercial companies whose records are quoted are Messrs Hackman, Finlayson, Fiskars and Malm. Swedish archives – especially *Riksarkivet*, *Krigsarkivet* and the Royal Library in Stockholm – also contain abundant Finnish materials.

Chapter 1

The geographical background to an appreciation of Finland is portrayed in a variety of publications sponsored by the Finnish Geographical Society – in particular its research publication *Fennia*, the successive *Atlases of Finland* (the latest published in Helsinki, 1960) and the *Handbooks of Finnish Geography* (the latest, Helsinki, 1952). R. R. Platt, *Finland and its Geography* (New York, 1955) is complemented by chapters on Finland in A. Sømme (ed.), *Geography of Norden* (Stockholm, 1960), R. Millward, *Scandinavian Lands* (London, 1964) and W. R. Mead, *An Economic Geography of the Scandinavian States and Finland* (London, 1958). An atlas of special interest is S. Jaatinen, *Atlas of the Finnish Skerries* (Helsinki, 1961). Complementary to the latter is the Guidebook to the Excursions of the International Geographical Congress, *Geographical Society of Finland* (Helsinki, 1960). Helmer Smeds and W. R. Mead, *Winter in Finland* (London, 1967) deals with a physical circumstance vital for the appreciation of the modern state: a specific study of summer frosts (with captions and summary in English) is Y. Pessi, 'Hallojen esiintymisestä ja niiden aiheuttamista vahingoista suomessa', *Acta Agralia Fennica* (Helsinki, 1958). I. Hustich, *Finland förvandlas* (Helsingfors, 1967) and Helmer Smeds and Paul Fogelberg, *Nyky-Suomi* (Helsinki, 1967) both convey the essentials of modern Finland's human geography (the latter focusing on air photographs with related maps, so that it has something to offer despite the language barrier).

There are two other valuable introductory books: Wendy Hall, *The Finns and their country* (London, 1967); Hillar Kallas and Sylvie Nickels, *Finland; Creation and Construction* (New York, 1968). Some pertinent observations are also to be found in the chapters on Finland in Donald S. Connery in *The Scandinavians* (London, 1966).

The publications of a number of Finland's learned societies have been freely employed – in particular, those of the Finnish Academy of Sciences; *Historiallisia tutkimuksia*, the series of the Finnish Historical Society and *Skrifter utgivne af Svenska Litteratursällskapet i Finland*. An invaluable reference book is J. Vallinkoski and H. Schauman, *Suomen historiallinen bibliografia, 1544–1900* (Helsinki, 1961). There has also been regular reference to the two standard histories of Finland – J. Jaakkola (ed.), *Suomen historia* (Helsinki, 1944–64), 10 volumes, and E. Juva (ed.), *Suomen kansanhistoria* (Helsinki, 1964), 3 volumes. In the field of systematic history, two definitive publications of E. Jutikkala have been indispensable – *Suomen talonpojan historia* (Helsinki, 1958; in Swedish, *Bonden i Finland genom tiderna*, Stockholm, 1963), and *Suomen historian kartasto* (Helsinki, 1949; an atlas with English captions). There are scores of Finnish parish histories. Among the excellent examples to which passing reference is made is K. Wirilander, *Savon historia* (Helsinki, 1962). *The Scandinavian Economic History Review* (Stockholm) is a journal with definitive articles on Finland's history. At a different level, but nevertheless containing a considerable amount of reliable information on Finland, are *The Norseman* (London), a quarterly periodical published from 1943 to 1958, and the *American Scandinavian Review*.

With the old-established Finnish Literary Society (*Suomalaisen kirjallisuuden seura*) to foster research into language, literature and folklore, it is not surprising that there should be fruitful publication in this field. Most volumes are in Finnish. Among those published in English, M. Haavio, *Väinömöinen, Eternal Sage* (Helsinki, 1952) gives some idea of the quality and inspiration evident in this type of work. Matti Kuusi, *Sampo-eepos* (Helsinki, 1949) belongs to the same school. The varied interests of K. Krohn are seen in such contrasted studies as *Die folkloristische Arbeitsmethode* (Helsinki, 1926) and the six volumes devoted to *Kalevala-studien* (Helsinki, 1924–8). There are several translations of the national epic, *Kalevala*. The best is that by F. P. Magoun Jr. (Cambridge, Mass, 1963). None rivals it in documentation and it also gives translations of Elias Lönnrot's prefaces to the original editions of the poem. The major survey of Finnish literature is M. Kuusi and S. Konsala (ed.), *Suomen kirjallisuus* (Keuru, 1963; in continuation).

There is a modest number of Lapps in Finland. The best study in English of this minority group is Björn Collinder, *The Lapps* (Princeton, 1949); the major contribution in Finnish is T. I. Itkonen, *Suomen lappalaiset*, 2 vols. (Helsinki, 1948). The series *Acta Lapponica Fennicae* contains a varied range of materials on the Lapps (some of it in English).

Chapter 2

The first part of this chapter leans heavily upon the standard work on Finnish archaeology. It is Ella Kivikoski, *Finlands forntid* (Helsingfors, 1965), also adapted and translated as Vol. 53 in the series, *Ancient Peoples and Places* (London, 1967). Reference has also been made to the publications of the Finnish Archaeological Society, *Suomen muinaismuistoyhdistys*, which include one especially handsome volume, A. Erä-Esko, *Germanic animal art of Salin's style I in Finland* (Helsinki, 1965). Perhaps the most readable publication on early Finland is by the French scholar A. Sauvageot, *Les anciens finnois* (Paris, 1961). The *Kalevala* quotations employed in the text derive from W. F. Kirby, *Kalevala, The Land of Heroes* (Everyman Series, London, 1956). The history of enquiry into Finland's prehistory and ethnography is illustrated by reference to the notebooks of C. A. Gottlund, *Antiquariska sammling*, in particular Vols. IV and V, in the National Museum of Finland, or to the Russian travels of M. A. Castrén, *Nordiska resor och forskningar* (Helsingfors, 1857). T. Vuorela, *Suomen sukuiset kansat* (Turku, 1960; with its counterpart in English *The Finnish-Ugrian People*, Bloomington, 1964) is a contemporary survey of knowledge about Finnish ethnographic relations. L. Hakulinen, *Suomen kielen rakkenne ja kehitys*, is a standard linguistic statement; Björn Collinder, *Survey of Uralic languages* (Stockholm, 1957), puts Finnish into its broader context. Much water has flowed under the bridge since L. Burnham, *Who are the Finns?* (London, 1939), but it indicated the direction in which Finnish thought was moving. A similar approach, in an up-to-date form, is found in Y. H. Toivonen, *Sanat puhuvet* (Helsinki, 1944). The introductory chapters by K. Pirinen to E. Jutikkala, *History of Finland*, are also directly relevant. *The ballad of the death of Bishop Henry*, the oldest manuscript in possession of the Finnish Literary Society, has been published in facsimile (Helsinki, 1967).

Chapter 3

There are illustrations of the first manuscripts referring to Finland in the standard histories edited by J. Jaakkola and E. Juva. Olaus Magnus, *History of the Goths, Visigoths and other Northern Peoples* (tr. London, 1656) is a readable blend of fact and fiction which epitomises the emergence from the Middle Ages to the Renaissance. The processes of land occupation are well described in G. Kerkkonen, 'Obygd-Erämark-Nygygd', *Historiallinen Arkisto*, 60 (Turku, 1966). The opening up of northern Savo is carefully treated in A. M. Soininen, *Pohjois-Savon asuttaminen keski- ja uuden ajan vaihtessa* (Helsinki, 1961). Of a more general character is A. M. Soininen, 'Burn-beating as the technical basis of colonisation in Finland in the sixteenth and seventeenth centuries', *Scandinavian Economic History Review*, VII, 2 (Stockholm, 1959). Location near Sweden encouraged early record keeping in Åland province and representative of earlier documents is Kaj Mikander (ed.), *Åländska handlingar, 1530–1634* (Helsingfors, 1959). A contemporary study having some direct relevance to the Finnish Lapps is J. Schefferus, *Lapponia* (Oxford, 1674). Place-name studies contributed to the understanding of the expansion of settlement. V. Nissilä, *Suomalaista nimistöntutkimusta* (Helsinki, 1962) is a representative volume. Aspects of the evolution of trade are discussed in S. E. Åström, *From Stockholm to St Petersburg* (Helsinki, 1962) and *From cloth to iron* (Helsinki, 1963). Some indication of the development of education is provided in J. Vallinkoski, *The History of the University Library of Turku* (Helsinki, 1948). One of the earliest biographies touching upon the period is E. Tengström, *Gezelii den Yngre minne* (Helsingfors, 1833).

Chapter 4

The extent to which the spirit of enquiry was abroad in eighteenth-century Finland is illustrated in the variety of the literature. E. Richter, *Geografins historia i Sverige intill 1800* (Uppsala, 1959) illustrates the wealth of available Finnish material; so do the volumes of *Åbo Universitets Lärdomshistoria*, published by the Swedish Literary Society. There is also a variety of maps. Å. Davidson, *Handritade kartor över Finland* (Uppsala, 1959) is a useful catalogue; but there is no printed catalogue of the great collection of hand-drawn maps in the Finnish Land Survey Office. S. G. Hermelin, *Atlas öfver Sverige*, II, *Storfurstendömet Finland* (Stockholm, 1799) is the first comprehensive atlas. The striving for order and organisation in the mapping and planning of settlements is illustrated in E. Jutikkala, *Tomtbesittningen och kampen om regulariteten i Sverige-Finlands städer* (Helsingfors, 1963). The origin and nature of Finland's statistical materials are shown in G. Fougstedt and A. Raivio, *Population of Finland in 1751–1805 by order and occupation* (Helsinki, 1953). The dynamics of this material are shown in E. Jutikkala, 'Finland's population movement in the eighteenth century', *Population in History* (London, 1965). R. Oja, 'Agriculture in western Finland in 1719', *Acta Agralia Fennica* (Helsinki, 1956) opens a window on the farming scene at the beginning of the century, while G. Cygnaeus, *Kungliga Finska Hushållningssällskapet, 1797–1897* (Åbo, 1897) shows the changing attitude among farming leaders a century later. A. A. Parvela, *Oulun läänin viljelyskasvit* (Helsinki, 1930) illustrates the dispersal of cultivated plants in northern Finland. The spirit of curiosity which carried natural husbandmen abroad is illustrated in M. Kerkkonen, *Peter Kalm's North American Journey* (Helsinki, 1959). Merchants also had their overseas experiences, as is illustrated in B. Lunelund, *Pehr Johan Bladh och Svenska Ostindiska compagniet åren 1766–84* (Helsingfors, 1940). The critical part played by Ostrobothnia in trading is brought out in E. E. Kaila, *Pohjanmaa ja meri 1600- ja 1700-luvulla* (Helsinki, 1931). The campaigns in eighteenth-century Finland are largely covered by the official Swedish military histories. *Svenska lantmäteriet, 1626–1928* (Stockholm, 1928) and *Suomen Maanmittauksen historia* (Porvoo, 1933) cover the story of the land survey. Travellers from abroad began to move to Finland and leave their records. Among the English travellers the fullest accounts are those of Edward Clarke, *Travels in various parts of Europe*, Vol. III (London, 1823) and Joseph Acerbi, *Travels through Sweden, Finland and Lapland, 1798–9* (London, 1802). John A. Atkinson and James Walker, *A picturesque representation of the customs and amusements of the Russians* (London, 1803–04) has a number of informative plates devoted to Finland.

Chapter 5

The developing social and cultural life of Finland is best appreciated by comparing the substance of E. M. von Frenckell, *Offentliga nöjen och privata i Helsingfors, 1812–27* (Helsingfors, 1943) and the picture books, *Vuosisatamme kuvissa*, 2 vols. (Helsinki, 1935), which cover the years 1899–1917. A picture book of a different character, which illuminates a brief phase in Finland's international history, is M. Hirn, *Från Bomarsund till Sveaborg 1854–55* (Borgå, 1956). The founding fathers of the state are the subject of a range of biographies from V. Tarkiainen, *Mikael Agricola* (Helsinki, 1958), through L. Castrén, *Adolf Ivar Arwidsson* (Helsinki, 1961) to E. W. Juva, *Rudolf Walden, 1878–1946* (Helsinki, 1947). P. Nyberg (ed.), *Zachris Topelius, självbiografiska anteckningar* (Helsinki, 1922) contains a mass of impressions from the mid-nineteenth century; *Boken om Gallén-Kallela* (Helsingfors, 1948) is an unusual autobiographical volume by the artist; and there is a rich series of memoirs published in the series *Ikivihreitä muistelmia* (Helsinki, 1967). O. Tigerstedt, *Huset Hackman, 1790–1879* (Helsingfors, 1940, 1952) and Oscar Nikula, *Malmska handelshuset i Jakobstad* (Helsingfors, 1948) deal with the merchants behind representative though contrasting trading houses in Viipuri and Kokkola. P. Schybergson, *Aktiebolags former genombrott i Finland* (Helsingfors, 1964) tells something of the age that witnessed their transformation. Hannes Gebhard, *Cooperation in Finland* (London, 1916) presents the emergence of another form of commercial enterprise. Two contrasting company histories are L. G. Bonsdorff, *Nokia osakeyhtiö 1865–1965* (Helsinki, 1965) and T. Svedlin, *Dalsbruks järnverk, 1686–1936* (Helsingfors, 1936). The strategy and economy of the Finnish railways are analysed in T. Polvinen, *Die Finnischen Eisenbahn* (Helsinki, 1962). Society was moved by philosophy as well as economy. M. Ruutu, 'De religiösa folkrörelserna och samhället *c.* 1750–1850', *Historiallinen Arkisto*, 62 (1966) analyses religious revivalism; A. L. Toivonen, *Etelä-Pohanmaan valtamerentakainen siirtolaisuus, 1867–1930* (Helsinki, 1963) looks at emigration from south Ostrobothnia; J. I. Kolehmainen and G. W. Hill, *Haven in the Woods* (Madison, 1951) and W. A. Hoglund, *Finnish immigrants in America, 1880–1920* (Madison, 1960) cover the receiving end of the movement. There were increasing numbers of European visitors to Finland. Xavier Marmier wrote for the French in *Lettres sur la Russie, la Finlande et la Pologne* (Paris, 1843); Angel Ganivet, for the Iberians, in *Cartas Finlandesas* (Madrid, 1961). J. Paterson, *A Book for every Land* (London, 1858) described journeys through the interior on winter missions for the British and Foreign Bible Society; Mrs Alec Tweedie left lively impressions in *Through Finland in Carts* (London, 1897); Rosalind Travers wrote well-informed *Letters from Finland* (London, 1911).

The Russian period opened with a fairly clear-cut international situation in the Baltic. Its features are identified in P. Tommila, *La*

Finlande dans la politique européenne en 1809–15 (Helsinki, 1962). S. E. Åström tells of the emergence of the planned capital in *Samhällsplanering och regionalbildning i kejsartidens Helsingfors* (Helsingfors, 1957). The constitutional struggle gave rise to one specific book in English, J. Fisher, *Finland and the tsars, 1809–99* (London, 1899); J. H. Wuorinen offers a synoptic view of *Nationalism in Modern Finland* (New York, 1931). The period ended with considerable confusion. Aspects of it are treated in J. Paasivirta, *Finland, 1918* (Helsinki, 1962); the same, *The Victors in World War I and Finland* (Helsinki, 1965); C. Jay Smith, *Finland and the Russian Revolution, 1917–22* (Atlanta, 1958); Geoffrey Bennet, *Cowan's War* (London, 1964); A. Agar, *Baltic episode* (London, 1963); K. von der Goltz, *Als politischer General im Osten* (Leipzig, 1963); J. H. Hodgson, *Communism in Finland* (Princeton, 1967); C. C. M. Maynard, *The Murmansk Venture* (London, 1928); K. H. Wiik, *Finland in der Krisenzeit* (1934); C. G. Mannerheim, *The Memoirs of Marshal Mannerheim* (London, 1953). The birth of independence was accompanied by stresses both on the east and the west. J. O. Söderhjelm, *Démilitarisation et neutralisation des Iles d'Åland en 1856 et 1921* (Helsinki, 1928) looks to the west; M. Jääskeläinen, *Itä-Karjalan kysymus* (Helsinki, 1961), A. von Gadolin, *Ostkarelien – das finnische Grenzland* (München, 1943) and *La question de la Carélie orientale*, I–III (Helsinki, 1922–4) look to the east.

Chapter 6

The climax of Finland's experiences as an independent state came between 1939 and 1944. There is a substantial literature dealing with the events leading up to the Winter War and on to the eventual peace settlement. The broader panorama is given in J. H. Wuorinen (ed.), *Finland and World War II, 1939–44* (New York, 1949) and W. H. Halsti, *Suomen sota, 1939–44*, I–III (Helsinki, 1957). Max Jakobson, *The Diplomacy of the Winter War, 1939–40* (Cambridge, Mass., 1961) is the classical statement on the war. A complementary and individual approach is provided by V. Tanner, *The Winter War* (Stanford, California, 1957). A diplomatic view of the war years and peace negotiations is provided by G. A. Gripenberg, *Finland and the Great Powers* (Lincoln, Nebraska, 1965). A French interpretation is M. Peltier, *La Finlande dans la tourmente* (Paris, 1966). The three years' war is looked at domestically in W. Erfurth, *Der Finnische Krig, 1941–44* (Wiesbaden, 1952). The final phase, against the Germans in Lapland, is described in T. T. Kaila, *Lapin sota* (Helsinki, 1950). Minority opinions are expressed in C. O. Frietsch,

Finlands ödesår, 1939–43 (Helsingfors, 1945) and O. Paavolainen, *Synkkä yksinpuhelu* (Helsinki, 1946). L. Lundin, *Finland and the Second World War* (Bloomington, 1957) and A. F. Upton, *Finland in Crisis, 1940–41* (London, 1964) adopt detached points of view and produce a liberal interpretation of the events. The relationship to the Russo-German War is analysed in A. Korhonen, *Barbarossa suunitelma ja Suomi* (Porvoo, 1960). The memoirs of J. H. Paasikivi, *Minnen 1939–40*, 2 vols. (Helsingfors, 1959) and C. G. Mannerheim (see Chapter 5) are directly relevant. O. Warner, *Marshal Mannerheim and the Finns* (London, 1967) is a rounded study of the national hero; E. Heinrichs, *Mannerheimgestalten* (Helsingfors, 1957, 1959) a definitive statement. There is a miscellany of autobiographical experiences by outsiders who were in Finland during the war years, examples of which are J. Byrom (James Bramwell), *The unfinished man* (London, 1957) and Constance Malleson, *In the north* (London, 1946). A different kind of observation is found in Geoffrey Cox, *The Red army moves* (London, 1941). The war years bred narrower as well as broader problems. Two examples are A. J. Schwartz, *America and the Russo-Finnish War* (Washington, 1960) and H. P. Krosby, 'The Diplomacy of the Petsamo question and Finnish-German relations, 1941', *Scandia*, 31 (1966), 291–320; 32, 167–211.

The social problems of the inter-war years are identified in J. H. Wuorinen, *The prohibition experiment in Finland* (New York, 1931); M. Rintala, *Three generations: the extreme right wing in Finnish politics* (Bloomington, 1962) and the complementary Ilka Hakalehto, *Suomen kommunistinen puolue ja sen vaikutus poliittiseen ja ammatilliseen työväenliikkeeseen, 1918–28* (Helsinki, 1966); M. Klöverkorn, *Die sprachliche struktur Finnlands, 1880–1950* (Helsinki, 1960). J. Hampden Jackson, *Finland* (London, 1939) still has a point of view to offer from the inter-war years. It is complemented by the well-balanced A. Mazour, *Finland between east and west* (Princeton, 1956).

There is a variety of autobiographies essential for the political understanding of the period – among them A. Tuominen, *Kremlin kellot* (Helsinki, 1957) and *Sirpin ja vasarantie* (Helsinki, 1957); C. Enckell, *Politiska minnen*, 2 vols. (Helsingfors, 1956); O. Tokoi, *Maanpakolaisen muistelmia* (Helsinki, 1947); *Sisu, even through a stone wall* (New York, 1957). Foreign visitors seemed unaware of the domestic disturbances beneath the outward tranquillity. Georges Duhamel, *Le Chant du nord* (Paris, 1931) is an idyll not even rivalled by William Sansom's chapter on Finland in *The icicle and the sun* (London, 1958).

Chapter 7

The English version of the 'Treaty of Peace between the Allies and Finland' was published by H.M.S.O. in 1947. Resettlement issues are dealt with in H. Waris, *Siirtoväen sopeutuminen* (Helsinki, 1952) and Axel de Gadolin, *The Solution to the Karelian refugee problem in Finland* (The Hague, 1952). Rural problems arising from the resettlement programme are considered in W. R. Mead, *Farming in Finland* (London, 1953). The broader sweep of domestic problems are identified in H. Pipping, *Finlands näringsliv efter andra världskriget* (Helsingfors, 1954), C. E. Knoellinger, *Labour in Finland* (Cambridge, 1960) and two valuable publications by the Finnish Political Science Association, *Finnish Foreign policy* (Helsinki, 1963) and *Democracy in Finland, studies in politics and government* (Helsinki, 1960). Integration with the other countries of Norden is covered by F. Wendt, *The Nordic Council and cooperation in Scandinavia* (Copenhagen, 1959). Foreign policy has been characterised by the so-called Paasikivi–Kekkonen line, a preliminary statement on which is found in L. A. Puntila, *Paasikiven linje* (Lahti, 1957).

Chapter 8

The contemporary problems of Finland emerge in one way or another from two helpful (and freely distributed) publications – *The Bank of Finland Monthly Review* (published since 1929) and *Unitas*, the quarterly review of the private bank Pohjoismaiden yhdyspankki. Government commissions also issue their reports with increasing frequency. They are usually published immediately in Finnish and eventually in Swedish. Examples of reports employed in this chapter are *Industridelegationens betänkande rörande industrialiseringens förutsättningar och åtgärder för dess främjande* (Helsingfors, 1961) and *Småkommunkommittens betänkande* (Helsingfors, 1965). The National Planning Board has its own publications, and Kai Palmgren, *Regional differences in the degree of development in Finland*, A. 15 (Helsinki, 1966) is among those more fully employed. Other economic studies to which this chapter refers are V. Holopainen, *60-luvun metsäpolitiikka* (Helsinki, 1967); O. Riihinen, *Teollistuvan yhteiskunnan alueellinen erilaistuneisuus* (Kuopio, 1965) and L. Wahlbeck, *Om inkomstnivånsgeografi, i Finland år 1950* (Vasa, 1955). Reviews of specific aspects of the Finnish scene include J. Uotila, *The Finnish legal system* (Helsinki, 1966) and J. Nousiainen, *Finlands politiska system* (Stockholm, 1966), the most comprehensive book available on the topic. O.

Ketonen and U. Toivola, *Introduction to Finland* (Helsinki, 1963) has continuingly useful chapters as has its logical ancestor, the substantial compilation *Finland, the Country, People and Institutions* (Helsinki, 1926). J. M. Richards, *A guide to Finnish architecture* (London, 1966) outlines the progress of an important aspect of applied art, A. Krohn, *Art in Finland* (Helsinki, 1953) is a succinct summary of artistic development over the last century and Denby Richards, *The Music of Finland*, (London, 1968) brings the story of musical composition up to date. An example of a private committee's report is the plan for agriculture published as *Maatilataloud-en peruskorjaukset vv. 1960–1980* (Helsinki, 1959). Revaluations are encountered in such studies as J. Paavolainen, *Poliittiset väkivalt-aisuuden Suomessa 1918*, I, *Punainen terrori* (Helsinki, 1966); Jörn Donner, *Nya boken om vårt land* (Helsingfors, 1967); Harold Johnson, *Jean Sibelius* (New York, 1959), which is now complemented by E. W. Tavastjerna's impressive biography (Helsinki, 1967). O. Mustelin, *Studier i finländsk historieforskning, 1808–65* (Borgå, 1957) conveys an idea of the changing interpretation of historical facts. J. Paasivirta, *Suomen kuva Yhdysvalloissa* (Porvoo, 1962) is the picture of Finland as seen in the U.S.A.

Finnish Fiction in English

A full list of Finnish fiction available in English translation down to 1953 is to be found in *Oversettelse til Engelsk av nordisk Skjønn-litteratur, Nordisk Kulturkommisjon*, 2 (Oslo, 1954). Among the earliest translations are those from the romances and fairy stories of Zachris Topelius. *The Surgeon's Stories* (Chicago, 1883–91) is the principal work available. It is strong on geographical setting. Alexis Kivi, *Seven Brothers* (Helsinki, 1952) is an undeniable classic and it comes through well in translation. J. L. Runeberg, *The Tales of Ensign Stål* (New York, 1938) is perhaps the best translation of the many varied attempts to deal with this popular Finnish narrative poem. Larin Kyösti, *Northern Lights* (Hämeenlinna, 1937) is a collection of short stories which retains a strong flavour of the original. Finnish backgrounds of varying regional character are found in F. E. Sillanpää, *Fallen asleep while young* (London, 1933), *Meek Heritage* (London, 1938), *People in a Summer Night* (London, 1966); Johannes Linnankoski, *The Song of the Blood Red Flower* (London, 1920); Jarl Hemmer, *The Fool of Faith* (New York, 1935); Unto Seppanen, *The House of Markku* (London, 1940). Sally Salminen, *Katrina* (London, 1937) still retains something of the romance of the Åland islands. Väinö Linna, *The Unknown Soldier* (London, 1957) looks to the Three Years' War: J. Talvi,

Friends and Enemies (London, 1959), also has a wartime background. Mika Waltari is the best known of the contemporary Finnish authors. Translations include *The Dark Angel* (London, 1953), *The Sultan's Renegade* (London, 1951), *Michael the Finn* (London, 1950), *A Nail Merchant at Nightfall* (London, 1954), *The Egyptian* (London, 1949), *The Etruscan* (London, 1957), *A Stranger came to the Farm* (London, 1953), *Moonscape and other Stories* (London, 1956). E. Tompuri, *Voices from Finland* (Helsinki, 1947) is a miscellany of translations of varying quality, but considerable diversity.

There is very little English fiction with a Finnish background. Much of it is listed in W. R. Mead, 'Finns in English and American literature', *Neuphilologische Mitteilungen*, LXIV (1963). Catherine Gavin, *The Fortress* (London, 1965) is an historical novel set in the Crimean period: Anthony Glyn, *I can take it all* (London, 1960), has a contemporary setting. Three memorable autobiographies about Finns are Ellis Carlsson, *Mother Sea* (Oxford, 1964), Pamela Eriksson, *The Duchess* (London, 1958), and T. Pekkanen, *My childhood* (Madison, 1967).

Index

Printed in Great Britain by
Western Printing Services Limited Bristol